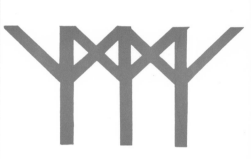

**Civic Garden Centre
Library**

THE GREEN GARDENER

ROY LACEY

THE GREEN GARDENER

*How to make your garden
environmentally friendly*

Illustrations by Tricia Newell

632
LII

DAVID & CHARLES
Newton Abbot · London

British Library Cataloguing in Publication Data
Lacey, Roy
    The green gardener
    1. Gardens. Organic cultivation
    I. Title
    635.0484

ISBN 0-7153-9862-8

Typeset by Ace Filmsetting Ltd, Frome, Somerset
and printed in Hong Kong by Wing King Tong Co Ltd
for David & Charles plc
Brunel House Newton Abbot Devon

CONTENTS

TURNING GREENER

This is a good time to be alive in the run-up to the twenty-first century. After the headlong industrial expansion, economic growth, and conspicuous consumption that have characterised this century, things are beginning to turn.

Perhaps it is the dawning recognition that mankind has never been in graver danger, that the problems he faces now, on this over-populated, over-polluted planet, are of such magnitude that unless they are solved human life on earth could become insupportable. The heartening fact is we are aware of the danger and are accepting the challenge to change our ways.

Up until about the mid-1970s those of us in the organic movement were whistling in the wind, trying to influence public opinion by pointing out the pitfalls of exploitive farming that measured production just in terms of maximum yield, by warning of the high price we were bound to pay for 'cheap' food. It was a pathetically fragmented effort by a relatively few impassioned people. It was environmental concern pitched against economic greed, and the message was unheard or ignored by the decision makers.

That's all changed. Greenpeace, Friends of the Earth, the Soil Association, World Wide Fund for Nature and other organisations have spearheaded campaigns that have alerted the public and forced politicians into motion, slow motion admittedly, but movement nevertheless.

We are no longer the silent minority. We can do something collectively and individually to move back from the edge. But we no longer have to wait on the outcome of tortuous talks in the places of power. We have real power ourselves, and we can demonstrate its effectiveness on our own immediate environment: our home and garden.

That's the purpose of this book. To offer guidance, based on long experience, of how to make the garden a greener place, because if we can garden without recourse to poisons, if we can work in harmony with nature instead of against it, encouraging natural pest control, then we can make our gardens havens for wildlife. And if we can recycle some of the waste from our kitchens to make our soil healthier, if we can grow some of our own food without chemicals, then we are demonstrating to the politicians, the polluters and plunderers that we are no longer going to be pushed towards the precipice. It's our planet, our earth, and our little bit of it is going to be tended with care, compassion and love.

THE GREEN GARDENING CODE

- Make your garden safe for all: children, pets, wildlife and yourself.
- Learn the limits of what you can do in terms of your soil, the weather in your district, your family commitments.
- Save materials that can be recycled. Start a compost heap, bin or other container.
- Do all you can to improve the structure and vitality of your soil.
- Don't forget that every pest has a predator, and that soapy water is one of the best insecticides.
- Peat is a non-renewable resource. Try to use composted bark instead.
- When buying bulbs make sure that they have been cultivated and not gathered from the wild.
- If you have space to spare, give over some of your garden to wildlife. Sow wild flower seeds bought from a specialist seed firm.
- Don't use weedkillers. Keep weeds under control by hand-weeding, hoeing, mulching or flame-gunning.
- Don't dig in raw vegetable waste, compost it. Put woody stems, like cabbage stalks, into a trench for composting, or at the bottom of your compost bin.
- Keep records of crop rotation, plant performance, quality and weather. Use a camera to record your successes with, for example, bedding schemes, hanging baskets and other containers.
- Start a worm farm and feed them the kitchen scraps.
- Shorten the distance between the vegetable plot and the kitchen. The fresher the food, the better.
- Learn the secrets of companion planting.
- Don't be in a hurry to sow, but do steal a march on the weather with cloches and a cold frame or greenhouse or both.
- Save water wherever and whenever you can.
- If you must mechanise, choose machines that will run on lead-free petrol, that are energy misers, quiet, long-lasting and safe.
- Don't ignore the good old varieties of vegetables: they are often more suitable for organic growing than the F1 equivalent.
- Test the pH level of your soil regularly.
- Don't expect miracles. Converting to organic growing is like giving up smoking: difficult at first but worth the effort.

WORKING
WITH NATURE

A garden should be much more than a piece of land that keeps houses apart. It should give pleasure, quietude, a chance to relax, an opportunity to forge a relationship with other living things. The actual content of the garden gives it its uniqueness. For some this could mean creating a showplace that is the envy of neighbours. For others it could mean laying a lawn with, maybe, a rose bush or two, and a bed for planting up each year with bought-in annuals. For a retired military friend of mine it meant marshalling all his energy into a regimental parade-ground of flowers, shrubs and a short-back-and-sides lawn.

For most of us our garden is neither a wilderness nor a weed-free vista of visual delight. It is something in between. Gertrude Jekyll (pronounced *Jeekall*), the great gardening writer who used her several acres of garden as a canvas, and the plants as a palette of colours and tones, said she spent half her long lifetime finding out what was worth doing with her garden, then the other half trying to find ways to do it. Another way of saying, perhaps, that you can't expect everything to go according to plan. Assuming you have a plan. Most of my gardens and, so far, we have had twelve different gardens up and down Britain, have just grown without any blueprint. The largest was nearly three acres, and as that had been a superbly cultivated garden for more than three hundred years we were more than content to allow it to dictate its needs to us, with ourselves making only minor suggestions to the overall scheme and a few renewals when necessary.

THE NATURAL GARDEN

Obviously, if you create a garden or change an established one something of your personality is expressed in it: flamboyance, laziness, expansive-ness, artistry are all recognisable in gardens by those observers who, like me, enjoy other people's gardens nearly as much as their own.

What may not be readily apparent is whether a garden is organically managed or not. Yet there are tell-tale signs. Tucked away discreetly will be a compost container of some sort. There will almost certainly be some vegetables, salad crops and fruit, however small the space available.

The choice of plants will indicate someone who is interested in the other creatures who share the garden, so provision is made for the birds, and thought given to attracting bees, butterflies, ladybirds, lacewings, butterflies, even hedgehogs. If there's enough space, there could well be a pond, with frogs, because farm ponds and village ponds are one of the disappearing features of Britain, and when the ponds go the wildlife associated with them also goes.

Hedges, too, have fallen victim to the demands of modern farming methods. Since the end of World War II farmers have removed nearly a third of all the hedgerows in England and Wales, a total of 7,250km (4,500 miles) a year, and yet, as Marion Shoard, author of *Theft of the Countryside*, points out, 'Hedgerows provide the framework of the English countryside.' If you live, as we do, slap in the middle of Suffolk, the barley baron county, the loss of the framework, the skeleton of the landscape, through the wholesale ripping out of hedges, has meant the loss of its flesh, its features.

There's another factor. Hedges, says Marion, have made England's wildlife richer by far than that of other lands: the primrose and the violet, the hedgehog and the dormouse owe their abundance to the hedgerow, and it is our network of bushy hedges which has made England, *par excellence*, the country of small songbirds.

Naturalist/farmer Robin Page, writing in *Country*

Living, adds, 'The agri-businessmen have created featureless prairies out of once beautiful patchworks of tree-lined fields and meadows. They don't mind, they drive BMWs and take winter holidays in Colorado and the Caribbean.' So much, therefore, is lost when a farmer or property developer grubs out a hedge.

Though the shrubs and trees that we gardeners plant cannot possibly compensate for the massive destruction of our hedgerows – in scale as devastating to native flora and fauna as the destruction of the Amazon rain forests – they do provide a refuge for some creatures whose very existence is threatened.

One of the endearing features of gardening is that there are few hard and fast rules. You can accept the advice of experts or do your own thing, but as a garden is a living, evolving thing in trust to you, it needs managing with care and respect, and the management skill involved in an organic garden is rather greater than one run in a conventional manner. It calls especially, I think, for a keener observation of plant behaviour, a better understanding of plant needs and a quick response to signs of pest and disease.

ATTRACTING THE BIRDS

Birds are by far the most familiar form of wildlife to share our gardens, and their companionship, and the help they give in controlling insect pests, more than compensate for the minor irritation of having to protect some plants and shrubs against damage. So when planning, or re-planning, your garden it is worth making special provision to encourage birds. The biggest danger to birdlife in suburban gardens comes from cats, who wander freely from garden to garden. There's absolutely no doubt that cats take a tremendous toll of birdlife in our towns and villages, with blackbirds, thrushes and robins the main casualties. They also kill small mammals such as shrews, young hedgehogs and baby squirrels.

So before embarking on the undoubted joys of cat ownership, remember that there are penalties. We keep dogs, and enjoy a full complement of birds, frogs, plus the occasional hedgehog in our small garden, while neighbours' cats tend to give the place a wide berth.

In a hard winter, just putting out scraps of food will bring birds to the garden, and, in fact, many urban birds rely on such hand-outs for their survival.

Bearing this in mind, you can increase your pleasure in their company, and make them more welcome, by planning where you feed them. A properly made bird table, or a tray suspended from a branch of a tree, will suit most bird visitors, while for those who prefer to feed on the ground, the food can be scattered near the table. An important factor is that the feeding site should be near enough to the house to be ministered to once or twice a day, from October to March. A central position on a lawn within sight of your kitchen or living room windows, yet out of immediate range from a hedge, or border plants, that could give cover to marauding moggies, should tempt even the shy feeders. A bird bath would provide further encouragement because water for drinking and bathing is appreciated by the birds as much as the food.

Give some thought to the type of food scraps you offer the birds and to the need to keep up a constant supply once you have started. Bird feeding equipment, tailor-made for the job, along with advice on what foods are recommended to attract the widest range of species, can be had from the Sales Department of the Royal Society for the Protection of Birds.

Feeding the bird visitors to the garden in winter is fine. It's even better if your garden can offer a safe haven for nesting and roosting, and warm shelter when the grip of winter tightens. In fact, with the loss of so many hedgerows, this has become desperately important to many species.

Some small birds, such as blue tits and nuthatches, will use nesting boxes in the garden, but it is important to position them at the right height and to ensure they are safe from cats. The RSPB has easy-to-follow plans for nesting boxes.

A much-loved feature of our town garden was a stretch of woven fencing, six feet tall, that over many years had become densely clothed in ivy. The October 1987 hurricane brought it down and now we miss the scores of wrens, tits and other small birds that used the ivy as a happy hunting ground for insect food, and the butterflies that haunted the ivy when the flowers appeared in late summer. We have partly made amends by providing lots of berry-bearing shrubs, such as pyracantha and cotoneaster, and plants, such as sedum, Michaelmas daisy and hebe, that attract both butterflies and hoverflies, and sunflowers whose seeds are a magnet to finches, especially the greenfinches.

*Attract birds to the garden with a
bird table and a regular supply of food*

GARDEN DESIGN

It isn't the intention here to give guidance on the detail of garden design. There are numerous excellent books for just that purpose and there are many good ones on wildlife gardening (page 147). But it is worth recalling some of the basic elements of garden design. Whether your garden is a tiny plot or part of a country estate, whether it is brand new or in need of rejuvenation, you'll find it easier to put your ideas into action if you first put them on paper. Make a sketch of the garden, preferably to scale, and mark the south- and east-facing sides. Then decide what you want your garden to do for you and yours.

- Keep your plan as simple as possible and don't try to cram too much into too little space.
- Most flowers benefit from as sunny a spot as possible, while the vegetables, on the whole, are not too fussy about some shade. So the south-facing area could be reserved for the flowers, particularly if you can have part of the lawn adjoining it. On warm summer days you can sit and enjoy the beauty of the flowers with, for company, the bees, butterflies and other insects that will share your enjoyment.
- Try to separate the children's play area from the planted parts so that you are not constantly having to nag them about keeping off the flower or vegetable areas. It's even more important if you have a greenhouse, cold frame or cloches because then you have the children's safety as a top priority, while remembering that replacement glass can be a costly item in the gardening budget.
- A lawn is usually the central feature of the small garden, but you may also want a paved area, perhaps a patio, near to the house for al fresco eating and for container gardening.
- Try to make room for at least a few fruit trees, apples and pears for preference. They can be bought on dwarfing rootstocks, trained as cordons or espaliers against south-facing fences or walls – or bought as columnar trees.
- If you are taking on a new garden, then a greenhouse or conservatory might not feature very high on your shopping list, but it is worthwhile making future provision for locating one or the other, or both, when you draw up your garden plan.

WEEPING TREES

When planting a weeping tree, such as a weeping willow, face the bare side away from the prevailing wind. This speeds up the growth on the leeward side to give the tree a balanced umbrella shape.

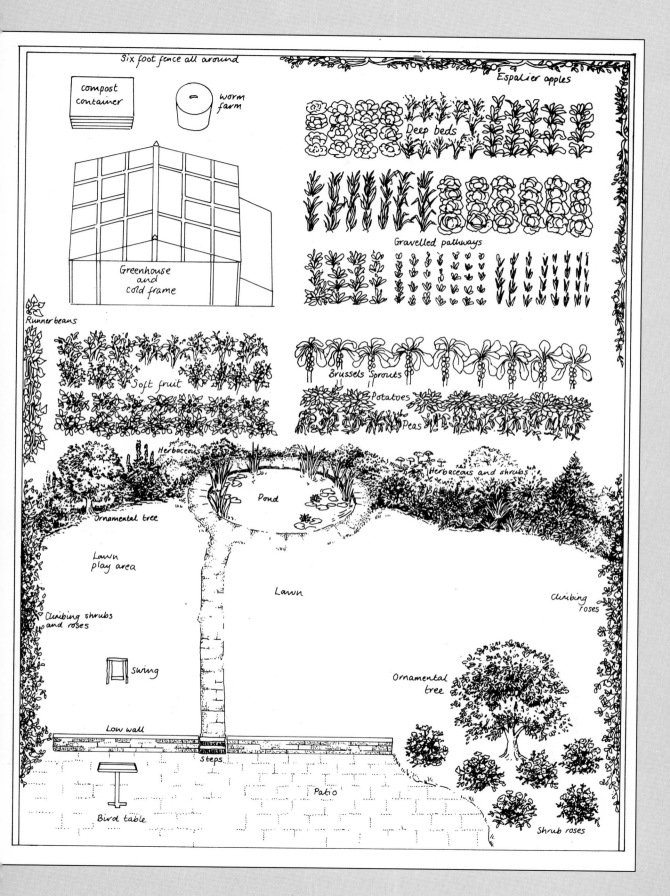

HOW TO MAKE YOUR GARDEN GREENER

If we were all able to start from scratch, making our gardens green would come naturally. That's not to say we would all have our own Garden of Eden. The pests would be a part of our plot because they have every bit as much right to a place on the planet as you or me. There would be plant disease, too, because that's part of the natural order also. But we wouldn't reach up for a bottle of something on the garden shed shelf the moment we spotted greenfly on the roses or caterpillars on the cabbages.

We should remember a cardinal rule of nature, that every pest has a predator. And when disease struck we would welcome the fact that some plants survived because the prospect would be that the survivors had gained a degree of immunity.

In practice, it is impossible to start from scratch, even with a new house and new garden on virgin soil. Put a fence or a wall around a piece of land and say 'This is my garden' and you have started to farm, to create order out of potential chaos. Anyone who has had to abandon their garden for a few weeks in summer will know exactly what is meant by chaos. It is astonishing how rapidly the jungle encroaches.

What can be done with a brand new garden, though, is to apply organic principles and practices from day one. Commercial growers who want to become organic to Soil Association standards often have a conversion period as long as two years, even longer if their land has had doses of the more persistent pesticides. It takes that long for the soil to be rid of the poisons. Providing the new garden is not a tangle of bramble, thistles, dockweed and couch grass, ridding it of weeds should not pose too serious a problem. The various options open to you are fully discussed on page 18.

There is no such thing as a safe weedkiller, in fact the herbicides are among the most dangerous chemicals in general use. However tempting it might be to kill the weeds chemically to make a clean start, avoid the temptation. If it kills the weeds, it will also kill many of the helpful organisms in the soil, the millions of minute creatures that give the soil its life and vitality, as well as the earthworms that are the organic gardener's best friends.

If you are taking over a sparkling new house with a garden to match, the chances are that it has topsoil imported from elsewhere or soil that has been bull-dozed into place. It may be weed-free; it may also be almost lifeless. Either way, the greening process begins with putting life into the soil, improving its fertility, encouraging it to become the life-support system for your organic crops, whether grass, flowers, fruit or vegetables. How you set about this is described in the next section.

If your land, instead of being pristine, is weed-infested, you can hire a cultivator with slasher blades that churn up the soil, a method that is relatively fast but should only be contemplated in late autumn or in the winter when the ground is free of frost and there is a minimum of weed growth. Even so, you'll almost certainly not get away with just one stint with the cultivator and, if there is a fair amount of couch grass, or twitch as some people call it, or those other pernicious horrors bindweed and ground elder, then rotavating is going to chop and spread the roots far and wide.

THE DANGERS OF BRACKEN

Bracken, one of the most invasive of plants, is also one of the most dangerous. It spreads both by rapidly growing rhizomes underground, and by the spores on the underside of the fretted leaves. The dust-fine spores are carcinogenic, while the fronds or immature leaves are poisonous to humans and to grazing animals. Although it provides cover for small mammals and some insects, its stems contain needle-like fibres which can tear the skin. In *Plant and Planet*, Anthony Huxley says of bracken, 'Horses which eat a few mouthfuls have their vitamin B destroyed and rapidly die. Cattle suffer something closely resembling radiation sickness and apparently linked with cancer: their bone marrow ceases to function, white blood cells cease to be produced and the blood is unable to clot; they die from internal bleeding, even weeping tears of blood. Sheep have their eyes severely damaged by what is called "bright blindness".'

At one time some of us reckoned bracken had its uses. Cut young, it could be composted or used as a mulch. Cut in July and burnt, the ash contains a good measure of potash. Now, I'm sure the only sensible thing is to eradicate it from cultivated land by a cut-and-burn operation, using the ash as a dressing for gooseberries and tomatoes.

By far the surest way of ridding the garden of perennial weeds is to dig them out, removing every tiny scrap of root or rhizome that, if left behind, will quickly become the outpost of another colony. Use a digging fork for this job so that you can lift and shake the weeds free of soil. Have a bucket or barrow with you and consign the contents to the dustbin or bonfire; don't add these perennial weeds to the compost bin because they have remarkable powers of recovery.

Be warned, however, that though digging will defeat even the most stubborn weeds, constant vigilance is required.

An alternative is to apply a dense mulch to the weed-infested area, utilising the theory that if you deny plants light and air they will die.

GARDEN TOOLS, GADGETS AND GIMMICKS

As with any other pastime, gardening is beset with gimmickry, and while some of the widely advertised gadgets are worth having, many are flash-in-the-pan products that are a waste of resources, energy and money. It isn't just the new gardeners who fall for these novelties. A neighbour of ours, common-sensical in every way, we thought, lashed out on a complicated cultivating tool, designed and made in the Far East, and claimed to be multi-purpose. As well as stirring the surface of the soil, its interlocking array of metal spikes were said to be capable of winkling out weeds and reducing lumps of soil to a fine tilth. In fact, on ground with any semblance of weed growth or modicum of stones and plant debris, the revolving spikes seized up and took an inordinate time to tease apart.

Some years ago I bought a little gadget to make seed sowing more precise. You filled the container with seed, set the aperture at what you considered to be appropriate and then allowed the seed to trickle into the already prepared drill. In theory it allowed the seed to escape at a steady rate, ensuring a thin, regular spacing. In practice, getting the right setting was easy enough for round seed like radish or cabbage, but very hit and miss with irregular-shaped seeds. A further complication was the frequent jamming of the exit. Freeing this meant taking off the container cover, a fiddly business that invariably scattered all the seeds.

Beware of the hi-tech products that are claimed to take all the guesswork out of gardening, particularly the electronic ones that tell you when your plants want watering, or predict the onset of a frost. They may do a lot to reduce the labour needs and mental input of commercial growers, but they don't add up to much in the average garden and can, indeed, diminish the enjoyment of gardening.

When to sow is an important factor in the successful germination of many seeds. The only sure way of knowing if the soil temperature is suitable is to use a soil thermometer

So, although the latest constant-reading digital thermometer, accurate to within a tenth of a Celsius degree, is probably the state of the art when it comes to measuring the heat at noon, I prefer my elderly, mercury-driven, maximum-minimum thermometer, even though it has to be reset every day. When it comes to testing the warmth of the soil, an essential operation prior to spring sowing, I wouldn't be without my soil thermometer, although there may still be some sturdy East Anglian characters who follow a regional practice of testing the warmth of the soil with their bare bottoms.

Another item I'd hate to be parted from is my seed organiser, a homemade contraption that consists of a long, narrow box with cardboard dividers and a hinged lid. Packets of seed are arranged in the box in alphabetical order as soon as they arrive from the seed firms. On the inside of the lid the seeds are

To simplify your sowing programme, make a seed organiser. Arrange the seed packets in alphabetical order, and on the inside of the lid list the seeds in order of sowing.

listed in approximate order of sowing, month by month. It's a neat way of keeping lots of seed packets tidy yet ready for use, although it would be helpful if all the seed firms stuck to the same size of packet.

When planning to buy new garden tools, here are a few points to bear in mind:

- Don't go for the bargain-priced stuff. Buy the best quality you can afford and ensure the tool is protected by a full manufacturer's guarantee.
- Stainless steel tools are the most expensive, but offer hard-wearing, long-life qualities that make them worth the additional cost. If you cannot afford stainless steel, choose a brand made from forged steel.
- Choose tools, especially a spade and fork, to suit your height and build. Heavy tools and light-weight people are not a happy mix. There are long-shaft spades and forks available, but don't buy until you have handled the tool to test it for weight and balance and compared it with others. Points to look for are a shaft that reaches well down into the socket without rough edges, and a strong, firmly-fitting handle, either strapped or T-bar, heavy-duty plastic or wooden.

- Choose a rake made from forged steel, with not more than twelve strong teeth and a length of handle that can be worked at a comfortable angle when you are standing upright. The same applies to hoes. Alternatively, choose a multi-purpose handle to which you connect a range of implements, buying them as the need arises.
- On an allotment or in a large vegetable garden you will need a spade, fork, rake or crome (see opposite), Dutch hoe and draw hoe, along with a wheelbarrow (preferably a builder's type with a wide body and pneumatic tyre), garden line for marking drills, hand fork and a good pocket knife. With a lawn and an ornamental garden you will need to add short-handled shears (maybe a long-handled pair for trimming the lawn edges), an edging tool, a spring-tined rake for removing thatch from the grass, a pair of good secateurs and, possibly, a pruning saw.
- Keep the receipt of any purchase you make and if you find a fault with the tool when you start to use it, take it back.
- Always clean your tools after use, scraping off soil and wiping off moisture. If they are going to be stored for some time – over the winter, for instance – clean and dry them thoroughly, then wipe over metal surfaces with an oily rag.

SNAGS WHEN YOU HIRE

Hiring DIY and garden equipment can be a convenient and economical way to tackle special jobs, such as rotavating, for example. But be sure to read the small print of the conditions of hire. If, for example, you finish the task quicker than you allowed for and let a friend or neighbour borrow the machine, you will be liable for any damage to the machine, or third party claim, even though you are not using it.

Buying secondhand Local auction rooms selling house contents can often produce excellent bargains in garden tools and equipment. They may well carry evidence of many years of hard use, with worn wooden handles and metal working ends honed to a fine finish, but in many respects they could still offer better value than their modern equivalents.

Look, for example, for sound galvanised metal watering cans, particularly the old-fashioned, long-spout, greenhouse type with a rim on the base that holds it off the ground. They are far heavier to hold than their modern plastic counterparts but will invariably outlive them.

The most successful garden tools are usually the most humble. Certainly that's true of the crome, a tool you won't find new in the garden centre, but might be able to snap up for next to nothing secondhand. Alternatively, if you know a black-smith, you can have an old garden fork converted to a crome by having the four prongs heated and bent at right angles to the handle which, in turn, is replaced by a length of ash shaft, so that it can be used like a rake.

might require spare parts. Too often the spares are no longer obtainable.

Secondhand timber and glass are potentially good buys, especially if you plan to make a cold frame and cloches, while used bricks are always useful for pathways, edging for deep beds (see page 97), for making a compost container, or a base for a green-house, or other DIY jobs in the garden.

Garden furniture Before forking out on bulky garden furniture and equipment, remember it will have to be stored somewhere for about six months of the year. If left outside during the winter months, wooden items can deteriorate quite rapidly, so if you haven't space in a shed, garage or cellar to store it, consider investing in units made of materials that are

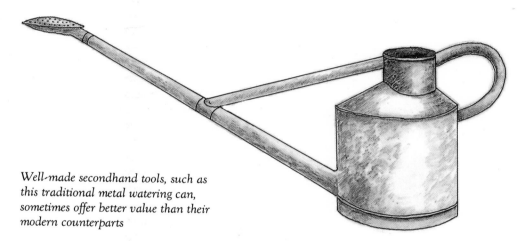

Well-made secondhand tools, such as this traditional metal watering can, sometimes offer better value than their modern counterparts

In practice, the crome is more useful than a rake. Pulled towards you, the tines will penetrate the soil a couple of inches to break up an overwintered pan or crust, and any stubborn lumps can be thwacked with the back of the crome. It can be used to tear out clumps of annual weeds, to spread manure and com-post, and to gather up leaves and other plant debris. It is a good tool for lightly stirring the soil in summer when rain and sun put a crust on the surface, and for lightly teasing in lime or organic fertiliser in early spring.

Other secondhand items worth watching for are clay pots and terracotta containers that are inordin-ately expensive when bought new, but are much more satisfactory in use than their plastic counter-parts. Don't be tempted to buy a secondhand green-house heater, lawnmower or flame gun, etc., which

durable enough to stand up to the worst winter weather.

If you choose teak, a wood famous for its strength and durability, ensure that it is made from sustainable plantation stock to protect the local ecology. Look for the Good Wood Seal of Approval awarded by Friends of the Earth. Alternatively, you could choose traditional cast-iron units, although these are usually very expensive, or cast aluminium. Even so, storage space in a damp-free place will have to be found for the cushions and hammocks. Heavy-duty plastic covers are available for covering the seats, sunloungers and benches, but in my experi-ence they tend to encourage a build-up of mould. Many of the products sold at ironmongers and gar-den centres to clean garden furniture and barbecues are drastically caustic.

WEED CONTROL WITHOUT CHEMICALS

There isn't an organic alternative to chemical weedkilling that is so quickly and dramatically effective. What the green gardener will do is to use one or more of these safer techniques.

Hand-weeding This is the method used since man started to cultivate crops. On land that has deep-rooted perennial weeds, hand-weeding can be a daunting task because you've got to dig deep and remove all trace of the plant. But it works and, in time, even the most stubborn weeds, such as couch grass, ground elder and horsetail, give up the ghost.

For clearing ground of perennial weeds you need a digging fork. This is a vital tool in the garden, so buy the best you can afford, preferably a stainless steel one. You need also a bucket or barrow to put the weeds in and a bonfire or dustbin bag to dispose of them because perennial weeds, particularly if they have seeded and have their roots intact, are not suitable material for recycling through the compost-making operation.

Later, when all the perennial weeds have been ousted, hand-weeding becomes far less of a chore as it involves removing the annual weeds before they take over too much space in the lawn, flower garden or vegetable patch. They can be pulled out by hand, or with a small hand fork or special lawn-weeding tool. I like weeding because it is a good reason to get down on hands and knees for the intimate contact with your plants and the soil that enables you to spot problems before they become critical. In the vegetable garden or allotment you can hand-weed and thin seedlings at the same time, adding the material you take out to the compost bin.

In an established garden, weeds have to be kept in check or they will compete with the plants you are raising for pleasure or for food, and, by their very nature, in a fight for space the weeds would invariably win. But not all weeds are unwanted in the organic garden. Some that are attractive to bees, butterflies, hoverflies, lacewings and other beneficial insects should be made welcome, if space allows, in a part of the garden set aside for the purpose (see page 65).

Mulching The theory behind this weed-control technique is that if you deny a plant light and air,

then, even though the seed germinates, it cannot survive. But the right choice of mulching material is crucial to success. My friend Bob Flowerdew, a professional gardener, took over what was a meadow and converted it into a high-output, low-maintenance organic garden of one-and-a-bit acres, and the conversion was done entirely with carpeting.

'Most people throw away their old carpets. I used them in the garden to rid it of weeds and improve the soil texture at the same time. I advertised for good, old-fashioned wool or cotton carpets and the response was amazing. The beauty about them is that they rot down after about a year and become humus.

'As well as excluding the light for weed control, the carpet offers ideal conditions for the earthworms. They can work right to the surface, safe from the birds and other predators.'

When the perennial weeds had been eliminated by the mulch the next stage was to plant crops through slits in the carpet.

If you are sensitive about the appearance of your garden, carpet mulching may not be for you. There are alternatives. Mulching with peat or forest bark not only successfully suppresses weeds, it also produces an attractive decorative finish for ornamental beds and borders. Both these materials are organic, although peat is non-renewable, and will eventually add humus to the soil.

Using these organic materials as a layer about 5cm (2in) deep on the flower beds, and around shrubs and trees, weed growth is checked, moisture is retained and the soil underneath the mulch becomes highly desirable to the earthworm population. In time, the earthworms will take the mulch into the soil, so an annual topping up is necessary, and a check should be kept on the pH level of the soil under the mulch as it may slowly become more acidic.

Forest bark is a relatively new garden material. It is produced from the bark removed from coniferous logs, and the Forestry Commission seems to have an inexhaustible supply. The bark is processed and composted without the use of chemicals, and this controls the pH and removes the phytotoxic substances. It is sold as a straight material for mulching, usually in a coarse grade, while finer grades can be used to mix with peat or loam to make a compost for potting or for DIY growing bags (see page 51).

Mulching is an excellent way of controlling weeds, conserving moisture and improving soil structure. Mulch with a thick layer of straw or bark (top left); old carpet squares (top right); a proprietary mulching sheet (bottom left) or thick layers of newsprint with an overlay of straw, bark or gravel (bottom right)

MULCHING GUIDELINES

- Whatever material is used for mulching, first clear the land of deep-rooted perennial weeds, such as horsetail, bindweed, docks, thistles and nettles. With carpet mulching, cutting off the top growth is usually sufficient.
- The mulch should be thick enough to deny light and air to the weeds.
- Wait for the soil to warm up before applying the mulch – it must also be moist.
- Organic mulches, such as straw, newspaper, peat and bark, are gradually incorporated into the soil by earthworms, so remember that an annual topping up is necessary.
- In the winter, draw the mulch away from the soft fruit canes and bushes to allow the birds to deal with pupating pests.
- Every other year check the pH level of the soil under the mulch. If it has become over-acidic (see page 33) remove the mulch temporarily and hoe in a dressing of calcified seaweed, dolomitic limestone or hydrated lime, then restore the mulch.
- Couch grass in pathways will penetrate into a mulched area. Better to use paving slabs or bricks next to permanent mulches.

GRASS CUTTINGS AS MULCHES

Grass mowings can be used as a mulch for weed control in, for example, the currant and raspberry areas, but you'll need a layer about 15cm (6in) thick to be effective against annual weeds. It would be ineffective against perennial weeds.

In the vegetable garden, there's a wider range of mulching materials, some of which would be less visually acceptable in the flower garden. Straw, newsprint, used peat from growing-bags, grass cuttings, leafmould, cardboard and brown paper, proprietary material such as Hortopaper or Plantex, black plastic sheeting, old carpets and rugs, and the end product from an electric shredder can all be used for weed control and moisture retention.

Between rows of raspberries you could use thick layers of newspaper overlaid with straw to check not only the weeds but also the suckers that spring up away from the parent canes.

Homemade compost can also be used as a mulch, of course, but as there is seldom enough of this marvellous material to spare for large-scale application, it generally has to be reserved for incorporation into the soil at sowing and planting times.

One of the newer techniques gaining favour with organic growers and gardeners is the floating mulch of a polypropylene fleece such as Agryl P17, which is a fine way of giving crops protection from the weather, birds and insect pests, but quite useless for weed control.

When the green garden is in full production with, maybe, deep beds for many of the vegetable crops, organic mulches become an important element in maintaining and improving soil fertility.

Flame gunning Purists argue that this is not an entirely agreeable method of weed control, using paraffin or bottled gas to burn off the top growth of the weeds and any weed seeds that have settled on the surface of the soil. However, used correctly, it is fast and efficient and does no harm to the soil or its residents. On our three-acre smallholding, a wheeled and hooded flame gun was an invaluable aid in establishing a weed-free (or stale) seedbed in early spring, and again for tidying up after harvesting the crops in late autumn. Now, my smaller, hand-held Sheen X300 flame gun is put to good use in the much smaller vegetable patch, and to keep the weeds under control on our paved pathways, the patio and driveway.

The trick with flame gunning is not to try to burn off the weeds in one sweep: use it in two stages. The first involves using the gun like a scythe, walking slowly forward and covering a strip about 2m (6ft) wide and holding the gun so that the almost invisible flame is no more than 15cm (6in) long. The intense heat causes the plant cells to collapse, and after an hour or so the weeds will have withered. Leave for another couple of hours, or even overnight providing rain isn't forecast, then make a second swift pass with the gun.

Hoeing This is a weed control operation mostly confined to the vegetable department or shrubbery in spring and summer, preferably during a dry spell. There are several types of hoe, but only one effective way of hoeing, and that is to sever the weed's top growth from its root system at a point just below the surface of the soil.

The hoe is a long-handled tool, so you stand upright and either push or pull it, although some types of hoe are easier to manage than others. My armoury of garden tools has four hoes. The **Dutch hoe** is pushed through the soil and therefore requires more effort for a less precise effect than the **draw hoe**, which you pull towards you, and which is the quickest way of earthing up potatoes. In fact, I never use the draw hoe for weeding because it drags the weeds from the soil, leaving them intact on the surface. Overnight rain will mean that the time you spent weeding was wasted because the weeds get an anchorage in the soil thanks to the rain.

The **onion hoe** is a little beauty, probably more than a hundred years old because it has been passed down the line in our gardening family and now has a tiny blade, honed to a very sharp edge, that can work close to rows of vegetables with the precision of a surgeon's scalpel.

My favourite, though, is the **Wilkinson swoe**, an ugly name for a fine tool. It has a working end that looks like a golf putter and, once mastered, is a joy to use, requiring very little effort for maximum effect. A big advantage of both the onion hoe and the swoe is that you walk backwards, leaving the soil neatly disturbed, and the weeds on the surface.

For the bigger vegetable garden or allotment there are wheeled hoes, such as the Jalo, which you push and which have adjustable blades set behind the single wheel. There are also powered hoes, specially designed for weeding large areas, such as the Roselea power hoe, and cultivators with hoeing attachments. As with everything in life, 'you gets what you pays for', so if your garden is small, your overdraft large and your willingness to hand-weed weak, small, electrically-powered cultivators are worth investigating. They are more environmentally

FLAME GUN SAFETY TIPS

When used correctly the flame gun is a fast, efficient and environmentally acceptable way of controlling weeds, especially on paved areas.

Follow these safety rules when using a flame gun:

- Avoid windy days. If the flame blows out, relighting can be a bit tricky.
- Do not allow children or animals near you while using the gun.
- Wear shoes, not sandals.
- Use only paraffin as fuel and keep it stored, clearly marked, in an outhouse, safe from children.
- If the flame goes out before the fuel tank is empty, close the control valve and relight with care. Have a spill of paper, matches or a lighter handy.

Whatever the type of hoe used for weed control, it is vital to sever the weed from its root system

bright golden flowers and prominent deep yellow stamens, is reckoned to be the more showy of the two. The flowers appear in early summer and, in full sun, attract butterflies, hoverflies and bees. One disadvantage is that the plants can become too fiercely possessive of ground space because the root system will work its way into every nook and cranny, and even make life-threatening demands on established trees and shrubs. So don't make rose of Sharon share a bed. You can grow the plants from seed or buy young ones from a nursery, spacing them about 45–60cm (15–24in) apart each way.

Established plants can be lifted and divided in autumn and spring, and growth should be trimmed back in March or April, with a further trimming if the growth becomes too rampant in late autumn.

Periwinkles are also difficult to control because they produce long trailing stems that can quickly find their way off limits, smothering the weeds in their progress and any less vigorous ornamental plants as well. *Vinca major*, the greater periwinkle, has purplish-blue, busy lizzie-like flowers in late April, with repeat flowering through to autumn. They look very attractive against the low-growing, glossy green leaves.

V. minor, the lesser periwinkle or trailing myrtle, is considered to be more hardy than the greater one and is available in several varieties, with white, double white, deep purple and sky-blue flowers, rather smaller than *V. major*.

The periwinkles are unfussy about soil or site, doing well in full sun or semi-shade. They give a very superior account of themselves at my home on the east coast, within yards of the salt-laden sea. The trailing stems root as they touch the soil and then throw up short vertical stems carrying the flowers. *V. major* establishes itself quite rapidly from nursery-raised stock, but *V. minor* may take up to three years before becoming an effective ground cover. To encourage bushy growth, trim back some of the trailing stems in April and May.

Ground cover roses have become popular in recent years. They are less vigorous than the periwinkles, and have resisted all my attempts to get a bed of them established among hybrid tea bushes. It

OK than the heavier, more powerful, petrol-engined jobs, being quieter, cleaner and cheaper to run. But they are lightweight both in poundage and in their ability to eradicate weeds.

Lightest of all is the Green Machine, which weighs 4kg (9lb), is electrically powered, yet does quite a respectable job of weeding land that is reasonably free of stones, bulky debris and deep-rooted weeds. A petrol-powered version is also available and both machines have attachments for lawn edging, trimming long grass and snow throwing.

Ground cover plants In the ornamental garden, you can use plants to smother weed growth, although you will first have to keep the area weed free until the ground cover plants have become firmly established.

Two fast-growing weed-smotherers that thrive virtually anywhere are rose of Sharon (*Hypericum calycinum*) and periwinkle in either its *Vinca major* or *Vinca minor* form. Both are evergreens with attractive flowers, although *H. calycinum*, with

*You can smother weeds with ground cover plants in the ornamental garden. Two vigorous, attractive subjects are the blue-flowered periwinkle (*Vinca major*), and the golden rose of Sharon (*Hypericum calycinum*)*

could be the occasional dosing with North Sea spray that makes them rather shy; normally they are quite happy even in poor soil.

As well as offering good opposition to weeds, these miniature prostrate roses will stop marauding moggies in their tracks since they are covered in wicked thorns. A good variety is the pale-pink Nozomi, which grows to about 45cm (18in) tall with a spread of up to 1.8m (6ft). It should be planted 60cm (2ft) apart each way. Other good varieties are Hansa, a reddish-violet double; the pink double Pheasant; and White Meidiland, a lovely white double.

POISONOUS BONFIRES

A garden bonfire burning weeds, leaves and vegetable waste produces smoke containing 350 times more cancer-producing benzopyrenes than cigarette smoke. That's not only dangerous to you and your neighbours, it's highly wasteful as well. Organic material should not be burned, it should be composted to return plant food and humus to the soil.

Scrap wood that has been treated with a wood preservative should be put in a public refuse tip, not burned on a bonfire. According to the Consumer Association, many commercially preserved woods are treated with a mixture containing arsenic compounds, which are released into the air when burned. Even the ash could be contaminated.

Pentachlorophenol is a common constituent of DIY wood preservatives, but timber treated with these can give off dioxins when burned. Woodsmoke itself is carcinogenic, add dioxin and you have a very unhealthy mix. In Sweden it has been illegal since 1978 to burn wood that has been treated with these preservatives because of the health risk.

Annual burning of the garden's pampas grass (*Cortaderia selloana*) was a way of ridding the clump of old growth. The smoke is both anti-social and carcinogenic, as well as a potential fire hazard in an enclosed space. Cutting back the growth to within about 30cm (12in) of the soil is far better for the environment and for the plant. Wear strong gloves when doing the job or you'll get badly scratched hands and wrists. The best time to do the cutting down is in early winter, after you have taken off the seed heads for a winter decoration indoors.

GUARD AGAINST LOCKJAW

Tetanus, or lockjaw, is a dangerous, sometimes fatal, disease. The tetanus spores live in the soil and can enter the human body through scratches or cuts, so gardeners are especially vulnerable. You can protect yourself by immunisation. It's a free service available from your doctor. One injection will give protection for at least five years, when you can have a booster.

Ground cover roses are planted from late autumn to early spring and should be given a good start in compost, enriched with some bone meal, in the planting hole. Aftercare consists of cutting out dead or disused branches and trimming back when growth looks like getting out of bounds.

Shady, damp parts of the garden often prove tricky to manage because, while discouraging herbaceous plants and annuals, they offer a refuge to all manner of weeds. Happily, damp shade or semi-shade suits the Epimediums, or barrenworts, extremely well and, although the flowers are nothing to write home about, the heart-shaped leaves that turn from bright green to bronze and red in autumn are very attractive.

Epimediums cover the ground quickly, even under the shade of trees and shrubs. You can help them along by giving the young plants a good mulch of compost, peat, leafmould or composted bark. Buy young plants in autumn and winter and propagate by division in the spring, allowing about 30cm (12in) between plants.

Another ground cover plant with similar shaped leaves is the dead nettle (*Lamium maculatum*), a member of the mint family, with a reputation for being particularly invasive. It isn't a subject that you plant and forget because it will make take-over forays into virtually any part of the garden, whether sunny or shady, dry soil or moist. Established plants will even climb round the stems of shrubs and trees, but are easily restrained by simply pulling unwanted bits off by hand. In June or July, when the deep-pink hooded flowers have finished, you can clip the plants with shears to encourage bushiness.

Easily the best dead nettle for ground cover work is Beacon Silver, which has shiny silver leaves edged with green. Buy and plant stock during late autumn or early winter, setting the plants 30cm (12in) apart each way. Increase your stock by division and replanting in late autumn.

Wild flower expert John Stevens recommends ground-ivy (*Glechoma hederacea*) as a good ground cover plant for a semi-shaded part of the garden. The plants are easily raised from seed sown in trays in spring or autumn and the seedlings are planted out when they are large enough to handle. The evergreen leaves are dainty and kidney-shaped on stems that hug the ground. Small, mauve, lavender-like flowers appear in spring and early summer and the leaves release a strong minty scent when crushed. John says that a tea made from the leaves is an old remedy for relieving coughs.

PLANT A HEDGE FOR WILDLIFE

If you are planning a new garden, or altering an existing one, try to make room for a hedge, particularly one that will be a haven for birds and other wildlife. You will not only help to fill the enormous gap created by the wholesale destruction of rural hedgerows by farmers and landowners, you will also enjoy, more vividly, the changing seasons as marked by the changes in the shrubs that form the hedge: the glistening red berries of dog rose, hawthorn and holly in autumn and winter; the fire-red bark of the dogwood; the bloomed beauty of the blue blackthorn fruit; the constantly changing palette of greens, gold, red and brown of the foliage.

Choose your hedging material carefully, taking into account the speed of growth, the height you want it to grow to, its function as a boundary marker or as a dividing line between parts of the garden, the

A DISAPPEARING CRAFT

Hedge-laying was the traditional way of producing a thick, stock-proof barrier. It took time, was labour-intensive and required the skill of a country craftsman, but the result was perfectly suited to traditional farming. Now hedge-laying is seldom seen. What hedges remain are slashed once or twice a year with a tractor-driven flail cutter. It's a quick one-man operation, and the result defies description.

For a laid hedge, different species were allowed to grow to become the main stems, called pleachers. In winter, the pleachers were cut partly through at an angle and then bent back into the hedge. They were woven through stakes driven at about 2m (6ft) intervals in the hedge, and secured by hazel or willow branches, called hedders.

The height and thickness of the hedge not only prevented sheep, cattle and horses from straying but also gave them shelter from strong winds, driving rain and snow. It was home to a rich diversity of wildlife.

species most suitable for your location, and the ease or otherwise of maintenance once the hedge is fully grown. The Leyland cypress conifer is widely used for hedging because it is quick growing in almost any type of soil, and gives a dense evergreen screen. Unfortunately, it doesn't offer much of a habitat to wildlife, although some birds will roost and nest in a mature conifer hedge.

Better by far to choose your hedging material from native species of shrubs, such as beech, hawthorn, hazel, field maple, alder, buckthorn, guelder rose, hornbeam, dogwood, dog rose and holly. They offer visual interest all year round, safe roosting and nesting (and some food) for a wide variety of birds, and will also attract bees, hoverflies, butterflies and other insects that feed on pollen and nectar.

Planting and aftercare Autumn is the best time for planting a hedge. The ground is still warm from the summer, and a warm soil is far more likely to encourage the production of a good root system. This process of root development is further helped by the shedding of leaves in autumn. Scientists at the Institute of Horticultural Research at East Malling, in Kent, found that fruit trees continued their root growth long after the leaves had fallen.

To create a dense hedge you will need to allow for about nine plants per metre/yard in a staggered row about 30cm (12in) wide. Place your order for bare-rooted young plants with a local nursery well in advance, and stagger the delivery if you have a fair stretch of hedge planned. You can carry on planting right up to the time the soil becomes gripped in hard frost. Mix the species in clumps of, say, three or four of the same kind rather than mixing single specimens.

The planting trench should be prepared with as much care as the planting hole of an individual shrub. This means taking out soil deep enough and wide enough to give the roots adequate room, adding plenty of organic matter, such as compost, well-rotted farmyard manure and leafmould, to the soil as you return it to the trench, along with about 450g (1lb) of bone meal per metre/yard run of trench. The soil should be moist but not saturated, and each plant should have its roots spread out and placed at a depth so that the soil mark on the stem will be level with the surface of the trench. Gently firm the soil around the roots as you plant, then thoroughly firm it after planting.

To create a strong hedge allow for nine plants to each metre/yard run, with the plants in a staggered row

Some nurseries will provide plants that have already been pruned. If not, you will have to cut them back immediately after planting. Beech, hazel and hornbeam are cut back by about a third of their growth, blackthorn and hawthorn are cut back to about 15cm (6in) from the ground, while conifers or evergreens simply have any straggly shoots trimmed.

After planting, if you can provide some protection from harsh northerly and easterly winds, all the better. A screen of polythene sheeting or plastic windbreak netting attached to canes will help the young plants to pull through the rigours of winter.

Buddleia in bloom attracts butterflies
to the garden, and carefully chosen
hedging material will prove a magnet
to friendly insects as well as a haven
for birds

HEDGE SENSE

The green gardener chooses hedge plants with extra care so as not to offer likely pests attractive quarters to spend the winter. The vapourer moth, for example, is fond of hawthorn hedges, and its caterpillar, one of the most commonly encountered in cities as well as rural areas, has a fearsome appetite for such garden shrubs as pyracantha. If you plan to grow apples and pears, don't have crab apples in your hedge, and avoid hawthorn because this could introduce fireblight.

Natural history expert Michael Chinery offers this advice to those planning a garden: 'Retain all hedges as living reservoirs of birds and ladybirds, and don't plant all your cabbages in one patch. It has been shown on several occasions that gardens with plenty of diversity yield far more than one-crop gardens.'

THE UNFRIENDLY WALNUT

A walnut tree in the garden is not good news to neighbouring plants. The reason is the walnut leaves contain the chemical juglone which, when it enters the soil, can have a toxic effect on plants. Some people reckon privet has the same effect because few plants flourish in the company of privet. However, privet doesn't exude any toxic substance. What it does is to poach the soil of moisture and nutrients to such an extent that there's little left for its neighbours.

In spring, when the ground is moist and warm, give the plants a mulch of compost, bark or peat to conserve moisture and discourage weeds. If rabbits are a problem, this is the time to give protection with, say, a Somerford sleeve for each plant.

You must give your hedge plants as much aftercare as you would any other plants in your garden. So in dry spells they will need watering, and after hard frost each plant should be checked to ensure that the frost hasn't lifted and loosened it. With a formal hedge of box or privet, maintenance consists of a twice-yearly clipping with the shears or electric hedge trimmer. Avoid doing this when there may be nesting birds in residence; wait until the end of May for the spring clip and late August or early September for clipping before winter.

Our wildlife hedge needs only one clip during the year, preferably after the flowering species have bloomed. The object is to cut out any dead or damaged branches, using secateurs or pruning saw, and to guide the plants to a shape that is slightly broader at the base than at the top. Remove all the prunings and put them through a shredder, if you have one, but in the autumn allow fallen leaves from the hedge to remain at the foot to give shelter to hedgehogs, voles, frogs and toads.

During the first three years of its life the hedge will need to be kept free of weeds and grass by hand-weeding and mulching. Not all the plants will grow at the same speed and any that romp ahead of the others should be cut back severely in the winter. After about four years your hedge should have grown about 1.2m (4ft) tall and have a good bushy base. You can now allow grasses and wild flowers to set up home at the foot of the hedge. The final height of the hedge is up to you, but a good height for the species mentioned is 1.5–1.8m (5–6ft).

KEEPING THE
GARDEN FERTILE

Giving up Growmore and the other man-made fertilisers will not result in an alarming decline in the quality and yield of crops. Man has been growing food crops, as farmer or gardener, for thousands of years and for only a tiny fraction of that time has he been using artificial fertilisers. It's a period that coincides with the worst pollution the world has endured.

The soil contains a vast reserve of all the nutrients needed to sustain human life: it is the Earth's most precious resource. We, as short-haul passengers on our planet's journey through space, cannot survive without a living soil, yet the experience of the past fifty years or so suggests that is precisely what we are attempting.

It was always considered to be good farming practice to husband resources, in other words to achieve a balance between what you give to the soil and what you borrow by cropping. It meant handing over your particular piece of land, whether farm or garden or allotment, in better heart than when you took it on.

But because of man's greed, the compulsion to exploit the soil for bigger and bigger yields, to take out those millions of years of investment in natural nutrients faster than nature can replace them, we are bankrupting the soil. In a natural ecosystem, such as a forest or permanent meadow, the cycle of fertility is maintained by the trees or plants taking the nutrients they need from the soil, and then returning them as dead plant material, with the help of living organisms that decompose plant litter so that its nutrients can be taken up again by plant life. But we, as farmers and gardeners, interrupt that natural cycle because we harvest the crops. Until the arrival of chemical fertilisers in comparatively recent times, soil fertility was maintained by animal manures in the mixed farming system, and they provided not only the nutrients but also a humus-rich environment. Parts of farmed land were allowed to lie fallow, enabling the earthworm population, and the countless millions of soil bacteria, to do their invaluable work of restoring the soil structure after cropping. Now intensive farming of arable crops is producing a soil condition that is almost lifeless and totally reliant on large inputs of nitrogenous fertilisers to sustain plant growth, supported by a regime of pesticide sprays that actually destroys vast numbers of the bacteria that live in the soil and decimates the earthworm population. In his customary forthright way, David Bellamy, in Stephen Nortcliff's book, *Down to Earth*, gives this warning:

Every minute the world loses 150 acres of forest, and with the trees go much of the soils, washed away to choke and clog rivers and estuaries with mineral salt. Today soil erosion and degradation is more widespread than ever. More than one-third of the Earth's arable land is at risk of becoming a desert because of human misuse of soil.

All this adds up to the appalling statistic that on average every acre of the world's surface loses eight tons of soil per year, while the maximum rate of soil formation is only five tons per acre per year. This is crass stupidity, international vandalism, 'resourcicide', call it what you will, and it cannot be allowed to go on.

The stock reply is that modern farming practices have evolved to meet a demand from a rapidly rising population for cheap food. If that is true, why is more than half of mankind teetering on the verge of starvation, while the favoured nations of the western world are overfed with junk food, over-taxed to keep mountains of basic foods in store, and unable to prevent the slow death of our living soil?

Happily, there are signs that the ultimate

stupidity will be halted as the green movement gains momentum. Green gardening is a practical way of demonstrating that there is an alternative to the 'crass stupidity' of soil vandalism. A tiny back garden that is run on organic lines might seem a pathetically small contribution to make to protect the Earth's most precious resource, but in Britain alone, if you add all those little plots together, you have more than a million acres, and that could become a very big factor in our survival.

It isn't easy for an arable farmer, dependent on his soil for a living, to switch from chemical dependence to organic farming. For the gardener it's a piece of cake, unless one has been so beguiled by the chemical companies' advertisements that running a garden without the help of their latest pesticide brew would seem suicidal. We do spend many millions of pounds every year on insecticides, herbicides and fungicides in our gardens, and most of it is money that could be better spent on other things.

SOIL TYPES

The first piece of information we need is the current nature of our garden soil: its texture, its free-draining or water-holding capacity, its acidity or pH level, its earthworm population.

All soils consist of mineral particles derived from the weathering of rocks, with the addition of water, air and organic materials in varying proportions, and it is the mineral content that is the key to whether a soil is light and open or close, wet and sticky. Most soils fall somewhere in between these extremes, but generally speaking the larger the mineral particles, the more open or sandy it is, while the finer the particles the more they cling together and the nearer to clay the soil becomes.

You can judge the clay content of your soil by making a simple test. Take a handful, moisten it and knead it to break up any lumps. Does it feel gritty and is it impossible to roll into a ball? If yes, then you have a **sandy** soil. If it can be made to form a ball, your soil is a **loamy sand** or a **sandy loam** and the difference isn't important. If the soil doesn't feel gritty but can be formed into a ball that easily breaks, it is a **silt loam** with more clay than sand.

The heavier or more clayey the soil becomes, the more the sample resembles dough or Plasticine. Clay is said to be a slow soil, difficult or impossible to work in winter and slow to respond to the warmer days of spring. In the hot, dry days of summer it can dry out, crack, and set in solid lumps, while if it becomes saturated with floodwater the air is driven out, and that is certain death to both plants and the living organisms in the soil. No wonder that heavy clay soil is heartily disliked by growers and gardeners. But it isn't entirely negative.

The good news is that clay soils are generally richer in plant foods than the lighter ones, they are slower to dry out during periods of drought, and they respond well to treatment with organic material to make them more open-textured. However, they do need regular dressings of calcified seaweed, dolomitic limestone or hydrated lime to maintain a pH value that is not over-acidic. Heavy soil also needs to be turned over in early winter so that frost, rain and snow can help to break down the clay lumps and make them more workable when the time comes to prepare a tilth for sowing and planting.

At the other end of the soil texture scale is the sandy soil, often called early but hungry. It's early because it can be worked on at any time and quickly warms up in the spring. It's hungry because these very light soils are usually poorly endowed with plant nutrients, especially potash. Another snag is that in dry spells they quickly lose moisture. The addition of large quantities of organic matter does wonders for light soils, improving texture so that there is greater water retention, and putting more food into the bank for use by the plants over a longer period. But it can be a long, hard slog, and all the time a watch must be kept on the pH level, because these light soils, too, are often quite acid.

WEEDS TELL THE STORY

When you take over a neglected garden or allotment, you can get some idea of the condition of the soil by looking at the weeds. Dock, thistle, daisy, plantain and creeping buttercup like acid soils, while clover and campion flourish on alkaline soils. Red campion, fat hen, nettles, chickweed and groundsel indicate a well-balanced soil that is neither too acidic nor too alkaline. Sedges can indicate patches of poor drainage, as does surface water with moss or slime.

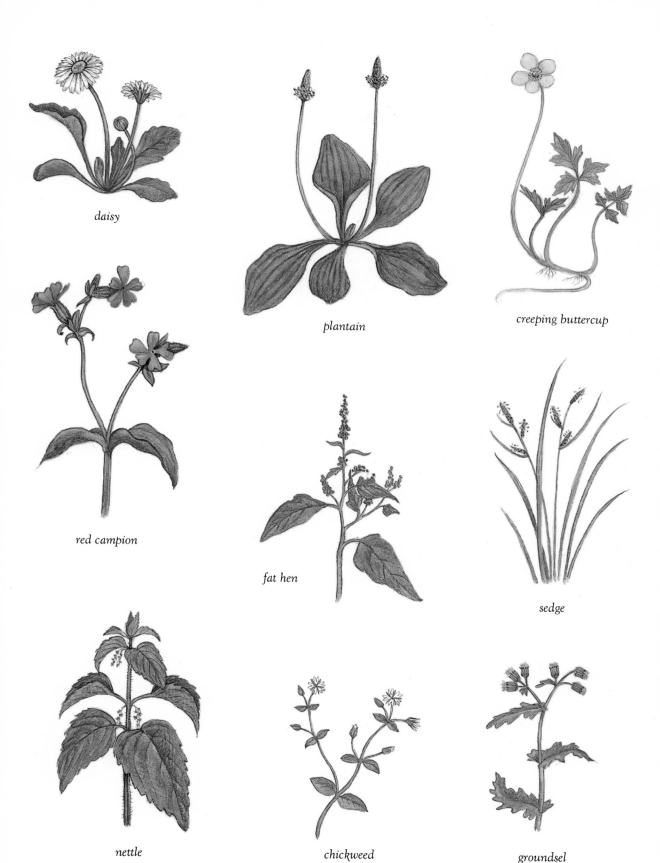

daisy

plantain

creeping buttercup

red campion

fat hen

sedge

nettle

chickweed

groundsel

In between the clay and the sand are the loamy soils, and a deep loam is every gardener's dream of a good working and growing medium. Loam is a blend of sand and clay with a crumbly texture that doesn't bind readily, that holds moisture well yet drains freely, is reasonably well supplied with plant foods and is easy to work at all times except when gripped by hard frost. To maintain an acceptable pH level in a good loam all that is required is a dressing every third year or so of calcified seaweed or lime, although a check should be made every year, because if loam is given large dressings of manure it can become over-acidic.

Humus The thing that readily differentiates loam from the extremes of sand and clay is its humus content. Humus is a truly wonderful material. It makes both sands and clays more crumbly and gives body to unstable soils where there is wind erosion or high rainfall. It holds nutrients and moisture in the soil, like water in a sponge, at a level where they can most readily be used by the plants, and helps them to develop a strong, searching root system which gives them both vigour and anchorage against wind rock.

Humus is an important factor in building a thriving earthworm community. Given the right organic conditions, there can be as many as eight million earthworms to the acre, and their contribution to soil fertility is impossible to over-estimate. Each worm can ingest about 4.5kg (10lb) of soil a year, and in the process produce worm casts that contain five times more nitrogen, seven times more available phosphates, eleven times more potash and forty times more humus than is found in the top 15cm (6in) of soil in which the worms are living. The use of chemical fertilisers, fungicides, pesticides and herbicides, on the scale we have today, reduces the earthworm population and so alters the soil structure that there is serious subsoil panning on heavy soils, and loss of topsoil through wind erosion and heavy rain, particularly on light soils.

The great thing about improving the humus content of your soil is that it doesn't have to be a back-breaking business of digging and turning in barrow-loads of farmyard manure. You can add organic matter to the surface and let the worms do the rest. They will take in the compost, leafmould, manure or whatever as part of their internal ploughing operation, and this willingness to co-operate with the green gardener can be put to very profitable use in the deep-bed, no-dig technique fully described on pages 97–104.

MANURES AND ORGANIC FERTILISERS

Making as much compost as possible makes sound sense for today's gardeners, not only to help to keep the soil's bank of nutrients in stock, but also to go on improving its structure. Pages 40–5 describe how to turn garden and kitchen waste into good, balanced plant food, but not all of us have the facility to make compost, and few can produce enough homemade compost to meet all our expectations. We do, after all, drive our gardens pretty hard, making the soil work overtime by almost non-stop cropping of plants, both edible and ornamental.

Fortunately, there are some sound organic answers to the problem of maintaining soil fertility. You can buy a load, or part-load, of horse or pig manure, or collect bags of spent mushroom compost from your nearest mushroom farm. If you live near the coast, you should be able to reap a rich harvest of seaweed at certain times of the year.

You can even grow your own manure by sowing a green manure crop whenever a piece of the garden becomes vacant, or you can simply buy a bag of composted animal manure, or composted straw and sewage sludge, or worm-worked compost, all now widely available as proprietary brands at garden centres.

If your soil is a good medium loam, easily worked with good water retention and a crumbly texture, you are indeed fortunate. Annual additions of manure aren't needed; just add the compost from the heap or bin with, maybe, a balanced organic fertiliser applied to the cropping area in early spring. If your soil is sandy it will need plentiful amounts of bulky organic matter, while heavy, clay soils will also benefit from regular dressing with organic material to open out the texture.

Manures are the best bulky products for improving soil structure, aiding better water retention and holding plant foods and trace elements at the right level for crops of all kinds. Compost, whether made in the garden or bought in bags, has the same benefits as manure for providing nutrients, both major and minor, although rather lower in humus content. For concentrated plant foods the inorganic gardener uses chemical fertilisers, such as

ACID OR ALKALINE

Mention has already been made of the need to know whether your soil is acid or alkaline, because this is an important factor in soil fertility. The measurement is made on a pH scale, pH being the abbreviation for the hydrogen ion concentration. Neutral on this scale is 7.0. A soil is slightly acid if the pH reading is 6.1 to 6.5; medium acid if the reading is 5.6 to 6.0; strongly acid from 5.1 to 5.5; extremely acid below 4.5. When the pH reading rises from 7.5 to 8.0 the soil is moderately alkaline; 8.1 to 9.0 it is strongly alkaline; 9.1 and above it is extremely alkaline.

Most soils in western Europe tend to be acidic rather than alkaline and, fortunately, most plants prefer a slightly acid soil of 6.0 to 7.0. If the soil becomes too acid, at pH 5.0 and below, key nutrients, particularly the phosphates, become locked up in the soil, and minor ones, such as magnesium and calcium, can be washed out of the soil. When the soil becomes alkaline, at 7.5 and above, essential plant foods are locked up and the crops show signs of chlorosis or other mineral deficiencies.

A complication today is acid rain, which adds to the natural acidity. So it is important to keep tabs on the pH value of your soil. Inexpensive chemical testing kits, such as the Rapitest, are widely available and give an approximate reading, but a more accurate value is given with an electronic meter. They are good value for money and should last a lifetime.

Changing the pH if your soil is rather acid is far easier than trying to correct an over-alkaline soil. Regular dressings of compost or farmyard manure usually keep the pH reading in the desired region for most plants of 5.6 to 6.5, although the vegetable plot in particular might need minor adjustment every third year or so. To do this you use hydrated lime, dolomitic limestone or calcified seaweed.

My choice is calcified seaweed, applied every three years at the rate of 113g (4oz) to the sq m/yd, although double this amount would be needed if the pH value of the soil dropped below 5.6. As well as providing calcium in slow-release form, calcified seaweed gives other benefits. It improves soil structure, particularly in heavy soils. It contains 46 per cent calcium oxide, 4.8 per cent magnesium oxide, sulphur, copper, zinc, iodine and cobalt, plus about 20 trace elements, all of which are important in determining the health and vigour of organically grown plants.

Calcified seaweed, ground limestone or ordinary chalk can be applied before planting or sowing a crop, but hydrated lime is best applied in late winter and lightly raked into the surface. It should not be applied at the same time as farmyard manure. More lime is needed to raise the pH level to 6.5 on clay soils than on sandy ones, as you can see from the table.

In the flower garden some plants, notably rhododendrons and azaleas, are lime-haters and must have an acid soil or the leaves turn yellow and the plant eventually dies. If you decide to grow any of these lime-haters, you should either have them as container plants growing in ericaceous compost, or reserve a site when you can adjust the pH reading of the soil to 6.0 or below.

Where the soil is moderately alkaline, annual applications of organic matter will help to make the adjustment, but if the soil is excessively alkaline at, for example, pH 8.0 and above, apply flowers of sulphur at the rate of 113g (4oz) to the sq m/yd on sandy soils, and at double that rate on heavy soils. Repeat the treatment annually until the required level is reached.

Kilogrammes/pounds per square metre/yard of hydrated lime needed to raise the pH level to 6.5

Starting pH	Sandy soil	Medium loam	Peat or clay
4.0	1.70 (3¾)	2.04 (4½)	2.26 (5)
4.5	1.36 (3)	1.58 (3½)	1.81 (4)
5.0	1.02 (2¼)	1.24 (2¾)	1.47 (3¼)
5.5	0.68 (1½)	0.90 (2)	1.02 (2¼)
6.0	0.34 (¾)	0.45 (1)	0.68 (1½)

TOO LITTLE MUCK OR TOO MUCH?

One of the arguments used by the agro-chemical faction against organic husbandry is that there is too little animal manure to sustain soil fertility. At a time when there was gross over-production of cereal crops that was probably true, but at modern levels it is no longer a valid assumption.

According to Charlie Pye-Smith and Richard North in their book *Working the Land*, Britain's farm animals produce about 190 million tonnes of manure a year. That's more than seven tonnes of manure available for every acre of land under crops, but about two-thirds of it is wasted. Disposal of animal manure has become a major problem for Britain's farmers and there have even been proposals that this natural, valuable material should be burned to produce electricity.

Animal manure used to be a mixture of dung solids, urine and the straw used as bedding. Now, with the trend away from straw, the manure is a liquid mixture of dung and urine, and it is this mixture that causes the huge problem of disposal. If spread as slurry in winter, it is rapidly washed away, causing polluted streams and rivers. If applied when the soil is dry, it can be quickly leached into the water supplies.

What is undoubtedly true is that too much manure is produced in the wrong places to make sane use of all the surplus straw, and transporting the straw to the muck would be a wasteful use of energy. What is needed is a far more diverse distribution of livestock farming, with a return to free-range pig-keeping as an integral part of farming in the major arable areas of Britain.

Growmore, Phostrogen and Vitax, while the organic gardener has a choice of naturally occurring minerals and organic fertilisers derived from animal farming and fishing.

Gardeners who oppose the use of animal manures and fertilisers such as dried blood, hoof and horn meal and bone meal, along with composted sewage sludge, must rely entirely on green manuring to maintain fertility in the soil.

MANURES AND COMPOSTS

Chicken manure A very rich source of nitrogen, best when provided by your own hens (see page 125) or from a poultry farmer who is wise and compassionate enough to keep his flock in free-range or deep-litter style. Poultry manure contains about four times as much plant food as horse or pig manure. You can use it fresh as a compost activator, or stack it until it is well rotted, then use it in the soil at the rate of about 2kg (4.5lb) to the sq m/yd. This manure is also available as a flash-dried and powdered product from battery hen and broiler chicken factory farms, when it can be used as a top dressing for leafy crops and onions at the rate of about 225g (8oz) to the sq m/yd.

Cow manure This also includes manure from bullocks that are yarded in the winter. It should be well mixed with straw litter and composted for six to twelve months. It contains a balanced amount of nitrogen, phosphorus and potassium and a full range of trace elements. It is used at the rate of 9kg (20lb) to the sq m/yd. Also available as proprietary brands, composted with peat and sold in bags.

Goat manure As with all other animal manures, this should be allowed to rot thoroughly, or composted with other organic material for about four to six months. It can be used fresh or rotted to make a good liquid manure by hanging a sack of it in a barrel of water and leaving it for a week. Dilute until it is the colour of weak tea, and top up the barrel.

Horse manure Now more widely available as riding schools proliferate: some are only too happy for you to bag up the stuff and take it away; others want a payment. Not all the stables use straw as a litter, some use wood shavings which are slow to rot down and may contain toxins. Do not use stable manure fresh, it must be composted or allowed to rot down in a heap and can then be dug into the top 15cm (6in) of the soil from October to March at the rate of 10kg (22lb) to the sq m/yd.

Leafmould Very little plant food is left in the dried, fallen leaves of autumn, but when stacked in a container for about a year, the resulting leafmould is a good source of humus, dug in at the rate of 2.25kg (5lb) to the sq m/yd autumn and winter. Not all leaves are suitable; avoid evergreens, for example, and any with signs of disease such as black spot. Leafmould can also be used as an ingredient of homemade potting compost (see page 51) and as a mulch for newly planted shrubs and trees.

Municipal compost If we were seriously green, every large town would have its own composting plant for recycling organic waste, saved in separate containers and taken away by the refuse collectors for eventual resale to us as a dark, friable compost, with value as a provider of humus and a range of plant foods. Some of the more enlightened councils already do this, others should be badgered until they follow suit. Municipal compost should be dug into the soil in autumn and winter at the rate of 1.5kg (3lb) to the sq m/yd. It might contain fragments of glass, so do not handle with bare hands.

Mushroom compost This used to be made of fresh horse manure, straw, chalk and gypsum. Today, it could be made mostly of straw composted with a chemical activator, or sewage sludge composted with straw. Some will contain the residues of insecticide and fairly hefty lumps of ground chalk. So, before you buy a load, or bag up some at your local mushroom farm, ask how the compost was made, and if it is basically just chemically activated straw, go somewhere else. Good mushroom compost should be dark and sweet smelling: the older the heap, the better because then any insecticide residues should have been leached out. Use it as a soil improver (it is particularly beneficial in clay soils), as a mulch, but not on any acid-loving plants such as rhododendrons and heathers, or as a lining for the pea and bean trenches. For digging in, allow 1.5kg (3lb) to the sq m/yd.

Pig manure As a matter of strongly held principle, I wouldn't use pig manure from a factory farm, any more than we, as a family, would eat pigmeat from such a place. The manure from properly farmed pigs is rich in plant foods and trace elements, but it should be stacked and rotted for at least eight months and not used more than once in two years. Dig it in over the winter at the rate of 10kg (22lb) to the sq m/yd.

Sewage sludge Digested sludge from the sewage plant, composted with straw, in a process developed by Hensby Bio-tech and Anglian Water, is free of any potentially dangerous pathogens. It is an excellent compost with a useful amount of plant nutrients and can be used at the rate of 9kg (20lb) to the sq m/yd in the top 15cm (6in) of the soil, dug in over the winter. Dried sewage sludge can also be bought in some areas in plastic bags. Mix three parts with one part of seaweed meal and use it as an activator for the compost, just covering the surface of the heap or bin every 15cm (6in) layer of vegetable waste. It can also be used at 170g (6oz) to the sq m/yd as a spring fertiliser anywhere in the garden, including the lawn.

Worm compost This is a truly wonderful organic product which you can produce yourself with the help of brandlings or manure worms, or buy as the end-product from commercial worm farms. All the help you'll need to set up your own worm farm is given on pages 54–5, along with advice on how to use the compost.

GREEN MANURES

The idea of sowing vacant land with a crop that can be turned in to increase soil fertility, prevent soil erosion through rain and wind, and improve its structure, was reckoned to be good farming practice in eighteenth-century Britain, but then fell out of favour. In mainland Europe, some Mediterranean countries and in China, green manuring, as it is called, has been in continuous use for centuries by both farmers and gardeners. Now, with the increased emphasis on non-exploitative agriculture and horticulture, many organic farmers, growers and gardeners are recognising that green manuring offers a viable alternative to animal manuring, or a useful adjunct to it.

The seed of crops grown for green manuring is inexpensive, so even if you don't want to commit yourself to a full-scale regime of this type of manuring, you can sow a patch of the garden or allotment when it becomes vacant, for preference in late summer and early autumn, and dig in the green manure as a normal part of winter cultivation. Some gardeners prepare the sites that are to be planted up with fruit trees, soft fruit or ornamental shrubs in this way, while others put a green manure crop into the annual rotation scheme for the vegetable patch.

A limiting factor until quite recently in the UK was the availability of green manure seeds for the gardener, but now specialist suppliers like Suffolk Herbs, HDRA and Chase Organics, list them, and even a major seed firm – Thompson & Morgan – offers a range of seeds for the purpose.

Alfalfa A deep-rooting member of the clover family, this is also called lucerne, and is so rich in plant foods that it is almost a complete natural fertiliser. A perennial, this is best grown for a whole year, and halfway through it can be cut back and the top growth either dug in elsewhere or added to the compost heap, then in late autumn or winter the new growth can be dug in. Sow from April to July at the rate of 15g (½oz) to the sq m/yd, and because this is a nitrogen fixing plant follow it with a leafy crop such as lettuce, spinach or cabbage.

Beans Broad beans are a good source of nitrogen and, having bought the seed for the initial crop, you can save seed for each subsequent one. The best plan is to sow a winter-hardy variety, such as Aquadulce Claudia, in October or November and dig it in at any time up to flowering, while allowing some plants to seed for saving. Alternatively, cut off the top growth in March or early April and use for composting, while leaving the root system in the ground for a following crop of cabbage or spinach. Sow the seed 15cm (6in) apart each way.

Buckwheat This is not one to be used routinely where space is limited because it is sown in spring and harvested in late summer. It has the advantage, though, that it is a tall, pretty plant with red stems, and small pink flowers beloved by hoverflies. Hoverflies are also very partial to greenfly, so buckwheat plants at the back of the border can really earn their living space. Scatter the seed and lightly cover, or sow in rows about 23cm (9in) apart at the rate of 30g (1oz) to the sq m/yd.

Clover, crimson This is a nitrogen-fixing crop, best sown in spring or early summer, scattering the seed at 30g (1oz) to the sq m/yd. The beautifully scented red flowers are a magnet for bees. Dig in the crop in late autumn. An alternative is Essex red clover.

Fenugreek This legume produces a mass of foliage within about ten weeks of sowing in the spring, before the tiny white flowers become seed pods. It can be left to self-seed. Some experts believe it doesn't fix its nitrogen, but I have cut the foliage for compost making and dibbled leek plants into the fenugreek roots, with excellent results.

Lupins This is not the garden lupin, but the smaller *Lupinus angustifolius*, a deep-rooting legume which grows well even in infertile, acid soil. Lupins have bacteria in their root systems that convert normally unavailable phosphates into available plant nutrients. Sow in April or May in drills 2.5cm (1in) deep, with the seed 5cm (2in) apart and the rows 15cm (6in) apart. Cut and compost or dig in before the stems get too woody, about twelve weeks after sowing. If sown after old turf has been turned under, this crop will stop the denitrification as the grass rots down.

Mustard Mustard is the most widely used green manure crop because it makes masses of organic matter in double-quick time, so it can be sown virtually anywhere land becomes vacant from early spring through to autumn. The snag is that it is related to the cabbage family and so will trigger dormant spores of the deadly clubroot. Sow at the rate of 30g (1oz) to 7sq m/yd, scattering the seed onto moist soil and gently raking in. Cut down the crop when the plants are about 20cm (9in) tall, before they flower, allow to wilt for a day or so, then turn into the top 15cm (6in) of soil. Mustard is a good crop for cleaning land that is wireworm infested, when the sowing rate should be increased to 30g (1oz) to the sq m/yd.

Phacelia This is a very attractive plant with delicate, fern-like foliage and bee-haunted, bright-blue flowers. Sow in May, thinly, in rows about 20cm (8in) apart. The dense mass of foliage can be used for sheet composting when cut in the autumn, or can be turned in during winter cultivation.

THE MAJOR PLANT FOODS

Nitrogen (N) is the leaf-making element that largely determines how big a plant will grow. It is produced naturally by the leguminous plants, but is readily leached from the soil. A deficiency will be apparent in stunted growth of young plants and yellowing of the leaves of older ones. Dried blood is a quick-acting source of nitrogen; hoof and horn a slow-release source.

Phosphorus or phosphate (P) is the root-maker, and so it, too, is vital for healthy plant growth. A deficiency causes stunting, with leaves developing a blue tinge. Bone meal is a good source of this important food and is released slowly, while rock phosphate, poultry manure and seaweed meal are also effective.

Potassium or potash (K) helps to determine the colour and size of flowers and fruits, so a deficiency can be recognised by undersized blooms and immature fruit. A dressing of rock potash lasts about three years and should correct matters.

Other important plant foods are:
magnesium, found in seaweed meal and foliar feeds;
calcium, available in calcified seaweed;
sulphur, a deficiency of which can be corrected by a dressing of gypsum;
iron, a lack of which can be put right by spraying with liquid seaweed extract;
boron, available in seaweed meal and homemade compost;
manganese and molybdenum, deficiencies of which can be corrected by spraying with a seaweed extract.

Most loams cultivated organically, using home-produced compost or composted animal dung, contain sufficient amounts of the major elements and trace elements without the need to add them as fertilisers. Remember that the main elements for healthy plant growth are oxygen (45 per cent), carbon (45 per cent) and hydrogen (6 per cent), and all you need do to provide them is to give your charges living and breathing space.

Rye, grazing One of the best choices for overwintering, rye produces a very extensive root system for improving soil structure. Sow in September at the rate of 30g (1oz) to the sq m/yd, scattering and lightly covering the seed. Dig in when the flower buds are forming at the base of the plants in mid-spring, but allow a few plants to form seed to save for the next sowing.

Tares, winter This is another excellent subject for overwintering. It will rapidly cover bare soil during the winter and give a nitrogen-rich start to the growing season in early spring. To do well it needs a good, moist loam with a neutral pH. Sow the seed in late August or September, in drills 2.5cm (1in) deep and 15cm (6in) apart. Turn in the crop before it flowers and follow with transplanted autumn or winter cabbages.

Trefoil Trefoil is a low-growing legume that does well even on light, dry soils, but it needs to be sown in spring and given twelve weeks to mature, so occupying land at the peak growing season. If that isn't a drawback, sow at the rate of 15g (½oz) to the sq m/yd, scattering the seed, or in shallow drills 10cm (4in) apart.

ORGANIC FERTILISERS

Organic gardeners don't indulge in the annual ritual of dosing their land with chemical fertilisers – these very quickly become soluble in the soil and are taken up by the plants, whether they need this type of force-feeding or not. The organic way is to feed the soil to feed the plants, a process that is enshrined in the belief that a healthy, fertile soil is the greatest asset we have. Feeding the soil with natural materials provides a wholemeal type of diet for the plants, as against the fast food of the chemical diet, and encourages the activity of that vast underground population of living organisms – nature's workers, recycling the material into nutrients for the plants.

The purist might argue that there is little difference between providing potassium to a crop as a straight chemical or in the form of the ground mineral rock potash. The argument has been summarised by Lawrence Hills, founder of the Henry Doubleday Research Association: 'The basic problem is the solubility of chemical fertilisers. This makes them available all at once, in massive concen-

trations, and they are leached away almost as suddenly. This criterion allows the organic grower to draw the line between chemical fertilisers like superphosphate and ground minerals like rock phosphate, or between sulphate of potash and rock potash.'

The following list of organic fertilisers is intended to indicate their value as wholefoods for the soil, and as supplementary feeds for plants indicating a deficiency of some sort. The availability of some of them is still haphazard, but improving month by month. They tend to be rather more expensive than artificial fertilisers, but it should be remembered that they are longer lasting, slowly releasing their nutrients over periods up to three years. Some, such as calcified seaweed, also contain a rich variety of minor nutrients and trace elements which can actually be locked out of reach of plant roots by the use of chemical fertilisers.

DIY FERTILISER

For those gardeners who prefer to use a single, well-balanced fertiliser, the organic equivalent of, say, Growmore, this is a good recipe:

Mix by weight:

1 part seaweed meal
1 part dried blood
1 part hoof and horn
2 parts bone meal

Use a trowel to do the mixing and wear rubber gloves.

This can be used for all crops, whether fruit, flower or vegetable, in early spring by sprinkling about 113g (4oz) to the sq m/yd and working it into the top 15cm (6in) of the soil.

Animal hair The hair we get from grooming dogs and cats should be saved and recycled in the garden to provide a good, slow-release source of nitrogen, or mixed thoroughly with other material and added to the compost heap or bin. If not composted, moisten the hair, spread it over the soil in winter and turn it into the top 15cm (6in).

Bone meal Bone meal is an excellent source of phosphates (up to 30 per cent) and nitrogen (about 3 per cent), both of which are released slowly over about two years, and some calcium. Apply 85g (3oz) to the sq m/yd in early spring on light soils where leaching of phosphates can lead to a deficiency, and at 113g (4oz) to the sq m/yd when planting shrubs, roses, fruit bushes, raspberry canes and strawberry plants.

Calcified seaweed This is a wonderfully versatile organic fertiliser that can be used to sweeten an over-acidic soil, as an activator in the compost heap, as an ingredient in the worm farm, and as a tonic for soft fruits and top fruits for all kinds. It is rich in calcium, magnesium and many trace elements, and although it has a lower neutralising value than lime, it lasts far longer. I use it every three years as a combined fertiliser and neutraliser at the rate of 113g (4oz) to the sq m/yd.

Dolomite Dolomite is an alternative to lime or calcified seaweed for altering the pH value of the soil and for preventing over-acidity in the compost heap. Dolomitic limestone, containing about 60 per cent calcium carbonate and 40 per cent magnesium carbonate, is valuable in preventing or correcting magnesium deficiency in tomatoes, potatoes and gooseberries, which shows up as yellowing of the leaves, or reddish-brown patches on the leaves. For general use allow about 225g (8oz) to the sq m/yd, but double the quantity where there is magnesium deficiency. Dolomite is used with gypsum as a soil conditioner for clay at the rate of 80 per cent gypsum (ground calcium sulphate rock) and 20 per cent dolomite. Apply 340g (12oz) to the sq m/yd in early spring and work it into the top few centimetres of the clay. Give a second application at the same rate in autumn and hoe it in. Repeat the treatment the following year. After that the dose can be reduced to just 85g (3oz) to the sq m/yd annually.

Dried blood Dried blood is the quickest-acting tonic for nitrogen-hungry crops, such as spring cabbage and lettuce, when applied in early spring, and best used in liquid form. Place 56g (2oz) in 1.12l (1 quart) of water and allow to soak for at least three days, stirring occasionally. First moisten the soil round the plants, then use the liquid feed through a watering can at 1.12l (1 quart) to each sq m/yd.

Feathers Don't throw away your old feather-filled pillows. Soak them in a bucket, then dig them into the soil over the winter at the rate of about 140g (5oz) to the sq m/yd to provide slow-release nitrogen and some humus.

Fish, blood and bone meal As with all fertilisers, always wear gloves when handling this organic equivalent of the chemical Growmore, or use a trowel and wash your hands afterwards. This is applied in early spring, preferably about two weeks before sowing or planting out, at the rate of 56g (2oz) to the sq m/yd, and repeat when the crops are about half grown, but not later than the end of August. Any fertiliser left over should be stored in an airtight container and kept secure from children, pets and stored food crops.

Foliar feeds Feeding plants through their leaves is in addition to, not instead of, the food taken up by the roots. The best of these foliar feeds for the organic gardener are undoubtedly those based on seaweed extracts, such as SM3 (Sea Magic), Maxicrop and Algoflash. They have good amounts of nitrogen and potassium and many trace elements, as well as alginates that seem to deter sucking insects such as aphids. Foliar feeding with seaweed liquid is a well-established remedy for trace element deficiency, sprayed or watered on the plants every fortnight until the symptoms disappear. You can make your own foliar feed from animal manure by hanging a sackful in a barrel or drum of water, or buy it ready-made as Farmura. Veganic gardeners say that you can also make a good liquid feed by soaking a range of weeds, roots and all, in a bucket or barrel for three or four weeks and using the liquid, diluted with an equal quantity of water. This brew is said to be particularly favoured by tomatoes.

Hoof and horn This is a rich, slow-release source of nitrogen, best applied at the rate of 113g (4oz) to the sq m/yd when turning over the soil in late autumn and winter. For house plants, add about 56g (2oz) to each bucketful of compost when repotting. Use at the higher rate when planting soft fruit stock and when transplanting Brussels sprouts.

Lime Acid rain and a natural tendency for organic soils to become acidic mean that a close watch should be kept on the pH level of your soil. Lime reduces acidity, but is continually being washed out of the soil and must be replaced, or reserves of plant foods will be locked up and unavailable to your crops. You can do this by spreading hydrated lime, quicklime, dolomitic limestone, carbonate of lime or calcified seaweed. If you use hydrated lime, do so early in the year at the rate of 225g (8oz) to the sq m/yd on heavy soil, and half that rate on medium and light soils. On very light soils carbonate of lime at 225g (8oz) to the sq m/yd is preferable because it is not so readily leached out.

Rock phosphate Rock phosphate is a slow-release source of phosphorus – one dressing will last for at least three years – but is seldom necessary except in areas of high rainfall. Apply at the rate of 450g (1lb) to the sq m/yd.

Rock potash This is sold as Highland rock potash or Adularian shale and holds 10 to 12 per cent potassium in minute particles, exactly as needed by potash-hungry gooseberries, tomatoes and potatoes. Spread over the soil at 225g (8oz) to the sq m/yd and lightly hoe in.

Seaweed Those who live near enough to the coast to be able to gather an annual harvest of fresh seaweed are very lucky. It is one of nature's finest fertilisers. Spread as a mulch it adds flavour to beetroot, helps to ward off the carrot fly, and is much liked by all the brassica family. It can be chopped and added to the compost-making materials, when the alginates speed the growth of the bacteria that promote aerobic decomposition. It is also available dried and powdered as a complete, easy-to-use fertiliser, at 56g (2oz) to the sq m/yd in early spring and again in early summer. On lawns use it in early April as a tonic at 113g (4oz) to the sq m/yd. The liquid extract of seaweed is sold under various trade names (*see* Foliar feeds).

Soot Highly regarded by our forefathers as a plant food and slug deterrent, soot is seldom available nowadays. If you still have your chimney swept, save the soot, allow to weather for at least six months and use it round plants likely to become meals for slugs in early spring.

Wood ash Save the ash from wood fires and store it in an airtight container, mixed with some charcoal.

It is rich in potash and can be applied in spring at up to 450g (1lb) to the sq m/yd onto moistened soil to feed gooseberries and tomatoes

DON'T WASTE YOUR WASTE

Everyone with a garden, however small, can and should make compost. All you need is the material, something to put it in while it is decomposing, and the know-how.

Making compost deserves to be treated seriously because it is one of the most enjoyable and rewarding of all gardening jobs. Books have been written on this subject alone, and there are high priests of the organic movement who invest the business of compost making with something of the myths and mystery of an obscure cult. Don't be put off by them. Good compost is easily made, and even badly made compost is worth having. It feeds the soil that in turn feeds your plants, and just as a cook can occasionally make a hash of things in the kitchen, so things can go wrong when making compost. The difference is that badly cooked food can be uneatable, but poorly made compost is still good grub for the garden.

COMPOST FOR SOIL HEALTH

Work at the Faculty of Agriculture, Hebrew University, Jerusalem, has shown that when properly made compost is added to potting media, harmful soil-borne organisms are reduced or suppressed. The germination rate of seedlings is also improved.

Types of compost There are two types of compost: **aerobic** and **anaerobic**. Aerobic compost is made relatively quickly, and when finished is dark brown, crumbly and with the fresh smell of soil after a summer shower. Anaerobic compost is the sort you get if you put all your vegetable waste into a plastic sack, or dump it into a corner of the garden and forget it for a few months. It rots down into a stinking, gooey mess. The key difference between the two methods is a micro-organism called the aerobe, which can only flourish where there is oxygen, and so a good oxygen supply is an essential feature of aerobic compost. It helps to set in motion a sort of biological bonfire in which the heat from the activity of countless billions of bacteria speeds the transformation of the waste material into nutrient-rich compost. At the peak of this transformation period the heat in the compost container will reach about 65°C (150°F), which is high enough to destroy weed seeds, pests and diseases. When the process is complete, each 5kg (11lb) of vegetable waste has become about 450g (1lb) of organic material, with a balanced amount of the nutrients required for strong, healthy plant growth. As well as the main plant foods, your homemade compost will contain many of the minor nutrients and trace elements, and a large volume of humus, the truly remarkable material that helps to improve soil structure, retain moisture, prevent soil erosion and maintain soil fertility. No wonder, then, that the compost heap or bin is the heart of the organic garden.

Suitable materials One of the problems about compost making, particularly for the person with a small garden, is that there never seems to be enough waste material to make a reasonable start, so some advance preparation is necessary. Start collecting waste material a couple of months beforehand and store it in plastic sacks, tied at the top to keep the rain out. Some experts say anything that has lived can live again if you compost it, but I draw the line at cooked meat and fish scraps and other kitchen waste that might attract vermin and flies. This is less likely to be a snag if your compost is made in a sealed composter, such as the Tumbler. Nevertheless, you

COMPOST CONTAINERS

You'll know best what sort of container will suit your location. It could be a purpose-made compartment or two that will make a tonne or more compost at a time and can become the power-house of the larger organic garden or allotment. Or, for the small town garden, the compost container could be a disused plastic dustbin, or a commercial composter, such as the Tumbler or other type of barrel composter, which will make up to about 100kg (220lb) of compost in from eight to twenty weeks, depending on the season.

may well prefer to feed kitchen scraps to the worms in your worm farm (see pages 54–5).

Lawn mowings, hedge clippings, potato peelings, cabbage leaves, even shredded newspaper are all suitable items for composting. Weeds, with excess soil shaken off the roots, should be saved, along with the hair from grooming your dog or cat and the litter from the rabbit, hamster or gerbil cage. If you live near the coast, collect as much seaweed as you can to add to your other compostible materials.

NETTLE COMPOST

Stinging nettles are a very useful crop. Use them as sheet compost by cutting them young and spreading them along the rows of your vegetables. They deter slugs and snails, help to conserve moisture in the soil and actually aid the growth of the neighbouring crops. Add them to the compost heap as a nitrogen-rich activator. Soak about 225g (8oz) of young nettles in a bucket of water for a week and use undiluted as a control for aphids on roses, or 50 per cent diluted as a liquid feed for pot plants and leafy vegetables.

Ask friends to save their waste for you; better still, ask your local greengrocer or supermarket to let you collect all the fruit and vegetable waste that they would normally have to dispose of through the refuse collection service. If your local park gardeners don't collect the grass cuttings and autumn leaves for composting, then shame on them. Profit from their ignorance by collecting as much as you want for your own compost making. Aim to have enough material to fill at least three-quarters of your container. If yours is a DIY effort of bricks, wood, corrugated iron sheeting or whatever, it should not be smaller than 1.22m (4ft) deep by 1.22m (4ft) wide by 1.06m (3ft 6in) tall. It should have gaps at the bottom to allow air to enter and should have a cover to prevent it becoming rain-sodden. Make one side readily removable so that when the compost is ready to be used it can be forked out without having to dismantle the whole structure.

In addition to the bulky materials, you will need an activator to give your aerobic compost a good start. This is a nitrogen-rich material that acts as a flame to set the bacterial bonfire going. You can buy an activator or devise your own (see page 42), or simply allow the aerobic compost to become anaerobic. When you use anaerobic compost in the garden the carbonic acid level can become too high, so you will need to keep a watch on the pH level and correct it, as necessary, with lime or calcified seaweed.

When you are building your heap, or filling your container, try to ensure that the compost-making materials are well mixed, and avoid adding too much soil. If you have bits of unwanted turves or lots of grassy weeds with the soil clinging to them, stack them separately and use the decayed product as loam for your homemade potting compost.

Large quantities of fallen leaves are also best kept separately to become leafmould. All you need for that is a square or cylinder of wire netting. Whether or not you add the contents of the vacuum cleaner bag to the compost depends on the composition of your carpets: the debris from manmade fibres is not suitable. Small quantities of animal manure, including the excreta from the family dog, can also be composted. In fact, fresh farmyard or riding stable manure makes an excellent activator. Fresh manure dug straight into the ground wastes the high nitrogen content, which evaporates as ammonia gas. Similarly, it is wasteful to dig raw vegetable waste straight into the ground because the slow decomposition will rob the soil of some of its nitrogen and phosphates. Newsprint, but not the colour supplements, is best added in shredded form and preferably moist, but not too much at a time as that could upset the carbon–nitrogen ratio of the compostible materials. So, also, would large amounts of straw, peat and shrub prunings, which are high in carbon and would have to be balanced by, for example, fresh stinging nettles, poultry or pig manure, pea or bean vines or stable manure, which are proportionately higher in nitrogen.

Reasons for failure If your compost fails to heat up, the carbon–nitrogen ratio of the materials may be out of balance in favour of carbon. You can improve matters by remaking and adding more activator. Another reason could be that material is too dry or too wet: it should be no damper than a well-squeezed-out sponge. So if it is in an open-topped container, add a square of old carpet or make a wooden cover to keep out the rain and snow. If it is too dry, add water or a dried blood or urine solution through a watering can.

MAKING THE BEST USE OF YOUR COMPOST

Compost is too good to be used wastefully, so it should be used where the plants want it, at the time it will be most beneficial.

If you are growing crops in deep beds (see page 97), the compost can be added to the surface as a mulch in early spring, or teased into the top few inches of the bed.

For all plants and seeds that are sown or set out in drills or shallow trenches, place a 2.5–5cm (1–2in) layer of compost in the bottom of the drill or trench and sow or plant direct into this layer.

When planting leeks with a dibber, put a small handful of compost in each hole, drop in the leek, then trickle water into the hole.

When planting seed potatoes in prepared trenches, use a generous handful of compost with each tuber. Brussels sprouts, cabbages and cauliflower plants can also be given a generous dollop of compost at planting-out time.

Brussels Sprouts

Before planting roses, ornamental shrubs, fruit trees and bushes and herbaceous perennials, incorporate as much compost as possible in the planting hole. This helps to encourage a good rooting system and so minimises wind rock, guards against drying out and provides a nutrient-rich environment for the young stock. Prepare the site at least a month before planting and use at least a bucketful of compost per tree or shrub, mixed half-and-half with soil. Water thoroughly after planting and, if you have it to spare, add a thick mulch of compost to complete the job.

If you have a greenhouse or conservatory, you can use your homemade compost as the main ingredient of potting compost (see page 51) as a substitute for peat, composted bark or coir fibre. However, for this purpose it must be friable well-decomposed aerobic compost, not wet and smelly anaerobic compost which should be dug in. It is also advisable to sieve the compost intended for potting so that any partly rotted material can be removed.

Remember that in the flower garden annuals would not benefit from a soil rich in compost. They would make too much leafy growth at the expense of flowers. In the vegetable garden you can start doling out the precious rations of compost in early spring, giving peas and onions priority, but avoiding the carrots and beetroot.

In mid-spring it could be the turn of the lawn with sifted compost applied as a dressing after rain. Then the strawberry bed, raspberry rows and the currant bushes have the compost applied as a mulch, followed by lining the drills, trenches or dressing the deep beds for the sowing of maincrop peas, dwarf beans and runner beans and when planting out celery, celeriac, Brussels sprouts, calabrese, cabbages, cauliflowers and leeks.

Later, from early summer to early autumn, the drill for the spinach can have a lining of compost, but not the spring cabbage.

Finally, in the calendar of composting, give the planting hole for each new tree, shrub and perennial as much compost as you can manage to give them a healthy introduction to your garden.

Fallen leaves should not be burnt. Collect them and store in a wire-netting enclosure to make leafmould. Moisten the leaves, cover and add a weight to compress them

Trench compost makes an ideal growing medium for runner beans, so in early winter decide where the beans will go and take out a trench a spade wide and as long as you wish. Dig out the soil to a depth of about 30cm (1ft), and over the winter and early spring fill the bottom 15cm (6in) of the trench with a layer of brassica stumps and the like. Add other vegetable waste and uncooked kitchen scraps, then tread it all in as firmly as possible and cover with soil to within about 5cm (2in) of the surface.

There will be considerable compaction after the winter's rain, and the remaining soil – or most of it – can be added in April. The runner bean seeds can be sown directly into the trench in May or June, or plants set out after the last frost. The ability of the bean roots to fix nitrogen will help the rapid decomposition of the brassica stumps, and any overwintering eggs of mealy aphids and cabbage whitefly will be destroyed.

Other reasons why compost fails to heat up include: failure to pre-mix the materials; too little air or too much (slats at the bottom of the container are sufficient); too much soil on the roots of weeds and other plants; it's too cold. In winter the decomposition process slows down, so try to organise your compost making so that it is finished in the early autumn. The compost can then be used as part of the winter and early spring programme of preparing the soil for the growing season.

Trench compost If you have a shredding machine, disposal of the woody prunings from roses and other shrubs and the stems of Brussels sprouts, cabbages and cauliflowers presents no problem. You simply feed the stuff in and add the chewed-up result to the compost heap, although don't use stumps infected by clubroot. If you haven't a shredder, these woody items can be successfully composted using the trench composting technique.

A shredder enables you to recycle prunings and other woody items such as cabbage stalks. Add the shredded material to the compost bin or spread it as a mulch that will eventually be incorporated in the soil

STEPS IN MAKING COMPOST

If you are erecting a DIY container, prepare the site first. It can be tucked away in a corner of the garden, but remember, there should be easy access for a wheelbarrow when you come to use the finished compost.

Fork over the ground and water well at least twenty-four hours beforehand to encourage earthworms towards the surface.

Build your container or place your ready-made structure in position. If you are not trench composting the woody stems of brassicas, they can go as a bottom layer, but don't expect them to have rotted down by the time the other material is ready.

Remember to allow for air to enter the container, preferably at the bottom. If the walls are solid, you will have to lay down an aeration layer of staggered bricks or rubble.

Save enough compostible material beforehand to half fill your container in 15cm (6in) layers. It should be moist but not sopping wet. After each layer add the activator. This can be dried blood, fresh stinging nettles, fresh farmyard or stable manure, seaweed or seaweed meal or urine diluted one part with three parts of water. Alternatively, you can buy a proprietary activator such as Compost Generator, QR herbal compost maker, Fertosan or Bio Recycler.

After the second layer of materials, a sprinkling of hydrated lime, dolomite or calcified seaweed can be added, but is not essential.

Continue filling the container in this way, but remember always to cover the compost to keep the heat of decomposition in and the rain out.

About a fortnight after the last layer is added, test to make sure the material is heating up. Use a metal rod as a probe to reach the centre of the container and leave it for a few minutes, then withdraw. The end of the probe should be hot to the touch.

Depending on the season, the material will have shrunk by about a third after five or six weeks (sooner in a barrel composter). Try to turn as much of the outside edges of the material to the inside as possible, and top up with more material, if available.

Test the heap now and again with the probe to check that the second stage of decomposition has got under way.

After each layer of compost-making materials, add an activator, such as Compost Generator or QR, to speed the decomposition

SAVE WATER WHENEVER YOU CAN

In temperate countries most of the rain falls during the six months of the year when our gardens need it least. That's the period from late autumn through to early spring when the annual flowers have finished, many trees and shrubs are dormant, and the spring growth is waiting to be sprung. Yet we do very little to conserve all that rain and, come the hot, dry days of late spring and summer, when our plants are dying for a drink, we have to rely on mains water and a hosepipe, although even that can't be taken for granted. In recent periods of intense drought, water companies have been quick to impose a ban on sprinklers. Once the soil becomes parched, heavy summer showers don't alleviate the drought significantly, because only a fraction of the rain penetrates. It is rather like pouring a jug of water over a dry sponge. Most of it runs off, but drip water onto a dry sponge and it slowly becomes saturated.

Increasing demand More cars means a vastly increased demand for water. It takes 200,000 litres (44,000gal) of water to make a tonne of steel, and 450,000 litres (100,000gal) to make a family car, but only 4.5 litres (1gal) to make a cabbage. More cars means more owners going through the Sunday morning ritual of washing the family saloon. By the year 2000 demand for water is likely to be double what it was in 1970, and supply is virtually certain to fall short of demand, so by 1999 we shall have to decide on our priorities.

The affluent 1980s saw a big increase in home swimming pools, making a major demand on domestic water supplies, and it is commonplace today for large houses to have several bathrooms and lavatories, all of which boosts the average total of 450 litres (100gal) of fresh water that each of us uses every day. Come the time when every litre of water is sold through a meter, we might see a more rational use of it. Meanwhile, conserving as much of the rainfall as possible makes sense for several reasons: it's free, it's available when it's wanted, where it's wanted, and it's generally a better product for garden use than tapwater because it has a neutral pH and has no chemicals deliberately added to it.

How much water Before considering ways to save water, there are points to be made about a garden's need for water. A lot can be done to ensure that the rain is used to maximum benefit by one's plants, and you will find advice on this at points through this book. Equally important is learning how much water food crops need for healthy growth and when that water should be given.

Excellent work has been done on this fascinating subject by research staff at the National Vegetable Research Station, summarised in *Know and Grow Vegetables* by P. J. Salter, J. K. A. Bleasdale and others. Their investigations discovered that watering unnecessarily may merely increase the growth of a plant, without increasing the edible part. It may inhibit root growth, and actually make the plant more susceptible to stress during dry spells.

So how do we decide when we should give water and how much should be given?

Plants take up water through their roots, and lose it through the pores in their leaves. How much and how quickly that loss takes place is determined by the sunshine, the air temperature, whether or not it is windy, and the relative humidity. During dry spells the plant sets in motion a survival process that actually restricts its water loss to a minimum.

In a summer with long, hot days and, hopefully, warm, wet nights, a vegetable crop whose leaves fully cover the ground will lose more than 5 litres (1gal) of water per sq m/yd of crop per day. In the shorter, cooler days of spring and autumn the loss may be under a litre (2pt) per sq m/yd per day. The passage of water through the plant is essential for photosynthesis, respiration, and the other life functions, such as the absorption of nutrients from the soil, to take place. The other important function of water absorption is sweating, as in a human. As the water evaporates from the leaf surface in hot weather, so it cools the plant.

The NVRS researchers conclude that the plant will only respond to watering under these conditions:

- If rainfall is inadequate to replenish dry soil.
- If the soil is so lacking in humus that it cannot hold an adequate amount of water.
- If there is competition for water from weeds or other neighbouring plants.
- If the root growth is too shallow or too immature to tap moisture reserves deeper in the soil.
- If the depth of soil is too shallow.

They confirmed that the critical stage in this business of watering is the 'wilting point' of the plant.

On sandy soils, with their coarse particles, wilting point is reached far quicker than on a loam packed with organic matter. In fact, a plant growing in such a loam has four times as much water available to it as a plant growing in coarse sandy soil.

So improving soil structure is the most important factor in improving water retention in the soil, and this means digging in composted farmyard manure, homemade compost, spent mushroom compost and leafmould. On poor, light soils at least 4.5kg (10lb) per sq m/yd will be needed, and it is very important that the organic material should be thoroughly mixed into the top 15cm (6in) of the soil, not buried at the bottom of the trench as is often recommended with double digging. If this treatment is impossible over the whole of the garden because of its size, or because of the lack of sufficient supplies of organic material, you could adopt the deep-bed system for your vegetable production (pages 97–104) to make maximum use of it.

Removing weeds as soon as they appear helps to ensure that available moisture gets to the crops you are tending, and this can be enhanced by putting a mulch of leaves, bark, peat or grass mowings around the plants after rainfall or thorough watering.

As a general rule, says the NVRS, whenever the soil dries out to an appreciable extent, say seven to ten days without rain, plants will respond to watering, but not always to the benefit of the gardener. For example, broad beans, dwarf beans and peas will make leaf at the expense of the edible pods, but once these crops start to produce pods then watering becomes beneficial. This means applying up to 54l (12gal) per sq m/yd on deeply dry soil, followed by 18l (4gal) per sq m/yd on already moist soil.

Root crops, such as carrots, beetroot and parsnips, respond to frequent waterings by extra leaf growth without a proportional increase in root, so with these crops watering is really only necessary at the wilting point. Watering onions as they reach maturity not only delays the ripening of the crop, but also has a detrimental effect on keeping quality.

Potatoes need a steady supply of water throughout the growth of the plants, but the critical point is when the tubers are about 2.5cm (1in) in diameter. A good watering at this stage undoubtedly increases the yield. With brassicas, celery, celeriac and lettuces, adequate moisture is needed at all times, but especially during the final three weeks before maturity.

Saving water Saving water falls into two parts: collecting as much rainfall as possible, and cutting down on the use of water from the mains supply. Obvious collection points for rainfall are the garden shed, garage, greenhouse and conservatory, all of which can be fitted with guttering, downpipes and rainwater butts, preferably of plastic and fitted with a draw-off tap. Washing-up water from the kitchen, provided it is not too greasy or over-dosed with detergent, can be used for watering shrubs and trees, while bathwater can be used virtually anywhere in the garden. You don't have to ladle it out by the bucketful. A siphon fitted to a length of hosepipe can take the water to where you want it in the garden. In countries where water is considered much more precious than it is in Britain, rainfall is collected from the roofs by fitting a junction to the downpipe from the guttering, and storing it in a tank.

SAVE WITH A SHOWER

The biggest use of water in the home is the lavatory. Each flush uses about 10l (2.2gal) of water. You can halve that amount by installing a dual-flush cistern, and don't flush every time you pee. Next most wasteful is the bath. If possible, take a shower, not a bath, and you will use 250 per cent less water.

When there is a drought and water supplies are restricted, the water wasters are fairly easy to spot. They insist on washing the car and having the sprinkler going all night to keep the lawn looking green. A garden sprinkler uses about 910l (200gal) of water an hour, an amount that could be a lifesaver to food crops, but is cosmetic on grass, which has a remarkable robustness in reviving from drought.

Anglian Water, supplying the driest region of Britain, established a drought garden to demonstrate how gardeners can cut down on watering their gardens, and full marks to them for their initiative. It's to be hoped they will also pass the word along to the farming conglomerates and golf clubs whose profligate use of water, even during severe drought, cocks a snook at the efforts of the rest of us.

MAKE YOUR
OWN COMPOSTS

Compost can be a confusing word because it means different things to different gardeners. To the organic gardener the word conjures up the fragrant smell – like soil after a summer shower – that comes from the rich-brown, crumbly material of a well-made aerobic compost container. It could equally mean the anaerobic alternative, often a slimy mess, that is also compost.

It can also mean the commercially produced organic compost, such as Stimgro, Morgro or Cowpost, often in multipurpose, potting or seed forms, while to the conventional gardener compost can mean one of the John Innes types, based on loam, or one of the versions with sphagnum peat or composted tree bark as the base.

Then there's the wonderful product of the worm farm, the worm-worked waste that has become clean, organic compost, rich in plant foods and trace elements.

John Innes composts were invented just before World War II, and they have largely been ousted by the peat-based ones. JI composts are not organic because their fertility derives from the addition of artificial fertilisers, along with the natural plant food in the loam.

Compost for seed sowing and potting is an essential material if you like to raise your own plants, and it is perfectly feasible, though only marginally cheaper, to make your own rather than buy it in.

GREENER IN GERMANY

By 1995 householders in Lower Saxony, Germany, will be separating their rubbish into two bins, one of which will be organic waste for municipal composting.

For the keen chrysanthemum grower, soil-based composts provide a more secure environment for mums in pots than peat-based ones. They are also more tolerant of over or under watering and are richer in the minor plant foods and trace elements. The snag is you need loam as the main ingredient of soil compost, and loam takes three years to make from scratch, although it is only fair to point out that some very successful organic gardeners make their own version of the JI composts using sterilised garden soil enriched with organic fertiliser. My friend Bill Skinner, of Great Waldringfield, uses the earth thrown up by moles in one of his meadows.

The danger of using unsterilised soil, particularly for seed compost, is that it could carry the organisms that cause damping off, a condition that affects young seedlings: they collapse and die quite suddenly or, when the first few leaves have formed, they fail to develop satisfactorily.

For sterilising soil in small amounts all you have to do is to heat it in the oven at 100°C (212°F) for fifteen minutes. Larger amounts have to be treated in a steriliser, such as the Nobles Soil Steriliser, which deals with a 9l (2gal) bucketful at a time. This sterilises very efficiently by steam, which circulates evenly through ordinary garden soil. It uses a 1.5kW electric element and the process takes about thirty minutes. If you have a large greenhouse and wish to have the soil sterilised organically, there are contractors with mobile steam sterilising units who will do the job for you. The nutrients in the soil and its structure are not affected by steam sterilisation unless the soil is acidic at pH 5.0 or less, when the recommendation is that you add lime first.

If you want to make loam, you need a supply of surplus turf, free from couch grass and weeds, which has been cut with about 5cm (2in) of soil. It is then stacked, grass side down, for at least a year, after which it breaks down into a humus-rich crumbly

Make your own small growing bag out of a strong plastic bag by filling it with compost, then sealing the open end. Cut out squares for the plants

GROW-AGAIN BAG

A growing bag used for an edible crop, such as tomatoes or cucumbers, can be re-used in a number of ways. Put it in a sunny part of the garden, or on the patio, and sow it with a mix of hardy annual flowers or everlasting flowers for cutting and drying. Or use the contents of the bag for storing root crops over the winter.

You can also re-use the compost in the bag for potting up spring-flowering bulbs, for mulching round newly-planted shrubs, for adding to the planting hole when setting out seed potatoes, or for starting off shallots and onion sets in trays.

In early spring you can sprinkle the compost from the bag over the surface of your seedbed. Its dark colour will help the soil to warm up. Peat from the growing bag is least valuable when it is dug into the soil because it will disappear within months: better to add it to the compost heap or your worm farm.

soil. If you have land to spare, then by all means sow grass seed specifically to make turf to cut for loam, but it will have to grow for two years before being cut, then stacked for another year.

You can make an extremely good compost out of worm-worked waste, the product of your worm farm, using half its volume with half of peat. This is good for potting up chrysanthemums and fuchsias. For other pot plants you will find it beneficial to add about one-eighth volume of sharp sand, gravel, perlite or vermiculite. In place of the peat (see recipes overleaf) you can use well-made leafmould, coir fibre compost or composted tree bark, but with these you should increase the volume of sand or perlite to open out the texture.

An important point to remember is that the plant food components in these soil and peat-based composts are non-renewable. Once the plants have taken up the nutrients, after about four to six weeks,

MAKE YOUR OWN COMPOST

For do-it-yourself composts the following recipes have worked well for me.

Soil-based compost

For sowing compost you'll need:
2 parts of loam
2 parts of peat, bark or coir fibre
1 part of coarse grit
Bonemeal and dolomitic limestone or hydrated lime.

For potting compost you'll need:
7 parts of loam
3 parts of peat or bark
2 parts of grit
Fish, blood and bone
Dolomitic limestone or hydrated lime.

To each 9l (2gal) bucketful of the peat, loam and grit mixture you should add 60g (2oz) of bone meal and 30g (1oz) of lime for the sowing compost. For the potting compost add 150g (5oz) of fish, blood and bone and 30g (1oz) of lime to each bucketful.

Peat-based compost

For sowing compost you'll need:
12 parts of peat, fine grade composted bark, or coir fibre
1 part of coarse sand
1 part of perlite or vermiculite
Dolomitic limestone or hydrated lime
Fish, blood and bone
Hoof and horn meal or seaweed meal.

To each 9l (2gal) bucketful of the peat, sand and perlite mixture add 90g (3oz) of fish, blood and bone, 30g (1oz) of hoof and horn or seaweed meal and 30g (1oz) of lime.

For potting compost you'll need the same ratios of peat or peat substitute, sand and perlite or vermiculite, but you should add three parts of leafmould or composted bark. In place of the peat you could use your homemade compost (page 43).

you will have to add more food to the compost as an organic liquid feed.

Another thing to bear in mind is that compost, whether bought or homemade, should be used as fresh as possible and not stored from one year to the next. So only make up as much as you need at a time, even though this might be difficult to judge. Store any surplus ingredients separately, keeping the fertilisers and lime in weatherproof containers, safe from the children.

You can use the potting compost not only for potting on seedlings after pricking out, for repotting established plants, and for filling outdoor containers such as troughs and hanging baskets, but also to make up your own growing bags. This is especially useful if you want to use a smaller-sized bag than the standard 95×35cm (38×14in).

Simply fill a strong plastic bag to the size that you want, then turn over the open end to form a seam and staple or tape it securely. Cut out a square or squares in which to put the plants, as you would a commercial bag, and you're in business. Instead of using one of the potting composts described here as a filling for your homemade growing bag, you can use the half peat/half worm-worked compost, or half peat/half aerobic compost mixture, if you are quite confident it has been properly made to eliminate any possibility of disease or pest carry-over. For the peat content you could substitute composted bark.

If you can't make your own compost or keep your own worm farm, there is a list of commercial suppliers in Useful Addresses.

MAKE YOUR OWN LIQUID PLANT FEED

When judging regional finalists in the National Allotments Awards a few years ago, one of the best plots I saw was at Thetford, Norfolk, where nothing but homemade compost was used to grow the most mouth-watering food crops and prize-winning dahlias and chrysanthemums. However, this green gardener also used the dark brown liquid that came from his compost bins during decomposition. It was run off into a container, diluted to the colour of good bitter beer and used as a liquid feed.

Making liquid manure was standard gardening practice up to twenty or thirty years ago. Now that supplies of horse manure are becoming more widely available because of the steadily increasing number

HOW MUCH COMPOST WILL YOU NEED?

Manufactured seed, potting or multipurpose composts are sold bagged by volume. The smallest size of 5 litres works out at about twice the price of the 40 litre size with many brands, so it obviously pays to estimate your need for the season and buy the biggest bag or bags that will meet that need without having too much of a surplus come the turn of the year.

The diagram will help you to estimate how many seed trays and pots of various sizes you can expect to fill from a 40 litre bag, but remember the precise numbers will depend on the density of the compost and how hard you pack the trays or fill the pots.

The Consumer Association recommends you should try to buy your compost from a shop or garden centre that stores its bags under cover and has a high turnover. Bags that have split and been taped or stapled should be avoided.

In trials by the association, reported in February 1989, the performance of multipurpose composts was compared, with surprising results.

Levington compost by Fisons, the peat pioneers, and Asda compost, sold as an own-brand by the supermarket chain, both scored the best ratings, but the Asda compost was about half the price of the Levington compost.

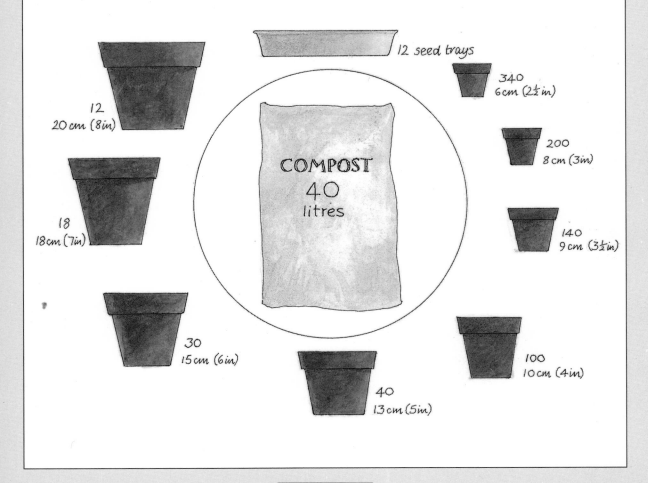

12 seed trays

12
20 cm (8 in)

18
18 cm (7 in)

30
15 cm (6 in)

COMPOST
40
litres

40
13 cm (5 in)

340
6 cm (2½ in)

200
8 cm (3 in)

140
9 cm (3½ in)

100
10 cm (4 in)

of riding stables, there's no reason why the practice shouldn't be utilised by the green gardener.

All that's needed is about 40 litres (half a sackful) of rotted horse manure, although pig, sheep, poultry or goat manure can also be used providing it has been gathered and stacked with straw litter, not wood shavings or shredded paper. The sack should be of hessian, not plastic, and before you fill it with the manure put a large stone in the sack. You'll also need a metal or plastic drum, such as those used for water butts, preferably with a draw-off tap.

Tie the sack with a double loop of plastic string or rope and dunk it in the drum, previously three-quarters filled with water. The stone will help the sack to sink. Then put the other loop over a length of wood so that the sack is suspended in the drum.

The liquid is ready to use after about a week, but it must be diluted. If it has been made with horse or cow dung, dilute one part of the liquid with two parts of water. If you've used pig, goat or poultry manure or pigeon droppings, dilute the mixture with three parts of water. As you draw off the liquid, you can top up the drum with water until the liquid has been replaced twice. After that the old manure in the sack should be added to the compost bin, or used for mulching, and replaced.

Use the diluted liquid as a foliar or liquid feed for plants in the garden, for crops in growing bags and for other greenhouse and house plants.

Dried blood also makes a good liquid feed for leafy plants, such as lettuce, spring greens and foliage pot plants: being high in nitrogen, it acts as a spring tonic. Use it at the rate of 30g (1oz) to 9l (2gal) of water.

Using liquid feeds It is better to use a liquid feed too weak rather than too strong. In fact, the plants benefit far more from a dilute feed twice a week than a strong feed once weekly. And always remember to moisten the soil or growing medium thoroughly before applying the liquid feed.

When you give a liquid feed use a fine rose on the watering can or, better still, a fine setting on a pressure sprayer and spray thoroughly until the liquid runs off the foliage.

Some people reckon that regular liquid feeding of edible greenhouse crops, such as tomatoes, cucumbers and peppers, is all that is needed to secure a good yield once the fertility of the growing bags has been exhausted. Others believe that a liquid feed is only a short-term answer to the plants' needs and should be supplemented with some solid food, such as fish, blood and bone or seaweed meal, or other organic plant food, added to the growing medium as a top dressing. It's what we used to call belt-and-braces caution.

Make your own liquid fertiliser by dunking a bag of animal manure in a barrel of water. You can use nettles or comfrey instead of the manure

HARNESS WORM-POWER FOR YOUR GARDEN

Even if your garden is too small to have a compost-making container of some sort, you can still save all your kitchen waste and have it converted to rich plant food by the willing help of worms. It's simple, clean and a worthwhile project whether your garden is a window-box in a high-rise block of flats or part of a country estate. What's more, you don't need a lot of gear to start worm farming. All you need to become a worm farmer is a plastic dustbin or some-

THE WONDER PLANT

Comfrey, made famous by the impresario of the organic movement, Lawrence Hills, is the ingredient of a liquid feed that is brimful with the main plant foods: far more nitrogen, potash, phosphorus and calcium than farmyard manure.

You will first have to grow your comfrey. Offsets or young plants of Russian comfrey can be bought or begged for planting at any time of the year except during hard frosts. Set aside a patch of your garden that you can spare in perpetuity and put the plants about 75cm (30cm) apart each way.

Comfrey grows vigorously and, once established, it's not easy to keep within bounds. Use the leaves as a mulch or dig them directly into the soil where they will quickly break down without poaching nitrogen, as would most other green material.

When the comfrey starts to flower in early summer, cut it back to make a concentrated liquid fertiliser, but, be warned, the smell is outrageous so the operation is best carried out well away from your living quarters.

Take a container, such as a disused plastic dustbin, water butt or similar, and fill it three-quarters full with the comfrey leaves. Then top up with water, cover and allow to ferment for about fourteen days. Then drill a hole in the container to allow the foul-smelling black liquid to seep into a container held at the ready. Use this concentrate, diluted one part to twenty parts of water, for all purposes for which you would use a proprietary liquid feed such as Maxicrop or SM3.

After about twenty days the concentrated liquid ceases to seep from the container. Use the mushy remains of the leaves as an activator on your compost heap. Your comfrey plants, meanwhile, will be making a forest of new growth.

---

thing similar, some peat (or peat substitute), a quantity of calcified seaweed, ground limestone or hydrated lime, and a regular supply of food scraps and waste vegetable matter plus, of course, the worms themselves.

The great thing about the worm farm is it utilises cooked kitchen waste that, if put on the compost heap or in the compost bin, would certainly attract rats, mice and flies. Worm-worked compost is rich in the main plant nutrients and all the vital trace elements. You can use it with soil, peat or bark for pot plants, hanging baskets and other outdoor containers, as a dressing for topping up the growing medium of pot plants, or as a plant food for the flower and vegetable plots, sprinkled over the surface of the soil and lightly hoed in.

The worms used in the worm farm aren't ordinary earthworms but manure worms (*Eisenia foetida*), or what anglers call brandlings, which occur naturally in any heap of decaying vegetation and can be bought from any angling shop. Unlike the aerobic compost-making operation, which relies on a combination of bacteria and heat to decompose the vegetable material, the compost produced by the brandlings is the product of the worms' digestive system.

WORM POWER

Starting a worm farm You'll need about a hundred brandlings to get your worm farm in a dustbin started, and to make it a suitable home for the worm colony it will need to have the right ventilation and humidity, plus a close-fitting lid to keep the flies out.

To ventilate the bin, bore holes in the lid using a drill or heated metal skewer. There will be some seepage, so, to allow this to escape and be collected in a drip tray for use as a liquid manure, make small drainage holes in the bottom 15cm (6in) of the bin. Fill this bottom section with a mix of pebbles and ordinary builder's sand, then add water until it seeps out of the drainage holes. This provides just the right level of humidity.

Place wooden slats on top of the sand and stones so that when you fork out the compost you don't disturb the bottom layer of sand.

Next add about 18 litres, or two bucketsful, of peat and well-rotted manure or spent mushroom compost and you are ready to introduce the worms to their living quarters.

Collect the worms from the angling shop, from your compost heap or a friend's, in a container of peat or moist soil and simply add them to the material in the bin. Then add the first load of well-chopped household waste, with a few sheets of moist shredded newspaper as a starter. This layer should be about 10–15cm (4–6in) deep and should be sprinkled with about a cupful of the calcified sea-

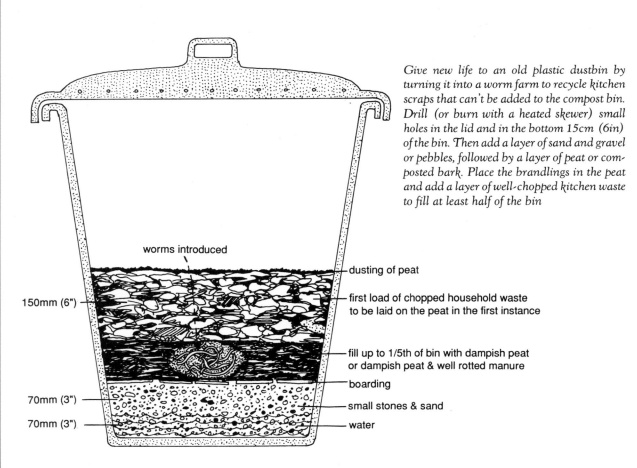

Give new life to an old plastic dustbin by turning it into a worm farm to recycle kitchen scraps that can't be added to the compost bin. Drill (or burn with a heated skewer) small holes in the lid and in the bottom 15cm (6in) of the bin. Then add a layer of sand and gravel or pebbles, followed by a layer of peat or composted bark. Place the brandlings in the peat and add a layer of well-chopped kitchen waste to fill at least half of the bin

worms introduced

dusting of peat

150mm (6")

first load of chopped household waste to be laid on the peat in the first instance

fill up to 1/5th of bin with dampish peat or dampish peat & well rotted manure

boarding

70mm (3")

small stones & sand

70mm (3")

water

weed or hydrated lime and then a light covering of moistened peat. Manure worms are very sensitive to acidic conditions so the calcified seaweed or lime is necessary to maintain a neutral pH level of 7.0. They will not survive if the compost dries out, so try to ensure that all the material you add to the bin is moist without being too wet.

Now all you need is patience as the worms get to work. Your starter colony of a hundred or so worms increases slowly at first, but after a few weeks, in spring or summer, there's a population explosion and myriads of the small red worms swiftly and efficiently convert your kitchen waste into compost.

Don't be in a hurry to add more waste to the bin after the initial loading; leave it for about three to four weeks, then add a little at a time. All organic waste and leftovers are suitable except those items that have been saturated in fat or vinegar. The more varied the diet, the better, but try to reduce everything to as small scraps as possible. The ideal worm's bite size is about two square millimetres.

Each adult worm produces two to five cocoons a week, each containing ten to fifteen hatchings which themselves mature in seven to eight weeks.

If you make your own beer, then add the spent yeast to the bin, along with crumbled stale bread, biscuits and cakes, sour milk and mouldy cheese. The more protein, the better. Jack Temple, in his booklet *Worm Compost*, reckons that if your kitchen waste is short in protein the first two layers should include generous dollops of chicken mash or similar meal. We feed our dogs on one of the proprietary complete foods and have found that the dusty scraps at the bottom of the sack, when moistened, make a good starter feed for the worms, but a stale loaf of bread would be equally good.

After about three weeks from starting you should be able to see signs of tiny, threadlike worms that have hatched from the cocoons of the starter colony. In cool weather you may have to wait longer, but once you see evidence of the population increase you can add further loadings of waste daily or weekly, but don't fill the bin right up to the top.

Every 15cm (6in) layer should be sprinkled with the calcified seaweed or lime and peat. Some people recommend that you churn the new material into the old, but I think this is unnecessary because the worms work their way up into the new material.

Worm compost The compost is ready when it has turned into dark, spongy, friable material, like sweet-smelling soil. This takes up to six months from starting – a little longer in cool weather. The contents of the bin can be forked into a plastic sack, or another bin, for storing, freeing the worm farm for a new colony. Use a little of the starter compost for the next colony, and so on indefinitely. Don't be concerned that your potting compost, made with the worm-worked waste, will be full of worms. It won't. Once they have exhausted the food supply they die and are themselves recycled.

When dry, the worm compost can be sieved and handled like any other compost. Because heat plays only a subsidiary role in the making of worm compost, don't add any garden waste containing weed seeds or the roots of such weeds as couch grass, ground elder or bindweed.

Winter quarters In winter the activity of the worms decreases as the temperature falls, until below 8°C (45°F) the worms simply rest up and wait for warmer times. If your bin is outside in the garden for much of the winter, your worms will not be operating, but the kitchen scraps will be gathering volume. You can encourage the worms to carry on working by moving your bin into a shed or garage and giving it some form of insulation, such as an old quilt or piece of carpet. Even better would be to make a purpose-built container, insulated with, say, expanded polystyrene, as the winter quarters for your worm farm.

If the idea of having your own worm farm doesn't appeal, you can buy worm compost in a variety of forms. See Useful Addresses.

GARDENING WITHOUT PEAT

Peat is a finite resource. Its extraction and use, both for horticulture and as a fuel, create problems of landscape degradation, habitat loss, erosion, and air and water pollution. Although alternatives have been sought, no commercially viable substitute has yet been developed.

Probably the most significant development in British research to find an economical alternative to peat as a growing medium has been the joint project by Hensby Biotech and Anglian Water using wheat straw and sewage sludge. These are composted to destroy all the potentially harmful pathogens while retaining all the major plant nutrients and many trace elements. The resulting compost is being marketed as Natgro by East Anglian Organic Products as a mulch, or for digging in, to replace lost organic matter, to improve soil structure, increase nutrient and water retention on light soils, and improve drainage on heavy soils.

Natgro compost combined with coir, a by-product of coconut production, is the filling for the first significantly new idea in portable growing units since the invention of the Grobag by Fisons. This is the Growbox, a compact 60cm (24in) long by 20cm (8in) wide and 15cm (6in) deep, which has a strong aesthetic appeal for use in the home, office, showroom and other public areas. It is peat-less, organic and even the box itself is biodegradable after use.

Whenever possible in this book I have given a reasonable alternative to the use of peat. Composted bark, for example, and leafmould can be used successfully on a garden scale in potting compost (see page 51) but not in commercial horticulture where enormous volumes of peat are used. The hope is that more municipal compost and composted straw and sewage will eventually be produced in enough bulk to become viable alternatives to peat. It is possible to buy organic growing bags, such as the Stimgro bag, which contain organic fertilisers instead of chemical additives. Certainly the use of peat as soil conditioner should be resisted by the green gardener. It actually breaks down quite rapidly and disappears within about eighteen months. The new Natgro compost or composted bark are better alternatives.

GETTING THE BEST FROM YOUR SEEDS

 Every seed is an embryonic plant waiting to get out. All it needs to turn from dormancy to a living thing are warmth, moisture, air and light. It even has its own food supply to see it through the earliest stage of development, that is, until it can grow roots to draw food and water from the soil.

Some seeds are so unfussy about conditions that they grow like weeds; others are so sensitive that getting them to germinate calls for considerable know-how. In general, though, most flower and vegetable seeds will germinate satisfactorily if a few commonsense guidelines are followed.

When you buy a packet of, say, lettuce seed it has this sort of instruction: 'Sow from mid-March onwards at three-week intervals in shallow drills. Thin seedlings to 23cm (9in) apart.' Such advice is unavoidably brief, but could spell disappointment for a gardening beginner. When the soil is cold and wet, you might have to wait quite a long time for the seedlings to emerge, if, in fact, they appear at all. If the soil is rough and ready, your seed might lodge in cracks and crevices too deep for the seedlings to emerge before it has exhausted its internal food supply. Anyway, what is a shallow drill?

SOWING

Before we so much as open a packet of seed for sowing outdoors we should check the soil temperature, and the accurate way to do this is to use a soil thermometer, an inexpensive piece of gardening equipment that can last a lifetime. The reading is taken 25mm (1in) below the surface. If it is below 10°C (50°F), hold your horses. In cold, wet soil seed is liable to rot before it has the chance to germinate. Particularly susceptible are French and runner beans, courgettes, ridge cucumbers, marrows, sweetcorn and tomatoes.

Whether the seeds are going into a seed bed or are direct sown where the plants will mature, it is important to give them a good start in life. The soil should be free from weeds, particularly of the deep-rooting perennial kinds. Ideally, it will have been dug and given a good dressing of compost or well-rotted farmyard manure during the autumn and winter. A week or so before sowing, scatter a balanced organic fertiliser, such as seaweed meal or fish, blood and bone, at about 56g (2oz) to the sq m/yd and rake this into the surface until you have a fine tilth without clods or stones.

SUCCESS WITH SEEDS

Some seeds can be pre-germinated very successfully, very simply. French beans, runner beans, broad beans and sweet peas are particularly suitable. Place the required number of seeds, plus a few extra for failures, into a clear polythene bag, add moist compost to cover them. Tie the top of the bag and shake it thoroughly to distribute seeds and compost. Hang it up in a light, warm place and examine daily. As soon as the seed radicle (the first spear-like root) appears, the seeds can be potted up individually or set out in trays of compost for subsequent hardening off.

For deep-bed sowing, where the crops are grown in blocks rather than regimental rows, the seed is scattered evenly and soil is sieved over them. Where the seed is sown in a seedbed, or direct into rows, first mark the row with a garden line. Then place the

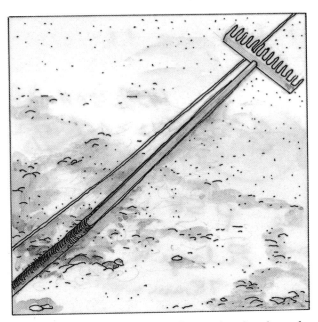

When sowing seeds in traditional rows, first fine down the soil and place a line along the row. Then make a drill by laying the rake along the line and pressing it into the soil. Sow the seed and gently rake earth over the drill

Use wire-netting to guard seedlings against birds

shaft of the rake along the row, teeth uppermost, and gently press it into the soil with your feet. Light pressure produces a shallow drill; increasing the pressure enables you to produce a drill 25mm (1in) or more deep. It is U-shaped, of even depth throughout its length and allows the seed to make good contact with the soil because there are no cracks or chasms. For best results the soil should be moist but not saturated.

A drill made this way enables you to space the seed thinly and evenly, and this is especially important with carrot seed where thinning of the seedlings would alert every carrot fly in the area.

If you are using your homemade compost, or half worm-worked compost/half peat mixture, you can form the drill rather deeper with the rake, then line it with sieved compost before sowing. Either way, after sowing, the seed is covered with soil eased from both sides of the drill and tamped down with the broad face of the rake. Final touches are to give the row a marker, with the type of seed sown and the date, and to give protection from the birds, if necessary, and some shielding from northerly and easterly winds if the site is exposed.

Most hardy annual flowers can be raised from seed sown direct into the garden where you want them to flower. Instead of sowing in drills, scatter the seed on the prepared surface of the soil and lightly rake them in, or sieve soil over them so that they are covered by about twice their diameter. Inevitably, you will find seedlings emerge in small groups and these need to be thinned out as soon as possible to give each little plant a fair share of space. Carry on thinning until the plants are spaced at the recommended distance for growing to maturity. Put the thinnings in the compost bin.

Half-hardy annual flower seeds, some biennial and perennial flower seeds, and some vegetable seeds need to be germinated under cover. Thanks to the development of inexpensive electrically-heated propagators this is no problem. Alternatively, a warm windowsill, airing cupboard or shelf above the boiler will provide the right temperature to get most varieties going. You'll also need seed trays, a seed or multipurpose compost, more trays or 8cm (3in) pots to prick out the seedlings into when they are large enough, and the space on a south-facing windowsill to stand the pots until the plants are ready to be transplanted outside once the spring frosts have finished.

WHY BUY F1 SEEDS?

When you buy F1 seeds you can expect to pay about twice as much as for seeds of ordinary open-pollinated varieties. Is it worth it? The first point to make is that we must do everything possible to ensure that the older non-hybrid varieties of flowers and vegetables are preserved in seedsmen's lists. Some are more suitable for organic growing than the newer F1 hybrids and are, anyway, intrinsically valuable as genetic stock.

Because of European Community regulations requiring rationalisation of national seed lists we have been losing vegetable varieties by the hundred every year since 1973. (See pages 120–1). However, it would be foolish to suggest that all those that were taken from the national list were worth keeping, or that the new F1 varieties are displacing the older ones merely to make more profits for the seed firms – now mostly in the octopus ownership of the oil companies and chemical conglomerates.

F1 seeds certainly carry a premium price and part of that is down to the higher cost of production. F1 means first filial, the offspring of a first-generation cross between two carefully selected parents. The pollination of the female plant by the male has to be controlled, unlike the open-pollinated types where nature is allowed to get on with it.

Every time the seed producer wants an F1 variety the identical crossing has to be made, and that's a laborious and therefore costly business. Additionally, royalties are payable to the plant breeder of F1 hybrids, a further on-cost to the seed buyer.

However, there are advantages in buying F1 hybrid seed over the open-pollinated equivalent. F1 seed has exceptional vigour and quality, so that the resulting plants are often stronger and more uniform in character than non-hybrid types. This is especially valuable in the early life of the plant when it is most vulnerable to attack by pests and diseases and has proved a strong selling point to commercial growers who are chemically independent.

A second factor is that you are buying a guarantee of performance. F1 seeds have a consistently high germination rate and the seedlings are true to type. In other words, they are precisely what you paid for in colour, height, growth rate, yield and other characteristics.

Thirdly, if you are growing a vegetable or salad crop the F1 varieties offer uniformity of size and time of maturity. So, for example, if you are growing a crop of Brussels sprouts for freezing, an F1 variety will give you plants reaching harvest condition together and buttons that are of uniform size.

However, not all F1 vegetable seeds are worth paying a premium for. Carrots are a good example. In trials by the Consumer Association's *Gardening* from *Which?* magazine, ordinary open-pollinated varieties of carrot were proved to give better value for money than the F1 types. In fact, the recommendation after the trials was that it wasn't even necessary to grow distinct early and maincrop varieties, just sow a good old variety like Early Nantes, pull them young as new carrots and allow the rest of the crop to mature.

Another factor is local conditions. If you are a newcomer to the district, or are just taking up gardening, it's always prudent to seek the advice of people who have had long experience of the local soil and climate. Ask them which varieties generally do well for them. The chances are that they will be the older varieties and that they will also do well for you.

TREATED SEEDS

Seed companies dress some of their seed with fungicide to minimise loss through rotting or other bacterial invasion, a practice that is condemned by the Soil Association. Seed that has been treated should be clearly marked in the catalogue and can be avoided if you buy by mail order. If you buy your packets of seed from a retail outlet, read the reverse side carefully. If the seed has been treated it should carry a warning. If you buy a packet of seed that has obviously been treated, but doesn't warn you, then send it back to the seed firm and ask for your money back.

Try to buy your requirements from seed suppliers who don't treat any of their seed, otherwise you will be sowing chemicals into your organic garden. Henry Doubleday Research Association, which supplies Heritage Seeds for organic gardeners, told me, 'It is becoming increasingly difficult to obtain untreated seed and, in some cases, we have had to do without a particular variety because chemical-free seed is not available.'

Chase Organics, Kings of Coggeshall, and Suffolk Herbs (*see* Useful Addresses) also supply untreated seed.

Bring the bag of compost into the room where you are going to raise your seeds for a few days prior to sowing so that it is warmed to the room temperature. For most seeds this should be 18–21°C (65–70°F), without too great a drop at night. Fill the seed trays to the top, gently tap the sides to remove air pockets, firm with your fingers, then level off the compost with a ruler or piece of card.

Next, thoroughly moisten the compost by standing the trays in a sink or bowl so that the water comes halfway up the sides of the trays, and leave until the surface changes to a darker colour and is just moist to the touch. Remove and let excess moisture drain away. Most seeds can be sown using finger and thumb or the dampened end of a matchstick, but very fine seed, such a begonia, needs special treatment. To ensure it is spread evenly pour a little dry sand into the seed packet, shake it and then allow the sand and seed mixture to trickle out, tapping the packet with your finger to ease it on its way.

Whatever the seed, try and sow as sparingly as possible to avoid waste and overcrowding of the seedlings. It's always better to have too much space between the seedlings than too little. Now add one of your homemade labels (page 142) giving the name of the seed and the date sown.

Wait for the first true leaves to appear before pricking out seedlings.
Place the tray of seedlings in a warm place out of direct sunlight

Check the instructions on the packet about the depth the seed should be sown, sieve compost over the surface and firm gently with a block of wood. Some seeds need light to germinate and should not be covered with compost. The trays can be covered with a piece of newspaper to keep out bright light, then put in the heated propagator or placed in a light, warm position indoors. Most seeds, however, need darkness, so, after adding compost to the surface, cover the tray with a sheet of glass or clingfilm, or put it in a clear plastic bag, and place in the bottom of the airing cupboard. If you are using a warm windowsill or shelf add a thick layer of newspaper, and remember to remove the tray from the windowsill at night when the sharp fall in temperature could severely delay germination.

Germination times vary considerably from as little as three days for some F1 hybrid geraniums to as long as three months for the Chilean bell flower (*Lapageria*). The longer the time taken to germinate, the greater the risk of the seed rotting or, having germinated, of the seedlings damping off. Spraying the surface of the compost with a liquid copper fungicide is a preventive and is organically acceptable.

Once the seedlings have emerged, the sheet of glass or plastic covering should be removed, the propagator temperature can be reduced to about 18°C (65°F) and the trays given as much indirect light as possible. This may mean moving trays onto a windowsill, out of direct sunlight, and turning them at least daily so that they do not lean towards the light, or use a light box. The first leaves to appear are the seed leaves. Wait until the first true leaves put in an appearance before pricking out (transplanting) the seedlings.

TRANSPLANTING

This is a delicate operation, but essential unless the seedlings are so widely spaced in their seed tray that they can be left to grow on. For pricking out use the same type of compost that they were sown in and have it moistened and at the same temperature. Very small seedlings can be lifted from the seed tray using a widger. This is an iced lolly stick with a notch cut in one end. Larger seedlings can be eased out of the compost using a pointed stick, such as a wooden skewer. Hold the tiny plant by the seed leaves, never by the stem, and take great care not to

MAKE A LIGHT BOX

A snag with raising seedlings on a sunny windowsill is that they are drawn towards the light and can become leggy. You can overcome this by putting the pots or trays in a light box. Make it yourself out of a cardboard box the depth of the windowsill, about 30cm (12in) tall and long enough to accommodate the pots or trays.

Line it on three sides with kitchen foil stuck to the cardboard, and cut away the fourth side which will face the window. Reflected light from the foil will help the seedlings to grow sturdily without leaning towards the window. Avoid having the box in direct sunlight which could cause scorching of the young plants.

To prevent windowsill seedlings becoming drawn and leggy, place them in a foil-lined cardboard box with the front panel removed

WHEN THE SOIL SAYS SPRING

Spring has arrived in the garden when the daily mean temperature, that's to say the average of the minimum and maximum temperatures, reaches 7°C (45°F). More important to the gardener, however, is the mean temperature of the soil, which should preferably be a little above the mean air temperature, at 10°C (50°F) before sowing seed outdoors.

SNOW SENSE

Snow on a cold frame during a spell of severe weather acts as an insulator, so leave it in place. But heavy snow can be damaging to shrubs, particularly conifers. It may look pretty, but brush it off.

damage the roots. Place the seedlings in ready prepared holes in their new trays or individual pots, and gently firm them in position.

After pricking out, the seedlings should be kept warm, out of direct sunlight, and moist, so after a few days they will need watering with a fine spray. When they have made two or three true leaves you can start liquid feeding with very dilute SM3, Maxicrop or your own brew (see page 50).

Hardening off is the final procedure before the plants are set out in their permanent quarters outdoors. This involves transferring the pots or trays to a cold frame about twenty days before the planned planting-out date. If you haven't a cold frame, they can be stood outside in a sheltered position for progressively longer periods during the day, and brought indoors at night, until the final four or five days, when they can be left outside night and day

WHAT THE INITIALS MEAN

For a long time the initials HB meant nothing more to me than a grade of pencil. Then, as gardening became a potent force in my life and the seed catalogues became required reading during the winter evenings, HB gained another, more interesting meaning.

GA (*Greenhouse annual*) These plants aren't hardy enough to be grown in the open ground and most of them are used as indoor flowering pot plants, including cineraria, cockscomb, hibiscus, lisianthus, Persian violet and indoor primula.

GB (*Greenhouse biennial*) Very much the same in character as the greenhouse annuals, but these plants require more than a twelve-month period to reach maturity. Calceolaria, one of the most popular pot plants, is in this category.

GP (*Greenhouse perennial*) Cactus, coleus and cyclamen all come under this heading of plants that go on maturing, possibly flowering, year after year, if protected from frost. This group also covers most of the popular foliage house plants.

HA (*Hardy annual*) This group of flowers complete their entire life cycle in one year, so a sowing made in early spring will give you flowers from midsummer until they make seed or die away. They do not need to be sown under glass or indoors, but outside where you want them to flower. Flowers in this group include acrolinium, agrostemma, anchusa, calendula, Californian poppy, clarkia, flax, godetia, larkspur, nigella, nasturtium, night-scented stock, scabious, sunflower, sweet pea and Virginian stock.

HHA (*Half-hardy annual*) These also germinate, flower and die in one year, but require a longer season of growth than the hardy annuals. This means the seed should be sown in a greenhouse or

unless frost is forecast. Those in the cold frame should be sheltered from strong sun but given adequate ventilation. Have a piece of sacking or old carpet handy to cover the frame lights against frost. Your local Weatherline phone service will inform you when the last frost can be expected.

After planting out, water well and regularly, and give some shelter from northerly and easterly winds which can damage young plants as severely as frost.

Biennials flower in the year after they were sown and then die, while perennials flower in the season after they were sown and go on flowering year after year. Some biennials and perennials can be raised indoors like half-hardy annuals, but it is more usual to raise them outdoors in a specially prepared seedbed in a sheltered part of the garden kept free of weeds and slugs. They are transplanted to their permanent position in the garden in early autumn.

SAVE ON BEDDING

Many bedding plants will self-seed if allowed to. Instead of dead-heading all the plants of, for example, alyssum, calendula, linaria, lobelia, nicotiana and pansies, let them go to seed. Then in the autumn, when clearing the beds, shake the seeded plants to spread the seed. Impatiens, the busy Lizzie, can be potted up and taken indoors for the winter. Small, compact plants can be allowed to go on flowering as house plants. Straggly ones should have the stems cut back to within a few centimetres and kept in a dry, cool place. They can then be replanted in the spring after the frosts have finished.

propagator, or indoors on a sunny windowsill with, maybe, a start in the airing cupboard.

These plants are all frost-tender and must be hardened off by gradually introducing them to the harsher climate of the great outdoors, so they are put outside for progressively longer spells during the day, then planted out into their permanent quarters when all danger of frost has passed.

Most of the popular bedding plants are in the HHA group, including antirrhinum, fibrous-rooted begonia, cosmos, dianthus, heliotrope, lobelia, marigold, nicotiana, petunia, phlox, salvia, tagetes, verbena, zinnia. Impatiens, or busy Lizzie, which has become probably the most popular bedding plant, is a half-hardy perennial, but is treated as a half-hardy annual.

HB (*Hardy biennial*) This is a group of plants, raised from seed, which require a longer period than one season to develop to maturity. The seeds are sown in late spring or early summer, and transplanted to their flowering position in autumn or spring to flower about twelve months after sowing. Some of the plants in this group are Canterbury bells, forget-me-not, honesty and wallflower.

HP (*Hardy perennial*) Many of our favourite border plants, such as lupins and delphiniums, are in this category. Sowing and cultivation methods are generally the same as for hardy biennials, although a safer way is to sow into seed trays for germinating in the greenhouse or propagator in March or April. The seedlings are transplanted when they are large enough to handle and will produce flowers in the autumn of the same year.

HHP (*Half-hardy perennial*) Two of the most widely grown plants in this group are geraniums and dahlias. If the seed is sown early in the year, in a heated greenhouse or propagator, half-hardy perennials will flower in their first season. This applies to gazania, geranium, gerbera, impatiens and mimulus which are normally treated as half-hardy annuals and are discarded after they have finished flowering. However, geraniums can be lifted before the first frost and kept over the winter in a cool frost-free place. Plants producing tuberous roots, such as the dahlia, should also be lifted in late autumn, labelled and stored.

CHOOSING AND CARING FOR BEDDING PLANTS

Bedding plants are big business and getting bigger all the time, with many hundreds of large nurseries, thousands of smaller ones and countless numbers of very small ones. Additionally, the major seed firms offer young plants by post, mostly species such as African violets, impatiens, begonias, geraniums and regal pelargoniums that are a bit tricky for the amateur to raise. They are despatched when only a few centimetres tall and are intended to be potted on and given protection until they are large enough to be moved to their final planting site.

Almost without exception, bedding plant producers have this much in common: having made the sale of carefully raised plants, their subsequent fate is in the lap of the gods. Or, to be more precise, whether those young plants survive the trauma of transplanting to become vigorous, healthy, mature plants is too often a matter of luck.

Here are a few tips on choosing and caring for your bought-in bedding plants:

- It is prudent to choose what plants will go where in the garden before making the trip to the nursery or garden centre. Most of the annuals and biennials come into flower from mid-May until late October and you can so organise it that you have a constant succession of blooms throughout that period.

- At the nursery choose sturdy-looking plants that are bushy rather than tall and thin. Plants that have pale green foliage and legginess are the result of greenhouse conditions that are too warm or too dark or both.

- Avoid plants that are in full bloom. They might look like the answer to instant colour in the bed or border, but plants that have been urged into early flowering to give them eye-appeal at the selling outlet will almost certainly have a shorter life than those that haven't been forced along.

- Hot, dry spells often coincide with the most critical time for bedding plants, that is, the first few weeks after planting out. So it is vitally important to nurse them through the trauma of transplanting by ensuring they are thoroughly watered in and, preferably, given a mulch of compost, peat or spent mushroom compost if daily watering is out of the question.

- After care consists of dead-heading the faded blooms and giving a gentle spraying with tepid water every few days, and a foliar feed of a seaweed fertiliser once a week.

Choose sturdy, bushy bedding plants with deep-green leaves

WILD FLOWERS, BEES AND BUTTERFLIES

 In ideal circumstances, each garden, however small, would have a part of it given over to wild flowers. That way we would be able to make some compensation for the wholesale destruction of our native flowers through modern farming techniques, road, house, factory and supermarket building, and the other methods we use to ensure that habitats for wildlife are lost for all time. We would also enrich our gardening experience because many wild flowers are too beautiful to be denied garden space. They bring with them the bounty of birds, bees, butterflies, helpful insects that act as predators of the pests, and small mammals that have every bit as much right to a home on this planet as you or me.

The reality is that, as gardens shrink, the pressure on available space is such that cultivated plants take precedence over wild ones. We'd sooner have a spring garden of daffodils and tulips than bluebells and violets, of hybrid tea roses in summer than the fleeting beauty of the dog rose. Yet it is possible to compromise, and here are suggestions designed to do just that, to give you a beautiful garden using a mixture of well-loved annual and perennial plants both wild and cultivated.

Wild flowers, and those becoming naturalised, don't require the extra feeding we give to cultivated ones, so, if you wish to reserve a part of the garden for them, the main task is to ensure that they are not overcome by the stronger wild plants that we reckon to be weeds. If, as I suggest, some wild subjects are blended into the beds and borders to share the living space with cultivated plants, you will probably find that the extra food available to them produces taller growth and larger blooms.

Seed of all the wild flowers recommended here for use in the beds and borders is available from Suffolk Herbs and John Chambers (*see* page 152-3 for addresses) and it's worth remembering that, having bought the initial stock, most of the wild annuals will re-seed at the sites you have chosen for them. Another point worth making is that wild flowers in among your cultivated ones will require you to be rather more relaxed about planting schemes – a fair degree of informality is needed. As John Stevens says in his beautiful book *Wild Flower Gardening*, 'Self-seeding will create informal and natural-looking associations that you could never achieve by planning. Your aim should be to guide things in the right direction and let nature do the rest. Surprises will abound: scarlet poppies will spring up in unexpected places; mulleins will appear towering above surrounding vegetation; and as if by magic the butterflies and birds arrive.'

Bird's foot trefoil Perennial, low-growing, with bright yellow flowers in late spring loved by butterflies and bees. Grows well in poor, sandy or chalky soil. Sow seed in situ in late summer or spring to form clumps at the front of sunny beds and borders.

Bluebell Perennial, grown from bulbs or seeds, that will rapidly colonise a wooded or shrubby area in semi-shade. Height to 30cm (12in). Plant the bulbs in the autumn 5cm (2in) deep; seeds take several years to become flowering plants. Some white and pale purple variations occur.

Chicory Perennial, with large blue flowers in summer. Growing to 1m (3ft) tall, this is an impressive subject for the border and is also grown as a green manure crop. Sow seed in situ and thin seedlings to 30cm (1ft) apart.

Clover, red Perennial that grows readily from seed to a height of 38cm (15cm). Order the seed of

Trifolium pratense, a true wild flower, as distinct from *T. incarnatum*, the agricultural legume used as a green manure crop, and sow in situ in spring.

Corncockle or corn campion Annual that readily self-seeds. It has brilliant red flowers in late summer and, growing to a height of 1.2m (4ft) makes a bold item for the back of a sunny border. Seed sown in situ in spring gives flowers in summer; seed sown in autumn gives flowers in the following summer.

Cornflower Annual for a sunny or semi-shaded position where it will have the support of other plants. This is because the brilliant blue, white, pink or purple flowers are often too heavy for the slender stems up to 45cm (18in) tall. Sow seed in situ in the autumn and allow the plants to self-seed.

Corn marigold Perennial, regarded with great dislike by the barley barons but a golden beauty in the garden, growing to 50cm (20in) tall. Sow the seed in situ in spring and allow to self-seed.

Cowslip Perennial that, for me, is the most beautiful of spring flowers. Easily grown from seed sown in trays in the autumn and overwintered in a cold frame. Give a position in semi-shade where the delicate beauty and fragrance of the flowers can best be appreciated. Height to 30cm (1ft). Divide established plants in the autumn to increase stock.

cowslip

Cuckoo flower Perennial that flowers when the cuckoo calls in spring. It is easily grown from seed sown in summer in a moist, partly shaded site, perhaps bordering the garden pond. Mature plants readily self-seed.

Foxglove Biennial that settles happily into any part of the flower garden where its tall flower spikes, up to 1.2m (4ft), can enjoy maximum sunshine. All parts of this plant are poisonous, but the flowers are loved by bees. Sow seed in situ in late spring.

Harebell Summer-flowering perennial with dainty blue flowers on delicate stems to a height of 38cm (15in). Sow in situ in spring and allow to self-seed.

Knapweed, greater Perennial, growing to about 45cm (18in), that attracts bees and butterflies to the large crimson blooms in midsummer, then finches to the seed heads in autumn. Sow seed in spring in trays and transplant when large enough to handle.

Marjoram Perennial, well worth growing as a herb for the kitchen, for its delicate rose-pink flowers and strongly scented leaves, and because it attracts bees and butterflies. When mature, it is 60cm (2ft) tall. Sow the seed thinly in situ in late spring.

Meadow crane's bill Perennial, its large purple-blue blooms rivalling any cultivated plant for loveliness and profusion. Prefers slightly alkaline soil. Sow in a seed tray in spring and transplant allowing plenty of space, because when mature the plants reach up to 80cm (2½ft). Self-seeds by catapulting seed away from the parent plant.

Mullein, dark Stately biennial that grows to 1.2m (4ft) tall, so group it at the back of a sunny border. Yellow and purple blooms mass on the flower spikes for weeks in the summer. Sow in situ in late spring.

Musk mallow Perennial that earns a place in my garden for its musk-scented, bright pink flowers that blend happily with annuals in the border. It makes a bushy plant to about 60cm (2ft) tall when mature. Sow seed in situ in early autumn.

Oxeye daisy Perennial, readily grown from seed sown in situ in autumn or spring. Most effective

Selection of wild flowers available as seed for sowing in beds and borders

bluebell

chicory

cuckoo flower

corn marigold

common dog violet

corn cockle

harebell

small scabious

oxeye daisy

WILD FLOWER RULES

- Buy wild flower seed only from a reputable source, preferably from a supplier who specialises in wild flowers.
- Ensure that full instructions on germination and dormancy are given with each species you buy.
- The seed should be of native species, indigenously grown and gathered, and so most suited to the climate and most attractive to native insects.
- The Wildlife and Countryside Act of 1981 (UK) makes it an offence to uproot, pick or collect seed from any plant in the wild on the schedule of protected plants. There are sixty-one species on the list and the penalty is a heavy fine. If you have spare seed from your home-grown plants, don't scatter it in the countryside. You could consign it to an early death if the land is sprayed with herbicide. Better to give it to a conservation group, such as your county's wildlife trust.

- More than 15,000 species of flowers grow wild in the UK, but 20 per cent are under threat. There are ninety-two plants on the protected list, including Adder's tongue spearwort, blue heath, branched horsetail, bedstraw broomrape, creeping marshwort, early star of Bethlehem, fen ragwort, fen violet, field cow-wheat, alpine, fringed and spring gentians, water germander, sickle-leaved hare's ear, red helleborine, lady's slipper, Lundy cabbage, pennyroyal, purple colt's foot, rock cinquefoil, rough marsh mallow, tufted saxifrage, sea knotgrass, rock sea lavender, spiked speedwell, stinking goosefoot, viper's grass, wild cotoneaster, wild gladiolus and downy woodwort.

PLANTS IN DANGER

The Resurrection Plant (*Selaginella lepidophylla*), or rose of Jericho, is sold as a novelty plant in Britain and other European countries. The plants are collected from their natural desert habitat in Central and South America and their numbers have been so reduced by traders that conservationists now want their export and import controlled by the Convention for International Trade in Endangered Species. The plant opens out to catch the morning dew, then closes up to conserve moisture. Sadly, the novelty of a unique desert plant in a British home quickly wears off: few survive for longer than a month or two. The National Council for the Conservation of Plants and Gardens at Wisley Garden, Woking, Surrey GU23 6QB will give advice on how the green gardener can help to protect many more species that are under threat of extinction.

when sown in meadow grass. Height to about 45cm (18in).

Oxlip Perennial, with flowers similar to the cowslip. Sow seed in late summer in situ or in trays, overwinter, then transplant to a moist, semi-shaded site. Height to 30cm (12in).

Pansy Perennial, but best treated as an annual. This miniature beauty has the country name heartsease, and will happily settle into the front of the border in full sun or semi-shade where it grows to no more than about 15cm (6in) tall. Sow the seed in situ in late spring.

Poppy Annual treated as a biennial that readily self-seeds in well-cultivated soil. A perfect companion for other flowers up to 60cm (2ft) tall in sunny beds and borders. Sow seed in situ in autumn.

Ragged robin Perennial for shady, moist areas in soil or grass, this has beautiful, rose-red ragged petals, the flowers appearing in late spring on single stems to 50cm (20in) tall. Sow seed in trays in spring and summer and transplant when large enough to handle. Mature plants readily self-seed.

Scabious, small Perennial growing to about 60cm (2ft) tall with a profusion of flowers that are a smaller and more delicate version of the sweet scabious or field scabious. It blooms over a long period of the summer and is a magnet to bees and butterflies. Sow the seed in situ in spring or late summer. The mature plants should be cut back hard after seeding.

Teasel Biennial, decorative giant grown for the large mauve flower heads that attract bees, followed by the seed heads that attract gold finches and, when cut and dried, make a striking winter decoration. Sow seed in situ in a damp spot, remembering that the mature plant will reach to 2m (6ft) tall.

Toadflax, common Perennial creeping plant for siting in grassland only. The yellow flowers, like small antirrhinums, are sought after by bees. Sow in situ in spring and don't let the plants creep into cultivated beds or borders. Height to 60cm (2ft).

Violet, sweet Low-growing perennial that spreads readily by runners, which can be replanted in spring to increase stock. Sow seed in pots or trays in autumn and overwinter in a cold frame. Prefers a moist position catching the early morning sun, such as an east-facing bank. The sweet-scented flowers appear as one of the first blooms of spring.

TOADFLAX AS A FLY TRAP

In summer soak a few plants, including the bright-yellow, snapdragon-like flowers of common toadflax, in saucers of milk. Leave for at least twelve hours, remove the plants and use as a fly trap, out of reach of children and pets. The flies settle in the milk and are poisoned.

Viper's bugloss Biennial, with flower spikes up to 80cm (2½ft) tall carrying brilliant bluish flowers, loved by bees. Sow seed in situ in late summer. Readily self-seeds.

Yarrow Perennial, with feathery foliage and flat heads of tiny daisy-like flowers throughout summer. Height to 40cm (16in). Good for seaside gardens, but spreads readily. Sow seed in trays in spring or summer, overwinter in cold frame and transplant in the spring.

CULTIVATED PLANTS

Many flowering shrubs attract bees and butterflies; some give the bonus of berries for the birds in autumn and winter, and a few offer roosting or nesting sites. Walls and fences can be clothed with cotoneaster, choisya, ivies, honeysuckle, *Kerria japonica* 'Pleniflora', the passion flower *Passiflora caerulea*, potentilla 'Gibson's Scarlet' which is very attractive to hoverflies, and pyracantha, while if you have room for a flowering hedge choose from lavender, *Cotoneaster lacteus*, berberis, escallonia, *Rosa rugosa*, *Prunus cistena*, chaenomeles, *Mahonia aquifolium* or *Olearia haastii*.

Shrubs for planting as specimens or in groups rather than as hedge material would include the butterfly bush, *Buddleia davidii* and *B. globosa*, *Berberis thunbergii*, daphne, hardy fuchsias, philadelphus, carpenteria, caryopteris, corylopsis, any of the

WILD FLOWERS, BEES AND BUTTERFLIES

*Reserve part of the garden for wild flowers
and plant it with seed from a reputable supplier*

extensive broom family, but especially *Cytisus burkwoodii, Cotoneaster franchetii* and *C. watereri,* the flowering currant *Ribes odoratum,* the male sallow *Salix caprea, Vibernum tinus,* rosemary, beautiful as a shrub, invaluable as a herb, and the winter jasmine *J. nudiflorum.* In my seaside garden the evergreen shrubby veronicas or hebes offer flowers for bees and butterflies from as early as March right through to Christmas.

In the flower garden proper the season for bees starts with the earliest spring-flowering bulbs – snowdrops, winter aconites, crocus, hyacinths, muscari and chionodoxas – the sweet williams, primroses and wallflowers, and the invasive but much-loved dandelions. Then follow the annuals, best planted in bold groups rather than scattered singly in the border, and perennials, that will provide a summer-long source of nectar and pollen for the bees.

Choose the cultivated plants for your sunny borders with their wild flower companions in mind: neither should overshadow the other and the finished effect should have the informality of the old-fashioned cottage garden. Particularly successful are the herbs that provide a rich source of nectar for the bees and butterflies as well as supplies for the kitchen: rosemary, sage, lavender, thyme and chives. In sunny island beds and borders select from marigolds, giant thistles, rudbeckias, Michaelmas daisies, golden rod (although this one tends to be rather invasive), lavatera, lupins, delphiniums. At the front of the border group the low-growing alyssum, catmint, rock roses, aubretia, thrift and campanulas, backed by clumps of candytuft, Canterbury bells, balsam, larkspur, nicotiana, nigella, pinks and aquilegia, while the tallest plants at the back of the border should include sunflowers, hollyhocks and the Scottish thistle.

SAFE WAYS TO CONTROL PESTS

 If you were to believe all the publicity put out by the pesticides people, the average garden is the stalking ground for every conceivable sort of pest, waiting in the wings to strike your carefully raised flowers, vegetables and fruit. Only the diligent use of an armoury of sprays will keep this multitude of pests at bay, they say.

In fact, a lot of this is scaremongering because unless there are exceptional circumstances, like prolonged drought, for instance, which weakens the resistance of plants, well-brought-up garden plants are able to cope with the minor attacks by assorted pests, aided by natural predators that will appear to challenge the attackers, if given the chance.

There are exceptions, however. The two most commonly encountered pests, aphids and slugs, can build up numbers very rapidly unless early preventive action is taken, so in considering ways to cope with pests without recourse to poisonous sprays, we'll put aphids and slugs at the top of the hit list.

JEYES FLUID

Many people swear by Jeyes Fluid as an essential gardening aid, particularly in warding off soil-borne disease and such pests as the carrot fly and cabbage root fly. But is it OK for the green gardener to use? The short answer is No.

Jeyes Fluid contains phenols which will kill not only harmful pests and disease organisms, but also those that are important to the soil's health and vitality.

However, Jeyes is certainly a very effective garden disinfectant and can be used, properly diluted, for cleaning the greenhouse, cold frame, glass cloches, trays, pots and tools.

APHIDS

The snag about aphids is that there are so many of them. Virtually every cultivated plant and weed in the garden is host at some time to its own species of aphid. Happily, this big family of pests is breakfast, lunch and tea to a fair number of predators, so control of the greenfly, blackfly and other aphids must be done without wrecking this natural balance of pest and predator.

The first job the green gardener must tackle in controlling aphids, or any other pest for that matter, is one of identification. Make sure that your target is a pest and not a helpful or benign insect. You'll find there are numerous books to help you identify insects, but one of the best is Michael Chinery's *The Natural History of the Garden*, which not only tells you where to look for pests and predators but also shows you how to recognise them when you have found them.

Aphids have mouths like miniature hypodermic needles, which they use to pierce the soft parts of plants and then to suck out the juices. This not only causes damage to the plants from the punctures but also weakens the plant as the food-laden sap is withdrawn. But there is another, possibly more important, feature of aphid attack, and that's the numerous virus diseases that aphids carry from plant to plant.

Greenfly Aphids multiply very rapidly, so early identification and control measures are needed. On the roses look for the first greenfly as soon as the new sappy growth appears in early spring. They will have hatched from eggs laid on the rose stems during the autumn, so control of greenfly among the roses can actually begin in the winter by encouraging birds to eat the eggs (*see* page 10). Small groups of greenfly can be destroyed between finger and thumb or, less messy, by directing a squirt of soapy water at them. Use a pressure sprayer and be sure to spray the plant thoroughly from top to bottom. One spraying is seldom enough; you may need several at weekly intervals.

Quassia, rhubarb spray, elder spray or one made from soft soap are also effective and safe, but insecticidal soap, such as Savona, is one of the safest organic insecticides you can buy.

Blackfly Anyone who grows broad beans knows they are Mecca to the blackfly or black bean aphid, which lays its eggs in the autumn on host trees such as the syringa and viburnum. In the spring, winged aphids emerge and fly off in search of beans, spinach, thistles, docks and all sorts of herbaceous plants. On the broad bean plants they head for the young pale-green leaves and flower buds first, followed a little later by the young bean pods. Numbers build up very quickly and badly infested plants become stunted and the crop ruined, so early control is vital. Use the same soapy water spray as for roses, ensuring that every part of every plant is thoroughly drenched. Alternatively, use insecticidal soap, quassia or derris (*see also* page 89).

Mealy aphid The cabbage or mealy aphid can be a serious pest in my part of the country where summers are frequently dry and hot, conditions that favour a rapid infestation before the predatory ladybird larvae arrive. The eggs are laid on the stems of brassica plants in the autumn and produce wingless aphids covered with white powdery wax. Winged aphids then appear and fly to the underside of the leaves of cabbages, Brussels sprouts, swedes and other brassicas. A small patch of mealy aphids speedily becomes a bigger patch. Leaves weakened by the sap sucking turn yellow and wilt. And there's an added complication: the aphids excrete excess sugar from the sap in the form of honeydew and this falls onto the sprout buttons and upper surfaces of cabbage leaves, and a black mould develops.

To minimise attack from mealy aphids, it is prudent to get rid of the brassica stems as early in the year as possible. Shredding them and adding them to the compost heap is one way. Another is to trench compost them (*see* page 44). Once the pest gets a grip on a crop, repeated spraying with insecticidal soap, pyrethrum or derris is necessary.

TAR OIL

Winter washing of fruit trees using tar oil was considered to be a good preventive because it killed overwintering eggs of aphids, as well as other pests. Now we know this can often do more harm than good because it may also kill the predators of the pests. A particularly successful biological control of woolly aphid is a parasite called *Aphelinus mali*. It was introduced from North America in the 1920s and is now widely established throughout southern England.

Woolly aphid Fruit trees are attacked by the woolly aphid, so called because it produces fluffy strands, like cotton-wool, to protect it from predators. If you tease away these strands you will find a mass of mauve-coloured wingless aphids on the new twigs of the tree. Small groups can be scraped off, but if the infestation is bad, spray with derris after petal fall.

SLUGS AND SNAILS

Slugs are snails without their shells, and there seems to be an awful lot more of them, but both are pests that gardeners must keep under control. Their numbers rise when a mild winter is followed by a wet spring, and they love the verdant conditions of the highly productive organic garden which gives abundant food and moist shelter without the interference of chemical fertilisers and pesticides. Someone estimated that under such ideal conditions there could be as many as one thousand slugs to the square metre.

In fighting such an army it pays to study their behaviour. They are nature's scavengers, living off dead and dying vegetation, as well, of course, as young living greenstuff. So one theory is that if you are meticulous in keeping your garden free of fallen leaves and other decaying material, you will provide fewer hiding places for them to breed and rest up. The opposing view is that if you deliberately place small mounds of decaying vegetable matter and dead leaves at strategic points, you concentrate the slugs' attention on these instead of on your plants.

Anyone who grows hostas, lupins or delphiniums will know the flaw in both ideas is that slugs have an

Four weapons in the fight against slugs: A container filled with beer or sugared water, a band of crushed eggshells round a target plant, (opposite) a barrier of coarse sand or sawdust and a ring of Slugtape

insatiable appetite for herbaceous plants, epecially the tender young growth of early spring, and given the choice will head for the hostas rather than a pile of old leaves.

Other features of slugs' behaviour are that they are slow movers, preferring to travel at night, and are very fussy about the surface they journey over. If you go into the garden after dark with a torch, from early spring onwards, especially during a damp warm spell, you will not only be able to see slugs and snails at their most active, you will also actually be able to hear them because they all feed by a rasping action of their toothed tongue. Take a container of salt water and a pair of tweezers and you'll have a field day but, regrettably, you will probably make little impression on the overall slug and snail population in the garden. In an experiment conducted over a week in a small urban garden, five people collected a total of more than 27,000 slugs and snails,

without any noticeable decrease in the damage to plants. One reason for this is that each slug lays about 500 eggs during its adult life, and, as both slugs and snails are truly hermaphrodite, lack of an available partner is no obstacle to breeding.

The eggs are laid in or on the surface of the soil and normally hatch within a few weeks during late spring and summer. Those that are laid in autumn and winter remain dormant until the warmer days of spring arrive, so gently stirring the surface of the soil during the winter months will invite the birds and ground beetles to help themselves. If you have mulches around plants, such as newly-planted shrubs, draw the mulch away for a time during the winter to expose overwintering slugs and snails.

As well as the new growth on herbaceous plants, slugs will eat cabbage and lettuce seedlings through to ground level in one sitting. In fact, few seedlings, whether from seed sown in situ or transplanted, are immune from attack. There's also a small black horror called a keel slug that lives and eats underground. Jerusalem artichokes are attacked, but the prime victims are maincrop potatoes, especially those grown organically: the keel slug will puncture the skin, work its way into the potato and munch its way through the flesh, safe from any predator. The damage is discovered when you harvest the crop and find potatoes, invariably the biggest and best, with telltale holes in the skin and a rather hollow feel to them.

A variety of control techniques is recommended. Those already mentioned should be backed up by placing traps near to susceptible plants. These can be small tins or plastic containers sunk to the rim in the soil and filled with stale beer or sugary water. Examine the traps every morning and change the beer or water every third day. Slugs can also be encouraged to congregate by placing halves of grapefruit or pieces of wood or slate around the garden.

Seedlings can be protected with barriers made from plastic bottles, and you can use the slugs' dislike of gritty surfaces by surrounding likely targets, such as the new growth of delphiniums, dahlias, lupins, and so on, with a band of eggshells, baked in the oven and then crushed, or coarse sand, or bark chips. Sawdust and soot can also be used although their effectiveness is diminished by rain.

The predators of slugs are ground beetles, toads, frogs, hedgehogs, slow-worms, centipedes and, of course, blackbirds and thrushes, all of which would be harmed to some degree by using some of the chemically impregnated slug controls sold in garden centres and shops. But there are safer chemical controls which can be used without fear of harming wildlife or soil micro-organisms. One I've found particularly effective is Nobble, based on aluminium sulphate. It acts as a slug and snail birth control by destroying the eggs on contact, so is best used very early in the season and at monthly intervals thereafter. Fertosan is another strongly fancied product which gives good control when used properly. It causes shrinkage of the slime-forming organs of the slugs.

Slugtapes, although based on metaldehyde, are not a threat to wildlife and are unattractive to pets because the active ingredient is incorporated in paper. The product can be bought in narrow strips for placing round plants or seedlings, or in square pads for use against keel slugs when planting out seed potatoes. Another answer to the curse of the keel slug could be a brew invented by a member of

the HDRA and reported in *Organic Gardening* magazine. It is a rather complicated recipe but has the bonus that as well as being effective against slugs it is also a good liquid feed for the potatoes and tomatoes, runner beans and sweet peas, with a particularly high content of potash.

Start by getting hold of a large plastic drum or a metal one which must be coated inside and out with black bitumen paint against rusting. Half fill the drum with weed roots, such as dock, convolvulus, couch grass, thistle, nettle, along with lawn mowings and kitchen scraps, excluding tea leaves, fish and meat scraps, but including plenty of orange peel. Fill the drum with tapwater so that you have a fifty-fifty mixture of solids and water. It will start to ferment after three to seven weeks, depending on the air temperature, and can then be drawn off and used.

The idea is to water it generously on the soil under the potato haulms throughout summer, but avoid splashing it on the haulms or on neighbouring crops as it can damage foliage. It can also kill worms as well as slugs, but as they move much faster than the slugs they should be out of harm's way by the time the liquor has soaked through the soil. As you draw off the liquid, you can top up with water until it no longer ferments, that is, when the bubbling stops. The mush as the bottom of the drum can then be used as compost for mulching, or added to the compost heap.

Another recommended slug repellent, although probably not for over-sensitive souls, is to collect as many slugs as possible using tweezers and a bucket of salted water, or a long nail on the end of a cane, like a litter spear. You will have to make your slug hunt at night or before dawn and your catch of slugs is left to decompose in a bucket of rainwater for several weeks. The gooey mess is then poured around those parts of the garden where slugs normally congregate and it is claimed that you will be free of the pests for several years.

CATERPILLARS

After the aphids and slugs, caterpillars are the next most commonly encountered garden pests, with ornamental plants of many kinds, fruit bushes and trees, and vegetables, coming under attack from a bewildering variety of the pests. Brassicas are the main target for the caterpillars of the large white and small white butterflies. If the cabbage white butterflies are a major pest in your garden, preventing them from laying their eggs is the simplest control and you can do this by covering the brassica plants from late spring onwards with fine mesh plastic netting or polypropylene fibre cloth, such as Agryl P17 or Papronet.

Control techniques for caterpillars on individual crops are given in the list that follows, but general advice is that keeping a sharp look-out for pests on a weekly tour of the garden is the best insurance against an infestation. Squash any eggs you see, looking especially at the underside of leaves, and pick off and destroy any caterpillars. However, there are undoubtedly times, if you are away on holiday, for example, when caterpillar numbers build up, and the damage to cabbages can be considerable. Fortunately there is a safe but very effective biological control now widely available in the form of a naturally occurring pathogen *Bacillus thuringiensis*, sold as Bactospeine, Dipel, Biobit or BT4000. It is a bacterial culture made from the spores of the bacillus and supplied in sachets. You simply add the contents to water and spray the solution onto the leaves where the caterpillars are eating. It will not harm insects, birds, fish, pets or humans.

It is usually necessary to repeat the spraying after about a week. Large caterpillars may take three to five days to die after the first spraying.

OTHER PESTS

Ants The harm ants do by stealing newly sown seeds and 'farming' aphids is outweighed by their usefulness in destroying pests and aerating the soil. But in the home they can be a nuisance – if you feel extermination is necessary, a proprietary ant-killer will do the deed. Alternatively, make your own by mixing 113g (4oz) of borax with the same amount of castor sugar and sprinkle it along the ants' route.

Apple sawfly This is the pest that causes maggoty apples and premature dropping of the fruit. Control is by spraying with derris a week after petal fall and destroying dropped fruit.

Asparagus beetle The adult yellow and black beetles and the grey larvae eat the shoots and leaves, so use tweezers to pick them off and remove the old stems to prevent them overwintering.

Bean weevil These little creatures look like beetles with snouts and the only harm they do is to give scalloped edges to the broad bean leaves, something you can surely live with.

Blackcurrant gall mite A pest to be taken seriously because it causes big bud and is the agent that passes on the virus disease that results in reversion. Limited control is effected by picking off the swollen buds in winter, but a badly affected bush may have to be destroyed. Seek expert advice on recognition of the problem before deciding on destruction.

Cabbage root fly All newly-planted brassica plants are at risk from this little pest, but cabbages and Brussels sprouts are the most likely victims at any time from April to July. The female fly lays its eggs in the soil against the stems of the plants, and sometimes actually on the stem. After a few days the eggs hatch and the larvae tunnel into the main roots of the plant, often eating the entire root system. First sign of attack is stunted growth with purple colouring of the leaves. Eventually the plant collapses and dies. Fortunately, a very effective control is to fit a collar around the plant when you set them out to stop the fly laying its eggs. You can buy special fibre collars or make your own, using old bits of foam-backed carpet or carpet underlay or thick brown paper. Cut squares about 10cm (4in) each side, or circles 10cm (4in) in diameter. Cut a slit to the centre and four short slits crossing through the centre. Thoroughly water the plant after planting out, then slide the stem of the plant to the centre of the collar.

Carrot fly This is another little horror from the same family as the cabbage root fly. It will also attack celeriac, celery, parsley, parsnip and fennel, using scent as its radar. It zooms in low and lays its eggs on the surface close to the carrots. The eggs hatch into tiny maggots that bore down into the soil, then up into the roots. First indications of an attack are the leaves of the plants turning from green to orange and red. The maggots are voracious feeders and cause major damage to maincrop carrots. There are several ways to prevent attack:

- Sow and raise the early carrots under cloches or under a floating cloche of Agryl P17 or Papronet.

Protect brassica seedlings from cabbage root fly attack with a collar cut from old carpet, or carpet underlay, and placed in position after planting out

- Because the female fly uses the scent of the crop to locate it, try scent-jamming by planting the carrots between onions or garlic, and avoid thinning the young carrots or bruising the foliage when weeding.
- Turn over the site for the carrot crop in October and again in November to allow the birds to feed on the pupae.
- Best of all, grow the crop behind a physical barrier because this offers the highest rate of control. I made panels 90cm (3ft) long by 37.5cm (15in) tall from clear polythene sheeting stapled to frames of secondhand roofing laths. They are positioned round the crop without any gaps and held in place by stakes pushed into the soil on either side.

Celery leaf miner This is the offspring of a fly which lays its eggs on the leaves of the celery plant. They hatch and the larvae then tunnel between the upper and lower leaf surfaces. When you see the

A physical barrier made from polythene sheeting stapled to wooden frames makes an effective barrier against carrot fly

used in May where there are several apple trees, while hessian sacking or corrugated cardboard tied around the trunks and branches from August onwards will attract the caterpillars, which can then be shaken out and destroyed.

Cutworms These live just below the surface of the soil and eat young plants at ground level. Hoe regularly to control them and wind a strip of kitchen foil round each plant stem when transplanting, with about 2.5cm (1in) of foil below the surface.

Flea beetle Turnips, radishes and swedes are the main targets for this tiny beetle, which jumps like a flea and is most active in May and June. The larvae pupate in the soil and a second generation hatches in the autumn and overwinters, so turning over the soil gives a first line of defence because the birds will eat the exposed larvae. The beetles eat small holes in the leaves and this can so badly check growth that the young plants die. At the first sign of damage spray with liquid derris or dust with derris powder. Alternatively, use a sticky board coated with treacle or wet paint. Hold it an inch or so above the crop and tap it. The flea beetles jump and become trapped on the board. It sounds a bit bizarre, but it really works.

tunnelling lines and yellow or brown blotches on the leaves, simply squeeze between finger and thumb or remove the damaged portion of leaf and destroy it.

Chafer grubs Large white grubs, with three pairs of tiny legs, which eat the roots of the raspberry canes and strawberry plants, causing wilting and collapse. The grubs live in the soil, especially in neglected parts of the garden, so detection isn't easy. As well as the raspberries and strawberries, the grubs and adult beetles attack potatoes, lettuce and herbaceous plants, and similar symptoms are shown after attack by vine weevils and leatherjackets. Happily, the pests can be eliminated by turning over the soil in autumn and winter.

Codling moth The white grubs of this moth eat into apples, feed for a month or more, then emerge and spin cocoons under loose bark and other hiding places, to reappear the next season. Pheromone traps, which act as decoys for male moths, can be

Gooseberry sawfly The small caterpillars eat the leaves of the bushes in late spring and summer and will entirely strip a bush in under a week. The creatures are green with black heads and black spots and should be hunted from late April onwards. Hand picking is seldom entirely successful because the pests seem to concentrate on the most inaccessible parts of the bush. Spray with derris and repeat at weekly intervals until June.

Leek moth This has become something of a problem pest in some parts of Britain in recent years. It is a tiny brown moth and lays its eggs alongside the leek plants in late spring and early summer. The small caterpillars eat into the leaves causing long slits that fray and tear. There is no entirely effective control, although some gardeners reckon that gently squeezing the plants in the early stages of development is as good a remedy as any.

Lettuce root aphid In dry, hot summers this can be a serious menace. Plants wilt and die and when

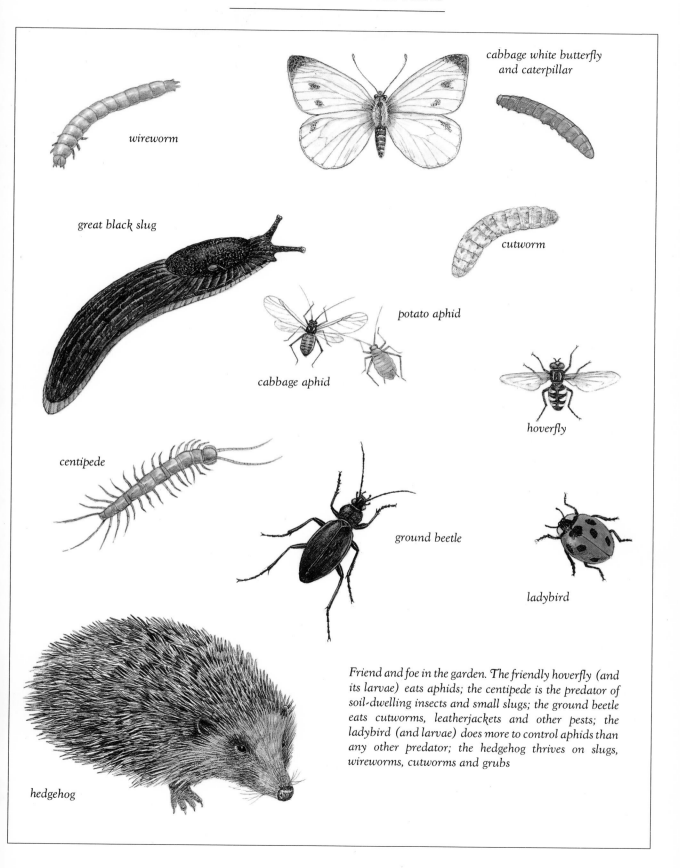

wireworm

cabbage white butterfly and caterpillar

great black slug

cutworm

potato aphid

cabbage aphid

hoverfly

centipede

ground beetle

ladybird

hedgehog

Friend and foe in the garden. The friendly hoverfly (and its larvae) eats aphids; the centipede is the predator of soil-dwelling insects and small slugs; the ground beetle eats cutworms, leatherjackets and other pests; the ladybird (and larvae) does more to control aphids than any other predator; the hedgehog thrives on slugs, wireworms, cutworms and grubs

dug up the roots are found to be covered in aphids and a white waxy deposit. Badly affected plants must be destroyed. The eggs of this aphid overwinter in the soil and on host plants, so it is wise not to grow outdoor lettuce on the same site more than once in three years. Don't leave any lettuce roots in the ground, give the soil a good turning over in the autumn, and in hot, dry weather give the lettuce crop plenty of water. If all else fails, grow a resistant variety, such as Avoncrisp or Avondefiance.

Mealy aphid This can be a serious pest on Brussels sprout plants in a dry summer, building up vast colonies on the undersides of the leaves, often defeating the attempts of predatory ladybirds to control them. The blue-grey aphids also colonise the developing buttons and because they are sap-sucking, sprouts and plants fail to develop properly. Early control by spraying with insecticidal soap is essential. Repeat every four days or so until the pest disappears.

Onion fly Another relative of the cabbage root fly, this tiny pest homes in on the onion crop to lay its eggs on the soil. The maggots feed in the stems and bulbs, causing young plants to wilt and die, and more mature bulbs to rot. Cultivating the soil in autumn gives the birds a chance to eat the overwintering pupae. Growing from seed in clusters and thus avoiding the need to thin offers fairly good control, but best control is achieved by growing onion sets.

Pea moth The small caterpillars of this moth eat the peas in the pod. A pheromone trap is available for commercial growers, while the amateur gardener must avoid attack by sowing before March or after April.

Pear midge The adult female midge lays eggs in the blossom buds in early spring and the larvae enter the baby fruits, which fail to develop normally and fall from the tree. Cut a fruit open and you'll find a white grub inside. The control is to destroy the fallen fruit and turn over the soil under the tree in late autumn to expose the pupating larvae to predators. Cottage gardeners would allow their hens into the orchard to do this commendable task.

Plum sawfly Similar in its habits and appearance to the apple sawfly, this lays its eggs in the blossom and the caterpillars then eat their way into the fruit. Telltale signs of an attack are the small entry holes, usually surrounded by a sticky black mess. Pick and destroy affected fruit. Control by spraying with derris seven days after petal fall and cultivate the soil under the trees during the winter.

Potato eelworm This is also called yellow potato cyst eelworm or golden nematode. It's a tiny pest that causes major damage and is difficult to eradicate once it gets firmly established in the vegetable garden. It causes stunted growth of the potato plant and when the tubers are lifted they are marble size. Examine the roots under a magnifying glass and you will see white or yellow cysts or tiny blisters on them. These each contain up to 600 eggs which will remain dormant in the soil for up to ten years, becoming triggered into life when the next crop of potatoes or outdoor tomatoes is planted. The eelworm larvae then feed on the roots causing the check to growth of the haulm and the tubers. After the crop has been lifted, many millions of the cysts may be left behind in the soil and there is no way of getting rid of them apart from denying them a host crop of potatoes or tomatoes. In effect, this means rotation of the potato crop, if your garden is presently free of eelworm. If eelworm has already attacked, there is no cure. You will have to refrain from growing spuds for at least six years. Some varieties are more resistant to eelworm attack than others and the early crop is not likely to be as badly affected as the main crop.

Raspberry beetle It is the grub of this small beetle that does the damage, eating into the fruit of raspberries, blackberries and hybrid berries. In June and July the female beetle lays eggs in the blossom and in about fourteen days they hatch into the grubs. They grow with the berries and after four weeks or so of gorging themselves the grubs fall to the ground, where they pupate over the late autumn and winter. The first line of defence is gently to fork over the soil during the winter to expose the larvae to birds. A second weapon is to spray the plants with insecticidal soap or derris as soon as the flowers open, with a second spray as the flowers die and a third when the berries turn pink.

Red spider mite Outdoors, this little pest has apple and plum trees and strawberry plants as its targets. In the greenhouse or conservatory, it will infest almost anything. In the greenhouse, regular misting is a preventive, while full control is achieved by introducing the predatory mite *Phytosieiulus persimilis*. Outdoors, the natural predators will normally keep the pest under control if they themselves are not killed by poisonous sprays. Symptoms of attack are mottling, then bronzing of the leaves, which become covered with fine silk webbing. In a severe attack the leaves shrivel and fall.

Scale insects These are sap-sucking insects which are rather difficult to detect on some plants because they concentrate on the stems and undersides of leaves. House plants are attacked as well as apple and peach trees and grape vines. Like aphids, these insects have a waxy coating that can be penetrated by a spray of insecticidal soap, such as Savona, or derris to which a little soft soap has been added. Outside, spray the trees or shrubs in spring, or as soon as the pest is verified, and repeat at fourteen-day intervals. On house plants, the first evidence of attack is the sticky honeydew excreted onto the upper surfaces of leaves and onto the polished table the plant is standing on. Small colonies can be squashed by hand or, if that's not your style, they can be painted with a fine brush or cottonwool bud dipped in Savona or derris. Badly infested potted plants that can be manhandled readily can be upended and dunked in a bowl or bucket of soapy solution at weekly intervals until the pest is cleared.

Strawberry aphid This is a dangerous pest because it transmits virus disease, and may be present on the leaves of the plant throughout the year, a good enough reason to burn off the leaves in late autumn. Keep a sharp lookout for the pest, which gathers on the undersides of the leaves, and spray with either pyrethrum or derris in April in the evening, when the bees are not active, and again in May.

Tortrix moth Three species produce caterpillars that attack apples, pears, plums and cherries, feeding on leaves, buds and fruit. Spray with *Bacillus thuringiensis* as soon as the caterpillars are seen.

Wasps Not a pest in the garden unless there is a nest of them. In fact, wasps do far more good for the green gardener than harm. The larvae feed on aphids and caterpillars. The adults will attack ripe fruit that has already been damaged by birds, for example, but are seldom the instigators.

MORE FRIEND THAN FOE

Wasps, like ants and earwigs, are pests only if they are in the wrong places. They are very efficient at clearing up waste fruit, so it's best to try to protect the ripening fruit from attack. But a wasp nest indoors is a problem that should be tackled swiftly. The loft is a favourite place, but wherever the nest is located, don't try to remove it yourself. Consult the pest control people in the local council's environmental health department.

In the garden you can deal with a wasp nest yourself using a non-poisonous organic technique. Put a pile of fresh grass cuttings over the entrance to the nest: as the mowings decompose, the oxygen in the underground nest is used up and the wasps die.

Weevils It is the little grubs of this beetle tribe that do the damage to apple blossom, pea and bean plants and the roots of turnip. There's also one, called the vine weevil, whose grubs destroy the roots of glasshouse crops, pot plants and outdoor garden plants. Another damages a wide range of soft fruit bushes, roses, clematis and other ornamental plants, while yet another concentrates its attack on strawberry roots. Control of apple blossom weevil is by wrapping a piece of hessian sacking or corrugated brown paper round the trunk in midsummer. This will trap the larvae as they descend the tree to pupate. Burn the sacking or paper and keep the base of the tree clear of fallen leaves and other debris. Crop rotation is the only effective control for the turnip gall weevil whose grubs eat into the developing root causing swellings. Lift affected plants very carefully and destroy them. The female pea and bean weevil lays her eggs in the soil near the plants, and the grubs eat the root nodules for about thirty days, then pupate in the soil. The adults emerge in June and July, feed on a wide variety of plants, then hibernate for the winter in plant debris until the warming days of spring bring them out. Good housekeeping in the garden by tidying up leaves and other waste vegetation is a first line of defence. The next is to give young plants a spray of derris or pyrethrum or a dusting with derris powder. Female vine weevils will each lay up to a thousand eggs in the soil, or in the compost of potted plants and glasshouse crops. The eggs hatch in spring and the grubs feed for about twelve weeks. They then pupate in specially prepared cells made in the growing medium. The pest in pot plants can be controlled by dunking the pot in a solution of derris liquid.

Whitefly Two types are commonly encountered: the greenhouse pest and the brassica whitefly. Mild winters in southern Britain have led to a build-up of the brassica whitefly on Brussels sprouts in particular. Both the larvae and the tiny, white, moth-like flies congregate on the underside of the leaves. The honeydew they excrete falls onto leaves and sprout buttons and a sooty mould develops. Spraying with

Yellow sticky traps can control mild attacks of whitefly in the greenhouse. You can also use an insecticidal soap spray, or a vacuum cleaner

pyrethrum or an insecticidal soap, such as Savona, gives good control, although it usually takes three sprays, at weekly intervals, to overcome an infestation. In the greenhouse, a mild attack can be checked with yellow sticky traps and a soft soap spray or two, but certain control is achieved by introducing a predatory wasp *Encarsia formosa* that lays its eggs in the whitefly larvae.

Winter moths It is the destructive caterpillars of a whole family of moths that cause damage to all the top fruit trees. They feed on the leaves and opening buds in spring, having hatched from eggs laid in the branches. The female moths are wingless and they emerge from pupae in the soil during the winter. To get up the trees they have to crawl up the trunk, so you can abort their egg-laying intentions by placing a grease band around the trunk in November, or smearing the trunk with a 15cm (6in) band of vegetable grease. The organic pesticides derris and pyrethrum will kill the caterpillars, as will the biological control *Bacillus thuringiensis*, although the use of these should only be necessary if the olive-green caterpillars are seen feeding on currant and gooseberry bushes.

Wireworm Old, neglected gardens and allotments are often infested with wireworms, which are the slender, smooth, tough larvae of the click beetle. They can do very considerable damage to root crops and flower bulbs and are active throughout the year. A good organic way to clear a badly infested area is to sow a green manure crop of mustard in April at 28g (1oz) to the sq m/yd. Dig this in during July and re-sow with mustard for digging in during October. The wireworms gorge themselves on the mustard, become click beetles and fly away. In well-cultivated gardens birds seek out the wireworms, so they shouldn't be a problem. You can check on the presence of this pest by putting pieces of raw potato onto sticks and pushing them about 15cm (6in) into the soil. Examine them weekly and destroy any wireworms that have eaten into the potato.

Woolly aphid Cottonwool-like patches on apple and pear trees in spring hide these grey-coloured aphids. You can scrape them off or cut out and burn them, but if the infestation is widespread, spray with derris after petal fall.

THE LARGER PESTS

Birds In country gardens wood pigeons can do an astonishing amount of damage, especially to winter crops. We once had a quarter-acre crop of Brussels sprouts stripped bare in the first hour of daylight following a heavy overnight snowfall. Pigeons do most damage in spring and early summer, however, eating leaves and buds from soft fruit bushes and taking peas, beans and other vegetable crops. Netting is the only certain safeguard against attack, although scarcely practical if there is a large area to be covered. Various scaring devices can be effective, but only in the short term because birds become accustomed to them. Some farmers use the very antisocial gas gun that scares not only the pigeons, rooks and crows, but also babies, pets, wildlife and passing horses.

The old-fashioned scarecrow is good if moved from place to place; so too is the kite in the form of a hovering kestrel. Strips of glittering foil hung from

THE GARDENER'S FRIEND?

The robin is Britain's best-loved bird, equally at home in town or country gardens and is noted for its tameness. Although its food includes earthworms and spiders, it eats many insect pests and some weed seeds. Naturalist W. E. Collinge analysed the average diet of the robin as 43.5 per cent beneficial, 48.5 per cent neutral and 8 per cent 'injurious' to man.

lines, humming tape stretched round susceptible crops, and whirligigs made from empty squash bottles and placed on canes at strategic points, all have their fans. There's also the theory that if you can interrupt a pigeon's flight path it will not attempt a landing. One way of doing this is to place empty wine bottles upside down on tall canes at intervals around the vegetable patch. Some control can also be achieved against birds that damage, for example, the buds of currants and gooseberries, by the use of a harmless repellent spray or dust containing alum or quassia.

Magpies have multiplied to the point where, in my part of Suffolk, and possibly elsewhere, they have become a threat to smaller birds, plundering their nests and taking eggs and fledglings. They seem almost indifferent to the usual scaring devices and are, of course, protected by law. How you protect your garden and its wildlife from them, I'm not sure.

Strawberries are a special case for protection because blackbirds seem to like them every bit as much as most people. Make sure the netting you use is well secured so that birds cannot gain entrance.

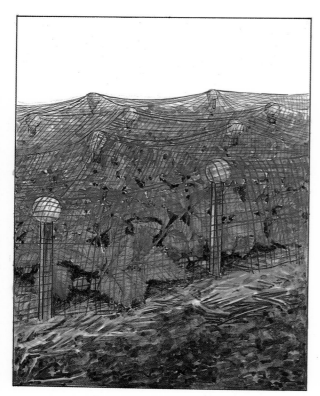

Net your strawberries securely against poaching by birds, but examine daily to rescue hedgehogs that might have become entangled. Old tennis balls on stakes prevent the net from snagging

---

DETER THE BIRDS

Birds, and particularly chaffinches and bullfinches, often take the buds of gooseberry and currant bushes in early spring. Dusting equal parts of weathered soot and hydrated lime over the bushes is often a successful deterrent.

Try to give the netting daily scrutiny: hedgehogs also have the knack of getting themselve helplessly entangled.

Cats To suggest that cats are a major pest is to invite a sackful of hate mail, but, lovable though they undoubtedly are to their owners, cats are a curse to the gardener and especially the green gardener. According to the Royal Society for the Protection of Birds, cats are responsible for the slaughter every year of vast numbers of young blackbirds, thrushes, robins and sparrows, along with shrews, baby hedgehogs and squirrels. The RSPB says that cats are the biggest danger to birdlife in suburban gardens. Not all cats wander from garden to garden, but most of them do, depositing their faeces and scattering earth to cover the deposit. This is more than a nuisance, it is a health hazard as well. Cats which have not been wormed regularly may pass larvae of the roundworm *Toxocara*, which can affect the optic nerve of a child who has accidentally handled, and ingested, cat's excrement while playing in the garden. Cats are most attracted to freshly cultivated soil, particularly seedbeds and newly sown lawns with a dry surface, so keeping the soil moistened is one deterrent. More effective is to net the likely target area because this will also protect newly

---

CAT AND MOUSE GAME

If you keep a cat, don't encourage birds to your garden. But, as Charles Darwin pointed out, a cat will keep field mice in check and that means more peas and beans will survive. Field mice also attack bumble bee nests and eat the young bees. So more cats means fewer birds in the garden but more bumble bees.

---

sown seed against the birds. We keep dogs, so neightbours' cats tend to steer clear of our urban patch. Even so, there are parts of the garden that are off limits to the dogs, and we try to debar trespassing cats as well. Proprietary repellents, such as Catoff, are harmless and quite effective for a while. So, too, is pepper dust, but these repellents also seem to deter the wildlife that we welcome in the garden. Just as with moles, there doesn't seem to be a satisfactory way of dealing with the problem of cats.

Deer Roe, fallow, sika and muntjac deer are troublesome in some country districts, eating plants in spring and stripping bark in winter, but only if the property is improperly protected. This means deer-proof fences or hedges, bearing in mind that an adult roe deer can clear a height of 1.5m (5ft). So where you are sure deer are responsible for the damage in your garden, you will have to erect a barrier at least 2m (6ft) tall. Alternatively, you could use an electric fence operating off a car battery of the type used by stock farmers, although there are regulations covering the use of this equipment.

Mice In the garden, field mice can be very destructive, taking bulbs, corms and newly-sown peas and beans for preference. My limit was reached when one sowing of peas after another was eaten, and instead of our usual feasting on fresh peas, the remnants of the sowings produced barely enough for two meals: only about one seed in ten survived the mouse invasion.

Mice have, or rather had, several predators, including owls, weasels, foxes, kestrels and cats, but in my part of barley baron Suffolk, all but the cats have declined in number through chemical farming and barn conversions. A succession of mild winters in the late 80s also had a part in allowing the mouse population to rise.

Setting traps in sheds, garages, greenhouses and other likely haunts over the winter months is a traditional preventive against mouse damage in the spring. Then, when susceptible crops such as peas and beans are sown, setting traps close to the rows is a second line of defence or attack. Unless you use the plastic box humane trap, ensure that the lethal breakneck trap is placed out of reach of children, pets and birds. The humane trap doesn't kill, so you have the problem of disposing of the terrified victim. In fact, unless you religiously examine the traps each

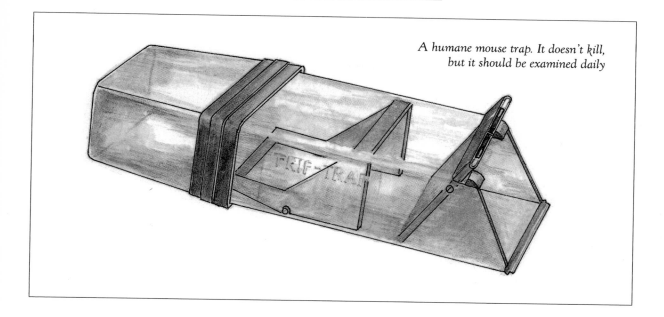

A humane mouse trap. It doesn't kill,
but it should be examined daily

morning, the chances are the trapped mouse will die of fright or of heat exhaustion within a few hours of being caught.

There are alternatives to trapping. Soaking the seeds, bulbs and corms in paraffin is one idea. Using garlic juice instead of paraffin is also said to be quite effective and infinitely preferable to the old trick of dressing seeds in red lead. Other mouse deterrents are: sowing dried holly leaves with the peas and beans, or lining each side of the sown rows with dried prickly prunings of, say, rose, gooseberry or pyracantha.

If none of this appeals to you, try using guards of fine mesh wire netting over the rows of peas and beans, or start off your crops under cloches.

DUCKS FOR SLUG CONTROL

If you have kept ducks, you'll know they are fine pest controllers, particularly of slugs and snails. Given grass to graze, a few ducks will keep a large garden clear of slugs while ignoring ornamental plants and vegetable crops, although their webbed feet are death to seedlings. In Far Eastern countries ducks are trained to go into the paddy fields and rid them of pests.

Moles If moles weren't such beautiful little crea-tures, many of us would feel less unhappy at trying to eliminate them from our patch of the planet. They are a nuisance at times: when, for example, they tun-nel under a row of newly-sown seeds or create may-hem under and over the lawn. Unfortunately for us, moles revel in the conditions found in the organic garden, its crumbly yet humus-rich soil with plenty of plump worms and other desirable items of food. The decline in barn owl numbers has seen a corres-ponding increase in moles, and in letters to garden-ing writers. Here are some suggestions that are worth consideration if you are reluctant to trap and kill moles and can square your conscience at sending them off to your neighbour's patch.

First, get the problem into perspective. Accord-ing to expert Michael Chinery in his *Natural History of the Garden*, moles are fairly solitary crea-tures, most abundant in woodland and permanent meadows. 'They do not usually take up residence in gardens unless there are large expanses of lawns or orchards . . . Mole hills are unsightly on the lawn, but the animals do no harm otherwise. They destroy large numbers of useful worms, but they make up for this by making their own drainage and aeration systems.'

● Sow a few plants of *Euphorbia lathyris*, the caper spurge or mole plant. It is quite an attractive plant and is said to be heartily disliked by moles.

- Get to know someone with a ferret, beg some ferret droppings and sprinkle them around the garden or down the mole runs.
- Flood the tunnels with water, or place elder twigs in the mole runs.
- An old technique was to place a few lumps of calcium carbide in the runs. This gave off acetylene gas which caused the mole to depart for distant lands very smartly.
- Whacking the soil or lawn with the back of a spade is said to scare the daylights out of the moles, but does no good to your spade, your soil or the grass.
- Bury empty wine bottles every few metres round the perimeter of the garden. The wind whistling over the mouth of the bottle is a deterrent. You can buy an electronic device that works in a similar way. It transmits ultrasonic sound waves and is powered by batteries.

If moles are a problem, try burying empty wine bottles round the affected area – the noise of the wind in the bottles is supposed to act as a deterrent

Rabbits The dreadful virus disease myxomatosis, introduced to Britain in the 1950s, almost wiped out the wild rabbit population. Since then generations of rabbits have gained immunity to the disease, or the disease has become less virulent, and rabbits are once again a commonplace feature of the rural scene. If your garden adjoins open land inhabited by rabbits, the only sure defence is a physical barrier of stone, bricks, wood or wire-netting, or an electric wire fence operated from a 12-volt car battery, which is also said to be effective against foxes. If you take over a garden that is already populated by rabbits, the best plan is to call in the experts to eradicate them: your local council offices should be able to give you advice on whom to contact. Until you are confident your garden is free of rabbits, newly planted shrubs and trees should be given the protection of a plastic or wire netting sleeve to prevent bark stripping and vulnerable plants should be doctored with a repellent spray, such as Hoppit which contains quassia. By the way, wire-netting as a boundary barrier against rabbits is only effective if it is buried about 30cm (1ft) deep.

Rats There are two species of rats in Britain, brown and black, and both came originally from Asia. The black rat, or ship rat, is the carrier of bubonic plague and is seldom found outside the great ports. The brown or common rat is larger, up to 23cm (9in) long with an 18cm (7in) tail, tougher and more aggressive. It will live anywhere it can find shelter and a source of food and is a carrier of serious diseases that can be fatal to humans and dogs and cats. There are usually seven young in a litter, and three to five litters a year are normal, so this is a pest of potentially fearsome destructiveness: too dangerous to be left to DIY eradication. If you have rats anywhere on your property, don't delay in contacting the Environmental Health Department of your local council.

Squirrels Britain's red squirrels are in decline not, as generally believed, because they are losing the fight for territory with the grey squirrel, introduced from the United States in the 1870s, but because of disease, so the chances are that any squirrels in your garden are grey ones, bigger and less shy than the native red squirrel. Landowners and officialdom regard the grey squirrel as a pest and there have been attempts at extermination by poisoning and shooting, although gardeners are more tolerant. If squirrels frequent your garden for the food you put out for the birds, they are unlikely to attack your trees for the sweet sap beneath the bark, although they may dig up your spring-flowering bulbs and raid the soft fruit. Protect the bulbs with wire netting and any newly planted trees with a plastic Somerford sleeve. To save your strawberries and raspberries from plunder you will need netting or a fruit cage.

COPING WITH PLANT DISEASE

When disease strikes a plant the pathogen will be either bacteria, a virus, or the spores of a fungus, and symptoms will be evident as a distortion of the plant, or part of it, damage such as discoloration of the leaves, rotting of the roots, or gradual die-back of the plant. Some attacks, like the common cold in human beings, are so mild that they can pass unnoticed in the plants.

Just as with humans, some factors in the environment can make plants more susceptible to ill health: overcrowding; too little light, air or water; a bad diet; cold, wet soil; rough handling, can all have an effect on the ability of a plant to fight illness. Organic gardeners believe that they give their plants the best possible help in warding off attacks, both by pests and diseases, by giving them a balanced wholefood diet throughout their life, not by force-feeding them with a chemical one. Through a more intimate and sympathetic understanding of our plants' needs in terms of soil conditions, sowing, siting, transplanting, feeding, pruning, harvesting and storing, we can minimise the frequency of disease attack, while at the same time remembering that disease in the plant world is as natural a phenomenon as it is in human terms, so there are bound to be occasions when we have to accept losses. The green gardener is not entirely alone in the fight against plant illness. There are a few natural medicines for some of the problems. More importantly, there's an enormous input of effort worldwide to give plants, particularly food crops, greater immunity to disease. For all of us with concern for a cleaner, safer planet, this work by hybridists and plant pathologists to use nature's controls, rather than chemical compounds, to fight plant disease offers tremendous potential. Biological control of plant diseases is in its infancy, but has already made some very significant contributions. Quite properly, the

The spores of apple scab overwinter on fallen leaves, so collect the leaves in the autumn and turn them into leafmould (see page 88)

Clubroot develops below ground as swellings and distortions on the roots of the brassica family (see page 88)

first to benefit from this research are the commercial growers, but we as amateurs are close behind in the queue.

Apple scab A common disease of apples that causes patches of corky skin. It is of far less concern to the amateur gardener than the commercial grower trying to meet the unreasonable demand for blemish-free fruit from the supermarket bosses. Fungal spores overwinter on fallen leaves, so in the autumn collect all fallen leaves and add to the compost heap, or turn them into leafmould. Some control is obtained by spraying at bud burst with one part urine and one part water, or with Bordeaux mixture at pink bud stage, and again four weeks later.

Blackcurrant reversion This virus disease is passed on by the gall mites that cause big bud. It severely reduces the cropping and the symptoms are not easy to recognise. Basically, the leaves of the bush get smaller and have fewer typical lobes. There is no remedy, but before passing the death sentence have an experienced eye cast over the bush.

Blackspot A fungal disease of roses, the symptoms of which are dark brown or black patches on the leaves. They turn yellow and eventually fall before their due time. Some varieties are more susceptible to blackspot than others and the disease always seems worse in hot, wet summers. Scrupulous collection and destruction of all infected leaves is a vital factor in controlling the problem, and some people swear by spraying with elder spray. Growing resistant varieties is one way of preventing the disease. It's interesting that in areas of heavy air pollution, blackspot is virtually unknown.

Botrytis Wet and warm summers also favour the development of this fluffy, grey mould which affects many types of garden plant. It can be particularly troublesome in small, enclosed gardens where the air movements are few and far between, and under cloches where it can cause terminal damage to early, covered strawberries, and in the greenhouse where the main targets are tomatoes and cucumbers. There is no cure, so destroy all infected leaves and fruit.

Clubroot Probably the disease most feared by the amateur gardener and allotment holder because it affects all brassicas. A slime fungus is responsible and there is no cure because once the spores enter the soil they remain there for many years. You can actually walk the disease from one garden to another on the soles of your shoes and on the scraps of soil clinging to garden tools. For this reason, it is unwise to buy plants of cabbage, Brussels sprouts, cauliflowers, sprouting broccoli or calabrese unless you are 100 per cent certain they are from a disease-free source. The disease spores can also be carried on stocks and wallflower plants. Symptoms of the disease are wilting of the plant during the day and a change of colour of the foliage from green to red or purple. Below ground, the roots develop swellings and distortions that, when cut open, have a foul smell. If you already have clubroot on your land, you have my deepest sympathy. You can lessen the effects by improving the drainage and liming the soil to raise the pH to 7.5, along with strict adherence to crop rotation. All infected crops should be burned or otherwise destroyed. On a small scale, cabbages can still be grown by sowing in small pots, transplanting to larger ones and finally into 22.5cm (9in) pots. Plant them out, pot and all, with the rim of the pot a good inch above the surface of the soil, and grow on to maturity.

Mildew, downy A greyish mould that penetrates the tissue of the plant, notably all brassicas, lettuce, onions and ornamental plants, including greenhouse plants. Remove all infected parts and destroy them, then spray with a solution of 113g (4oz) of washing soda in 4.5l (1gal) of water and 56g (2oz) of soft soap or Lux soap flakes. Try to keep a buoyant atmosphere in the greenhouse and avoid having pools of water lying about the place.

Mildew, powdery A white, powdery fungal growth which attacks the leaves, flowers, buds and fruit of a wide range of garden plants. It can be most serious on apple trees, gooseberry bushes and roses. On apple trees sulphur is the traditional control, but it is damaging to many varieties. Affected shoots should be removed in the winter, spring and early summer, and a further precaution against spread of the disease is to spray at pink bud stage, and fortnightly thereafter, with a solution of 21g (¾oz) of potassium permanganate in 13.5l (3gal) of water.

On gooseberry bushes it is called American gooseberry mildew and appears in spring as a white coating on the young shoots, eventually spreading to the stems and the berries. Pruning to keep an open, inverted-umbrella shape, and avoiding a site that is damp and sheltered, are precautions. If the disease appears, spray with Bordeaux mixture in the winter, and in spring with a solution of 84g (3oz) of washing soda and 28g (1oz) of soap flakes in 4.5l (1gal) of hot water. Use it when cool.

Mildew on roses appears in early May and can spread very rapidly. It is worst in small, enclosed gardens where there is little air movement. In such locations it is advisable to plant only resistant varieties and to avoid using nitrogenous fertilisers. Control with a solution of 56g (2oz) of carbolic soap in 4.5l (1gal) of water, sprayed on the bushes every three weeks from May to September, except in wet summers.

Onion white rot Like clubroot, this is another much-feared disease because once it gets into the garden there is no organic remedy other than resting the land from onion growing for at least eight years. Leeks, shallots, chives and garlic may also be affected, so all these members of the onion family should be rotated as a precautionary measure. First symptoms of attack are yellowing of the leaves and stunted growth. Eventually the plant keels over, revealing a mass of cottonwool-like white threads of the fungus. Sometimes all the roots will have rotted away. Infected plants must be burnt and not put on the compost heap. Current research is directed at producing a biological control for this very damaging disease.

Potato blight This fungus disease, which also affects outdoor tomato plants, first shows as dark brown patches on the leaves, often with a white mould on the underside. The blotches rapidly spread to the stems until the whole of the haulm turns dark brown. At this stage it is pretty certain that the spores have reached the tubers, having been washed into the soil by rain. Infected tubers rapidly rot and are useless for storing. In damp summers don't wait for the disease to appear, start preventive spraying with Bordeaux mixture fortnightly from July, and don't forget to include your outdoor tomatoes. The disease is spread from diseased tubers left over from a previous crop, either in the ground or in seed tubers. Spores can be wind blown to infect a new crop and are produced and dispersed in vast numbers in damp, misty weather.

Potato scab This is a corky growth on the skin of the potatoes which looks unsightly but does not affect the keeping or eating qualities. It is most prevalent on light, hot soils and on land that has recently been limed. Adding liberal amounts of organic material to your potato patch is a precaution, while the addition of a generous handful of lawn mowings when planting the seed potatoes will create local acidity and give a scab-free result. An alternative is to use spent peat from growing bags in the planting trench. Try to avoid planting your potato crop in land that has recently been limed.

ORGANIC PESTICIDES

Organic pesticides are safer to use than the agro-chemical sprays because they are naturally occurring substances that are non-systemic and non-residual. That means they neither harm the environment nor enter the food chain, and break down harmlessly once they have done their work. Nevertheless, whenever possible, use an alternative control technique and always follow the instructions on the label. To avoid harming bees, always spray in the evening, and keep containers of pesticide out of reach of children. Sometimes the label on the bottle of a pesticide becomes stained or damaged, so it is a good idea to copy the basic instructions on its use into your gardening notebook immediately after buying the product.

Bordeaux mixture A fungicide made from copper sulphate and lime that has been in use since 1885. It is non-systemic and non-persistent and is the most important control for potato blight. It is best applied as a preventive spray on the maincrop potato plants and outdoor tomato plants fortnightly from July.

Burgundy mixture Much the same as Bordeaux mixture, but the lime is replaced by washing soda, and it is used in January as a preventive spray against mildew on roses and gooseberries.

Derris This is derived from the roots of a tropical plant and has as its active ingredient a powerful alkaloid, rotenone. It is used as a powder or liquid to control aphids, red spider mite, weevils and caterpillars. It is harmless to warm-blooded animals, but deadly to fish, so never use it near to the garden

---

ATTRACTING THE PREDATORS

Mealy aphids can be a problem pest in my dry part of East Anglia. Derris kills them but may also kill predators. An alternative is to plant marigolds or the poached egg plant *Limanthes* among the Brussels sprouts and winter cabbages. They attract hoverflies and parasitic wasps, the main predators of mealy aphids. The parasitic wasps also eat young cabbage white caterpillars.

---

pond, lakes or rivers. It breaks down quickly and is non-persistent.

DIY sprays There are any number of homemade sprays that can be used with varying success in place of proprietary pesticides. Try them by all means, but remember that even these homespun recipes, some handed down over many generations, are potentially dangerous in the wrong hands, so keep them safe from children. Bracken spray is reasonably effective against blackfly on broad beans. Gather the bracken when brown and dry. Crush the leaves and store in paper bags until wanted. Measure out 125ml (4fl oz) and pour on 400ml (14fl oz) of hot water, stir and soak for twenty-four hours. Strain off the liquid and bottle it in airtight jars. Dilute 25ml (1fl oz) of the liquid with 4.5l (1gal) of water and spray each day for three days. Elder spray can be used instead of Burgundy mixture to prevent mildew on roses and gooseberries. It kills aphids and small caterpillars, having hydrocyanic acid as the toxic agent. To make up the spray gather 450g (1lb) of leaves and young stems of elder in the early spring when the sap is rising. Place in an old saucepan and add 3.3l (6pt) of water. Boil for half an hour, topping up as necessary. Strain through muslin or old tights and use the liquid undiluted when cool. Bottle it tightly while still hot and it will keep for about three months. The common stinging nettle is cursed by many gardeners, but blessed by those who appreciate its value in the green garden. Gather the leaves and stems in spring and early summer to use as an activator in the compost-making operation, as a good liquid feed and as a spray to control aphids and celery leaf miner. Soak 225g (8oz) of the nettle leaves in a bucket of water for a week, strain

and use undiluted. Put the gooey remains from the bucket onto the compost heap. Rhubarb leaves contain oxalic acid so can be used as a safe spray for aphids on roses. Chop up 450g (1lb) of rhubarb leaves and place in an old saucepan with 1.1l (2pt) of water. Boil for half an hour, topping up as necessary. When cool, strain off the liquid and add a dessertspoonful of soap flakes, dissolved in a little warm water, to serve as a wetting agent. Use this spray undiluted.

Insecticidal soap Soft soap, which can be bought from some chemists or from HDRA, has good insecticidal properties, and ordinary household soap is very effective against aphids. Dissolve 56g (2oz) of flaked soap or soap flakes in 4.5l (1gal) of hot water and use undiluted when cool. A proprietary insecticidal soap is Savona. It is effective against aphids, whitefly, red spider mite and scale insects and is harmless to people, pets, bees, ladybirds and other predators.

Potassium permanganate Buy the granules from your local chemist and mix 28g (1oz) in 9l (2gal) of water for use against powdery mildew on roses, delphiniums, chrysanthemums and other plants.

Pyrethrum This is made from the flowers of *Chrysanthemum cinerariifolium* and can safely be used on all food crops to control greenfly, blackfly, strawberry aphids, thrips, sawfly, weevils, leaf hoppers, flea beetles and capsids. It is harmful to fish, ladybirds, ladybird larvae and bees, but non-toxic to people and other warm-blooded creatures.

Quassia Sold as chips of wood from a tropical tree, it is made up into a spray to control small caterpillars and aphids. It is harmless to bees, ladybirds, ladybird larvae, people and pets, although it is used as an ingredient of such products as Catoff and Hoppit to repel cats, birds and rabbits. As a caterpillar spray, simmer 28g (1oz) of chips in 1.1l (2pt) of water for two hours, topping up as needed. Strain, then add 28g (1oz) of soft soap or soap flakes. Against aphids, dilute the mixture with five parts of water, while for small caterpillars and sawflies, dilute it with three parts of water.

Sulphur Flowers of sulphur dusted on dahlia tubers prevents them from going rotten while in store over the winter. When mixed with lime it is used as a winter wash on fruit trees and for controlling big bud on blackcurrant bushes. It is also sold as a fungicidal spray to control blackspot on roses and powdery mildew on ornamental plants. It can harm parasitic wasps and predatory mites.

Urine Our ancestors used the chamber pot's liquid neat as a winter wash for soft fruit bushes and top fruit trees. It is effective against mildew on gooseberry bushes, when 0.5l (1pt) is mixed with 3.9l (7pt) of hot water into which 84g (3oz) of washing soda and 28g (1oz) of soap flakes have been dissolved. Urine is also an excellent activator, used neat, for the compost heap.

POINTS ABOUT PESTICIDES

Organically acceptable pesticides, such as derris and pyrethrum, are short-lived and work by contact with the pest. This means they must be sprayed or dusted directly onto the pest to be effective. Because these pesticides are active for only a few hours, repeated applications are necessary where pests are in various stages of development. Special attention should also be given to the underside of leaves. Remember that derris and pyrethrum can kill helpful insects such as bees, ladybirds and hoverflies and are poisonous to frogs, toads, tortoises and fish. Always follow the instructions on the manufacturer's label.

THE GARDEN POND

A pool in the garden does much more than provide a focal point, with reflected light, movement, colour and, maybe, sound. Properly prepared and managed, it can play a major role in attracting wildlife to your garden, including dragonflies, damselflies and newts, along with frogs, toads and hedgehogs which, as well as being delightful creatures to share the garden with, also earn their residency by keeping slugs under control.

However, if you have a toddler in the family, ask yourself whether it wouldn't be better to wait a while before installing a pool. There have been too many accidental drownings that could have been avoided if more thought had been given to the potential danger ponds present to very young children.

Constructing a pond has been made relatively easy these days with pre-formed plastic pond liners and PVC or butyl sheeting, but there are a number of points that need to be established in the planning stage.

- The location of the pond is the most important factor to determine. The site should be in a quiet part of the garden, not one where there is constant traffic. It should be a peaceful spot both for you and the wildlife.
- The site should be free from the shadow of tall trees or fences, because a pond needs more sun than shade, preferably two or three hours of sunshine a day, and the roots of trees can cause problems with a pond liner.
- If the pond is to have a fountain, remember you will need to have a pump and an electricity supply to power it.

- Try to arrange a location where there is air movement. Too sheltered a site can cause problems in establishing a biological balance in both the water and the surrounding vegetation.
- The bigger the pond, the easier it is to keep the water clean, and aim for a minimum depth of 45cm (18in). If it is much shallower than this it will heat up rapidly in summer, the oxygen will quickly be lost, and that would be fatal for fish and other aquatic creatures. Ideally, the pond

FITTING A FOUNTAIN

The green gardener will question whether adding submersed coloured lighting bulbs to the pond is going to add substantially to the pleasure it gives. It might well prove detrimental to the pond's attractiveness to wildlife. Less questionable, maybe, would be a fountain which, in addition to adding gentle sound to the visual delights of the pond, actually assists in oxygenating the water, and that benefits the fish.

Plan the fountain as an integral part of the pond, don't add it as an afterthought. The electric cable powering the submersible pump will need to be laid before the landscaping of the border is completed. Any job like this, involving the supply of electricity to an outside source, is best carried out by a professional contractor. If you feel skilled enough to tackle it yourself, the finished job should be approved for safety by an electricity official.

PLANTING YOUR POND

Try to plan your pond building so that everything is ready for planting in early spring. For the deep end of the pond choose from the large family of water lilies, the lily-like plants, floating plants and the oxygenating plants. Your local water garden centre will be able to advise you which of the water lilies will be most suitable for the depth of water and surface area of your pond.

Oxygenating plants suitable for water depths of 30cm–1m (1–3ft) are essential aquatic plants, especially where there are fish as the plants absorb some of the carbon dioxide exhaled by the fish. This group of plants, once established, should be thinned out every autumn. Avoid the Canadian pond weed (*Anacharis densis*) which is over vigorous, and choose from hornwort (*Ceratophyllum demersum*), milfoil (*Myriophyllum*), water violet (*Hottonia palustris*), curled pond weed (*Potamogeton crispus*) and water buttercup (*Ranunculus aquatilis*).

Floating plants for water depths of 30cm–1m (1–3ft) include the surface floating fairy moss (*Azolla caroliniana*), frogbit (*Hydrocharis morsus-ranae*), water chestnut (*Trapa natans*) and water hyacinth (*Eichhornia crassipes*) and the submerged water soldier (*Stratiotes aloides*) and bladderwort (*Utricularia vulgaris*).

For the shallow water or marginal zone of your pond there's a wide choice of plants which will be happy in as little as 5–10cm (2–4in) of water. Stock plants can be bought from water garden centres and thereafter propagation is by division.

Arrowhead (*Sagittaria sagittifolia*) has distinctive arrow-shaped leaves and white flowers. It grows to about 60cm (2ft). Bulrush or reedmace (*Typha latifolia*) grows to 2m (6ft) tall, which can be overbearing. Smaller versions are *T. minima*, 30–45cm (12–18in) or *T. stenophylla* 1m (3ft) tall. The true bulrush (*Scirpus albescens*) grows to about 1.5m (5ft).

There are some lovely irises among the marginal aquatics, flowering in early summer and growing to about 60cm (2ft) tall. Look for the varieties of *I. laevigata* which are especially suitable for small ponds, while for its most attractive foliage the sweet flag (*Acorus calamus variegatus*), up to 1m (3ft) tall, is worth a place.

Other marginal plants with their approximate heights are water forget-me-not (*Myosotis palustris*) 23cm (9in); water musk (*Mimulus luteus*) 30cm (1ft); and marsh marigold (*Caltha palustris*) 23–30cm (9–12in).

---

should have a deep end of at least 80cm (32.5in) to ensure a frost-free winter home.

- Plan the surroundings of the pond at the same time as the pond itself. That means working out the relationship of the plants bordering the pond, including a suitable area for sitting and enjoying the pleasures of pond life.

- Not least in your planning should be deciding what you are going to do with the soil that is excavated. Early spring is the best time to construct the pond and to dispose of the spoil. The easy way is to use the heap as a rockery bordering the pond, but take my tip and forget this idea unless you are prepared to spend a lot of time and money on proper terracing and planting schemes. Even then you run the risk that the first heavy rainstorm will see soil being returned to the pond. Alternatives are to use the spoil to make a rockery elsewhere in the garden or to distribute it as evenly as possible over beds and borders.

A pond lined with plastic sheeting is the easiest and least expensive method of making a pond. Polythene is not a good choice because it has a life of only three or four years. Nylon-reinforced PVC is much stronger with a life at least twice that of polythene. The best material for lining is undoubtedly butyl, widely used for lining reservoirs and with a lifespan of at least fifty years.

Ready-formed pond liners are made of resin-bonded glass fibre and are available in many shapes and sizes, but generally are too shallow and too small for fish to survive a warm summer or a freezing winter. However, in very small gardens a pond of this type can be incorporated quite readily into another feature of the garden such as a raised bed or rockery.

To work out the lining size of your pond first sketch the shape you want onto graph paper, then use this formula:

length of pond + twice the deepest depth ✕
widest part of the pond + twice the depth.

A pond will attract wildlife, including dragonflies, frogs, toads and hedgehogs

Then add 60cm (2ft) on both the width and the length to allow for the lining to be buried at the edges.

Mark out the shape of the pond on the site using a trickle of fine sand or flour, then start digging. You'll find it easier to maintain a level surface for the lining if the soil you excavate is either thrown well clear or is barrowed away. You will need to dig out about 2.5cm (1in) more soil than the depth of the pond to accommodate a cushion for the lining. If you use PVC, this cushion could be old carpet or a thick layer of newspaper, but with butyl the hole should be lined with a layer of fine sand. Don't forget to provide shelving around the edge at about 15cm (6in) from the surface to accommodate the marginal aquatic plants.

Next step is to lay out the lining. Prepare for this by laying it out in a warm room for a day or two beforehand, or choose a spell of warm weather when the plastic becomes more flexible than at cool temperatures. Weigh down the edges with bricks or lengths of timber and start filling with a hosepipe. As the pond fills up, the lining will stretch to follow the contours of the hole.

When setting out aquatic plants, do so in zones and choose varieties recommended for the size of your pond. If water lilies are included, they should not cover more than one-third of the pond surface

When the pond is full, no part of the lining should be visible. The next task is to lay the edging. For preference use paving stones or decorative paving blocks and allow an overhang of about 2.5cm (1in). Depending on the size of the pond, leave a few gaps in the overhang as escape routes for hedgehogs or other small animals that might fall in. One of the manufacturers of ready-formed liners actually builds in rough-finished steps to make escape easy.

ICE ON POOLS

In winter, if ice persists, fish in the garden pool might die through lack of oxygen. Melt a hole by standing a saucepan of boiling water on the surface. Float rubber balls in concrete-lined pools to prevent cracks in the concrete from the pressure of the ice.

Don't be in a rush to start planting up the pond; allow at least a couple of weeks for the liner to bed down. Meanwhile you could be landscaping the borders of the pond with such plants as irises, hostas and ferns. If you want to use groups of reeds and bulrushes, don't plant them directly into the soil of the banks because the roots are very invasive. Instead plant them into large containers, such as old stone sinks.

If you intend to stock your pond with fish, go to the local water garden centre and seek expert advice on the sort of fish to buy, the stocking rate and the most suitable plants to use in the pond. Be warned that where there are fish, sooner or later there will be a heron, unless your home is in the heart of a city, and in next to no time the entire fish stock will have been eaten.

Instead of providing a bed of soil and gravel in the pond for the deep-water aquatic plants, sink the plants in their own baskets filled with loam and some bone meal and then mulch with gravel. Oxygenators are necessary and you should allow for one of these plants for every square metre/yard of pond surface. These plants can be set in trays of coarse sand and gravel and placed directly on the bed of the pond. Marginal aquatic plants can be positioned in their containers on the shelf round the pond, using bricks if necessary to bring them to the correct level.

The disappearance of so many village ponds, and the pollution of many others by chemical run-off from farmland, have been the principal factors in the decline of the smooth newts and common frogs, so that garden ponds are increasingly important refuges where they can breed. Out of the breeding season, frogs will roam the garden working as very successful slug destroyers. We no longer have a pond in the garden, but we do have frogs for much of the year, finding them in damp, shady places at the height of summer and in secret cubby-holes in the rockery in the autumn.

FIRST FIND YOUR SPAWN

If you want to introduce frogs and toads into the garden, get in touch with your local wildlife trust in early spring. They should be able to tell you where to get spawn. If you keep fish, adding spawn to your pond would be pointless because as soon as the tadpoles emerge from the eggs, the fish will eat them.

When you bring the aquatic plants back from the water garden centre, transplant them into larger pots, or the special baskets sold for the purpose, using ordinary garden soil covered with a layer of gravel. If you decide to include one of the water lilies as a feature of the pond, choose a variety recommended for the size of your pond. The lily pads provide resting places for frogs and shade for fish, but in total they should not cover more than one-third of the surface of the pond. Even so, you must be prepared to lift and divide the water lily plants about every three years.

GETTING MORE FROM LESS SPACE

Every green gardener, with however small a garden, should try to make space for some home-grown food. Growing one's own crops is a deeply satisfying experience that brings rewards far beyond the saving in money and, while one must always be prepared for disappointments, especially when starting out, one quickly discovers that raising good wholesome vegetables, salads and fruit without the intervention of chemical fertilisers and poisonous sprays is a craft, not an art.

Two of the best ways of making the optimum use of the restricted space for food growing in today's smaller gardens are deep beds and interplanting, and both systems can be equally applied to large gardens.

The great benefit of the deep-bed method, which, by the way, has been practised by the Chinese for many hundreds of years, is that the beds become no-dig areas requiring a minimum of hard work to maintain the soil in a tip-top fertile condition. All the work of aerating and draining the soil and ensuring that its nutrients are made available to the crops is done by earthworms, helped by the teeming underground population of insects, bacteria and fungi that inhabit a healthy organic environment.

You can't achieve this very satisfactory state of affairs overnight, of course, and to start with there's a stint of hard digging involved, but it is a technique that has a lot to recommend it:

- It saves space by growing the crops in blocks rather than in traditional rows. This means that you can expect to get double or even triple the yield from a deep bed compared with the same area of rows.

Deep-bed crops are grown in blocks rather than the traditional rows

- There's a saving of time because the bed system is far easier to manage than conventional rows. The work of sowing, planting, weeding and harvesting is all done from the pathways, which can be given a weatherproof surface. There's freedom of access even after heavy rain.
- Seed is saved because crops grown on the block system require less thinning than those grown in rows.
- Rotation of crops to avoid the build-up of pests and diseases is a simple aspect of management because of the clearly-defined boundaries of the beds.
- The soil is never walked on after the initial preparation of the bed. It starts off as a highly-fertile, well-structured growing medium with a high humus content and gradually improves as more organic material is added to the surface. Free drainage yet good moisture retention, with nutrients at a level where they are readily available to the plants, are other important features.

Adopting the deep-bed system involves three phases best done in late autumn and early winter. They are: marking out the area for the bed or beds; digging out the bed; and planning what to grow on a rotation cycle.

DON'T OVERDO IT

It is very easy to overwork a garden, especially a small one. The lawn, for example, can be mown too often. In fact, one cut a week, even at the height of the growing season, will keep it stronger and healthier than two cuts a week.

Don't be tempted to stir the soil constantly around plants and shrubs. By all means hoe to keep the weeds in check, but close to border plants, shrubs and roses and along the rows of onions and leeks it is better to hand weed.

When it comes to pruning, decide what you want to do and why before you start with the secateurs. Pruning to keep growth under control is necessary to us, the gardeners, but isn't nature's idea. Left to their own devices, fruit trees will crop well, though irregularly, while the famous Lime Kiln rose garden at Claydon, near Ipswich, is a remarkable demonstration that roses in the right setting don't need pruning or spraying, ever.

MARKING OUT

Each bed should be about 1.2m (4ft) wide so that it can be worked easily from pathways on either side, once the bed has been prepared. The length of the bed can be tailored to suit your garden layout, but for convenience you will find that 4.5m (15ft) is about the maximum length, to avoid too much time spent trekking up and down the pathways.

Use strings and pegs to mark out the boundary of the bed and, if you are planning to have adjoining deep beds, remember to mark out the paths. They should be about 60cm (2ft): just wide enough to take size ten wellies and a wheelbarrow.

When planning where to site your beds, try to align them so that the length of the beds is on a north–south axis to give the crops maximum benefit from sunshine. But a quick word of warning at this stage. Deep-bed production is ideal for most back garden vegetables, but if you have enough space to

Secondhand bricks make attractive hard-wearing pathways, and edges for borders, islands and deep beds

A CROPPING GUIDE FOR VEGETABLES SOWN IN BANDS IN A DEEP BED

	RECOMMENDED VARIETIES	SOW or PLANT	DEPTH and SPACING	SUCCESSIONAL SOWINGS	CULTIVATION	HARVEST	FEEDING + SPECIAL CARE
BEETROOTS	Avonearly Boltardy	April	½" deep in bands. 3" between seeds	May, June	Pull alternate roots when golf-ball size	Late July to November	Appreciates mulch of chopped seaweed
BROAD BEANS	The Sutton Bonny Lad	March	2" deep. 15" apart each way	Mid April	Pinch out growing tips to avoid blackfly	Late June to August	Support with string + canes
FRENCH BEANS	The Prince Tendergreen	March in pots	Plant out in May, 18" apart each way	May, direct sowing 2" deep	Appreciates twiggy supports	July to Late August	Watch out for slugs when young
RUNNER BEANS (BUSH)	Gulliver	May	2" deep, 15" apart each way	June	Mulch with lawn mowings before plants flower. Water well	August to October	Pick crop from pathways
BROCCOLI, SPROUTING	Purple	April in seedbed	Plant out 18" apart each way	—	Encourage side shoots by cutting centre first	January to May	Use felt collars to guard against cabbage root fly
BRUSSELS SPROUTS	Peer Gynt Monitor Rampart	March in seedbed	Plant out 18" apart each way	—	Stake each plant in exposed places	September to end February	Do not tread on bed when gathering buttons
CABBAGE, SPRING	Avoncrest April	August	Late September 9" apart each way	—	Cut alternate plants as greens	As required February onward	Rotate this + the other brassicas
SUMMER	Minicole Hispi	March	Late May 15" apart each way	—	Water well after transplanting	Late July to November	Use felt collars to guard against cabbage root fly
WINTER	January King Aquarius Jupiter	May	Late June 15" apart each way	—	Provide some protection from pigeons	November to March	Felt collars
CARROTS	Jurawot Autumn King Mokum	March (early) April (main)	½" deep in wide bands	May, June, July	An excellent subject for cloches	June onwards. Store maincrop in peat over winter	Try dusting bed with soot to deter carrot fly
CAULIFLOWERS	All the Year Round	April in seedbed	Plant 24" apart in late June	May, June	Use Australian varieties for succession	September-December	Felt collars
CELERY	Lathom Self-blanching	February under glass	Plant out 10" apart each way in May	—	Must never be short of water	September-December	Will not do well in long, hot summers
LEEKS	Argenta Herwina Snowstar	March in seedbed	Plant out 6" apart each way	—	Can be blanched using plastic or paper collars	October onwards	Give a second feed fertiliser in August
LETTUCE	Little Gem Salad Bowl Avondefiance	March in seedbed	Plant out 6" apart each way	May June	Water well at planting out and during dry spells	Late June onwards	Good subject for cloche production
MARROWS, COURGETTES	Bush varieties Zucchini	April in pots	Plant out in June, 30" between plants	—	Keep well watered at all times	Late July onwards	Appreciates liquid feeding
ONIONS, SETS	Sturon, Stuttgart Giant	Late Mar. early April	Plant 4" apart each way	—	If you want larger onions, increase spacing	September	Ripen thoroughly before storing
PARSNIPS	White Gem Avonresister	April	Station sow 3 seeds. Thin to one plant 6" apart	May	Slow to germinate, but be patient	October onwards. Flavour improved by frost	Recommended varieties resistant to canker
POTATOES, EARLY	Maris Bard Pentland Javelin	Early April	Plant out 4" deep, 12" apart each way	—	Do not attempt to earth up	July onwards	Mulch with lawn mowings
RADISHES	Cherry Belle French Breakfast	April	Broadcast seed in wide bands	May, June	Good under cloches	June onwards	Grow quickly to avoid woodiness
SPINACH	Perpetual	March or April	Station sow 6" apart each way	August or September	Keep well watered	July to December	Given protection, the crop can be overwintered
TOMATOES	The Amateur Sigmabush	Late March in heat	Plant out early June 20" apart each way	—	Mulch with peat or straw to protect fruit	Late August to October	Liquid feed once a fortnight
TURNIPS	Early Snowball Golden Ball	March August	Broadcast seed in broad bands	April, June	Thin seedlings to 6" apart for late sowings	Early crop - June. Maincrop Sept. onwards	Lift and store main for overwinter use

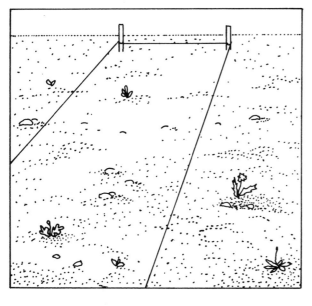

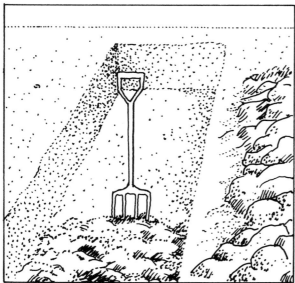

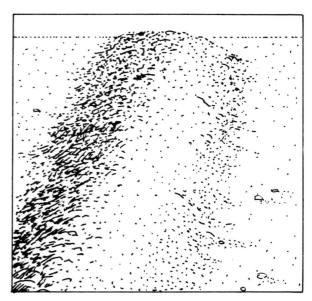

grow potatoes, peas and runner beans, don't include them in your deep-bed cropping plan.

The pathways will have to be kept weed-free and accessible whatever the weather. If funds allow, you could put down permanent paths of secondhand bricks or paving slabs. Grass is not a good idea unless you are confident you could stop it creeping into the rich environment of the beds. My technique is to cover the paths with a weed-inhibiting barrier of heavy-gauge black polythene over which goes a layer of coarse bark chips, although coarse gravel would work just as well.

Prepare the deep bed by first marking out the site. Then, double dig, forking over the bottom before returning the soil to the trench, and adding the well-rotted manure, compost or leafmould. Concentrate most of the organic material in the top 15cm (6in) and finish off with a dressing of balanced organic fertiliser

Another point to consider is what to use as retaining walls because, when finished, the surface of the bed will be proud of the paths. An edging certainly stops soil from being washed by heavy rain onto the pathway. Depending on how much you want to spend, and how attractive you want this part of the garden to look, you could provide 10–15cm (4–6in) high walls of brick, breeze blocks, railway sleepers, corrugated plastic or secondhand timber. Alternatively, you could simply make the bed slightly wider to allow for a shallow trench between it and the path.

DIGGING OUT

This is the toughest task because the section you have marked out has to be dug to twice a spade's depth: the double digging beloved by so many of the older generation of gardeners. Digging out about 50cm (20in) of soil is necessary for two reasons. All weeds must be removed, especially the deep-rooting perennial ones, such as bindweed, couch grass and horsetail. When the soil, minus the weeds, is replaced, large quantities of organic matter are added to the trench.

Digging out and weeding at the same time is a slow, tiring job but worth doing as thoroughly as possible. My technique involves putting the soil from the trench to one side and reserving the other side for barrowing in the compost, farmyard manure, leafmould, mushroom compost, seaweed, etc, that provides the organic heart of the deep bed.

Coarse items such as Brussels sprouts, cauliflower and cabbage stalks can go into the bottom of the trench, mixed with shredded newspaper, scraps of wool or cotton, soft prunings and plenty of lawn mowings. This layer should be no thicker than about 23cm (9in) and should be thoroughly trodden in. Then the soil and compost or well-rotted manure, leafmould and so on are mixed with the soil that you return to the trench. Be generous with the manure or compost, preferably in the ratio of half a barrowload to a barrowload of soil, and try to ensure that the finest textured material is reserved for the final few centimetres so that you don't have large lumps in the tilth when it comes to seed sowing.

Because you have added more to the trench than you took out, the finished bed will have a gently rounded profile and you will, in fact, have marginally increased the growing area. If all your preparation has been done in good time for the start of the sowing season, a final touch will be to tease into the top two centimetres or so of soil a balanced organic fertiliser, such as fish, blood and bone or seaweed meal at the rate of 113g (4oz) to the sq m/yd.

WHERE TO BUY PLANTS

When buying plants resist the temptation of the bargain-basement stuff at the corner shop or local supermarket. You could be very disappointed with the result. For preference, go direct to a nursery where the plants are propagated, then you will not only be assured of value for money, you will also be able to take advice on the aftercare of your plants.

There are other sources of supply. As part of student training, horticultural colleges propagate a wide range of trees, shrubs, bedding and house plants and these are usually available for the public to buy at attractive prices. National Trust properties also derive some of their income from the sale of plants, while many private gardens open to the public under the National Gardens Scheme have plants for sale. Watch out, too, for the annual plant sales organised by the local branch of the World Wide Fund for Nature.

An excellent way of increasing your garden stock, bedding plants excepted, is through the friendship of other gardeners. If you join your local gardening club or allotment association you'll find plenty of opportunities for swapping plants and know-how. You may also find that you can buy seeds, organic fertilisers and gardening tools at special discount prices. Some allotment associations I have visited even have their own plant-raising units so that members can be assured of getting healthy young plants at cost price.

INSIST ON YOUR RIGHTS

If you buy plants from a garden centre or nursery and they die, despite being properly cared for, you are entitled to compensation under the Sale of Goods Act. This could be a replacement of the plant that died (not an alternative variety or species) or your money refunded in full.

Similarly, if you sow seed and the plants that emerge are not as described on the packet, you are entitled not only to replacement but also in some instances to compensation. For example, a vegetable gardener bought a packet of seeds of an F1 variety of marrow, raised the plants in his propagator and planted them out in early summer. When the fruit formed he discovered they were not marrows but ornamental gourds. The seed company offered their apologies and a replacement packet of marrow seed. He demanded (and got) compensation.

Remember always to keep receipts from shops and a record of your order when buying by post.

FIGHT THE TRADE IN WILD-DUG BULBS

Many millions of wild-dug bulbs are imported annually, mainly from Turkey, and gardeners may unwittingly buy them believing them to be cultivated.

More than 70 million bulbs are dug from the wild every year in Turkey, Portugal, India and Japan. Some 22 million of these end up in British gardens.

According to the Fauna and Flora Preservation Society this trade is not illegal because very few of the wild bulb species are protected. Even those that *are* named in legislation, such as the Convention on International Trade in Endangered Species, are still in danger because the regulations are almost impossible to enforce. Very few customs officers know how to differentiate between wild bulbs and those that have been commercially propagated.

In the ten years 1978 to 1988, Turkey alone exported 71 million anemones, 20 million cyclamen, 111 million winter aconites and, in one year alone, 30 million snowdrops. Almost all were dug from the wild because the only bulbs which are entirely, or mostly, artificially propagated in Turkey are the madonna lilies, crown imperials and snowflakes.

There's no doubt that if the trade in wild-dug bulbs continues at these levels their natural populations will be decimated, even wiped out. Some bulb retailing firms have announced that they will avoid selling any bulbs which have been dug from the wild and will only deal in those that have been nursery-propagated. As well as protecting the dwindling stocks of wild bulbs, this will also benefit the gardener because such bulbs are more likely to perform better.

PLANNING WHAT TO GROW

The crops are grown in blocks in a deep bed; this not only increases the yield but also enables the size of some of the vegetables to be regulated. It also allows the gardener to make good use of a floating cloche, such as polypropylene fibre cloth (Agryl P17 or Papronet), which can be spread over sections of the bed after sowing or planting out to give the crop protection from the weather, even from several degrees of frost, and from birds and insect pests.

You can also get an earlier start by covering the bed, or part of it, with black polythene sheeting a fortnight before sowing. This will warm up the soil, but ensure that you have first worked the surface to a fine tilth for sowing and that the bed is thoroughly moist before the sheeting goes over it.

Regulating the size of the vegetables by close spacing calls for experimentation, because the fertility of the bed, the district, the weather and the varieties you grow all have a bearing on the crop's performance. Spacing a roundhead autumn/winter cabbage such as Celtic at 35cm (14in) each way should give the highest yield of heads at the family size of about 1kg (2.2lb) with very little waste of outer leaves. Increase the spacing to about 45cm (18in) each way between the plants and you should find the individual heads come a little earlier and about a third more in weight, while the total yield is about the same.

With both early and maincrop carrots, radishes, turnips and parsnips the seed is sown in bands, with the seed covered by about 1.25cm (½in) of soil. You will probably find the best way of doing this is to broadcast the seed by trickling it through the fingers across the width of the bed and then sieving soil over the seed to the required depth. Although the block system of sowing and planting out crops makes best use of the deep bed, don't feel that this bars you from using rows of cloches. Just adapt the method so that the seed is in narrow bands lengthways along the bed.

The DIY buff can quite easily and inexpensively make a frame, covered with clear plastic sheeting, to place over the full width of the bed for protected cropping of bush marrows, courgettes, melons and bush tomatoes. Similarly, sowings of early and maincrop carrots can be guarded from attack by the carrot fly by using a barrier of polythene sheeting stapled to scrapwood frames (*see* page 77).

INTERPLANTING

The second way of securing extra space for growing food crops in a small garden is to interplant them with your ornamental shrubs and flowers. The effect can be quite awful, but if care is taken in choosing decorative salads and vegetables they can take their place with great success. Other factors must also be taken into account. For example, the mature height of the crop in relation to its neighbours, the timing to maturity, and the space required to grow a worthwhile amount of a particular crop.

Runner beans were once grown solely for the beauty of their flowers, and they are still worthy of a place in the garden on that count alone. Grow them trained up a bare fence or wall, preferably where they will catch the sun, and you will be rewarded with the daylong company of bees when the plants are in full flower, followed by the delight of being able to pick succulent beans for weeks on end. A single row 3m (10ft) long with the plants spaced 30cm (1ft) apart will give a family of two adults and one child plenty of meals.

The techniques of inter-cropping and catch-cropping require some juggling with space, careful selection of the crops and planning the sequence of sowing and planting. Inter-cropping involves growing a fast crop, such as radishes or baby turnips, between rows of a slower one, such as Brussels sprouts. The quick maturing crop is taken to the kitchen well before the slower one reaches maturity.

Catch-cropping means using parts of the vegetable plot, as they become vacant, for quick-growing crops. Suitably fast-maturing crops for both techniques are early carrots, baby beetroot, radishes, lettuce, spring onions, early turnips and spinach. Plan your cropping programme on paper early in the year and sow the crops to take full advantage of vacant land as a crop is cleared.

By raising some of the plants indoors or in the greenhouse instead of direct sowing outdoors, you can introduce far more flexibility into your programme.

As well as interplanting edible crops with flowers in the ornamental parts of the garden, you can interplant quick and slow growing crops in the vegetable section. Here lettuce and leeks are growing closely together – the lettuce will be taken to the kitchen well before the leeks need more growing room

Rotation of the crops in a deep-bed system presents no problem, unless you have so many beds that you would need to keep a card index of the cropping plans. But here, crop rotation is used more as a preventive against soil pests, such as the lettuce root aphid, rather than for the conventional purpose of protecting against the depletion of nutrients. In the well-balanced organic environment of the deep bed there is little chance of a greedy crop poaching too much of a particular plant food, to the detriment of other crops.

Try to give your deep beds an annual dressing in the winter of compost or well-rotted farmyard manure, and every other year a dressing of a balanced organic fertiliser. The tendency will be for the soil to increase in acidity, so check the pH every year and adjust as necessary with dolomite or calcified seaweed (*see* page 33). I said that the structure of the soil steadily improves and this is nowhere better demonstrated than when it comes to harvesting root crops such as carrots and parsnips. There will be no need to fork them out: they can be eased out of the soil by hand.

A final important point about the management of the deep bed. Weeds love the rich stock of goodness in the soil every bit as much as the edible crops, so learn to recognise seedling weeds and whip them out to add to the compost heap before they compete overmuch with the legitimate seedlings.

GROW YOUR OWN ORGANIC FOOD

 Gardens are shrinking and attitudes to gardening are changing so that now we expect even smaller spaces to yield more. I hope the ideas discussed in this book, such as taking on an allotment or someone else's neglected garden, will inspire readers to make the decision to grow good, wholesome food the organic way, while others will set aside part of the garden for some edible crops. If you haven't already done so, I can guarantee that growing your own food without the use of artificial fertilisers or poisonous sprays brings a reward far in excess of the shop value of the crops. The seasons and their role in the gardening cycle have a deeper interest when you are growing food. Even in the doldrum days of winter you can involve the family in planning next season's output.

With that in mind, this section gives guidance on those crops that should be given priority where space is limited, pointing out where the dietary or flavour values of the organically grown version of a crop beg for it to be included. However, there are other equally important considerations and, at the top of the list, are the likes and dislikes of your family. There is, after all, very little satisfaction to be had from growing fine organic parsnips if that's a vegetable the children heartily detest.

Another factor is the nature of the soil you are working with. It may be fine for, say, cabbages but too flinty for carrots. The local climate, too, is ignored at your peril, and to decide how best to use this in planning your crop production might involve drawing on the experience of older hands in the neighbourhood. Late frosts, biting easterly winds, regular spells of drought and well below average rainfall are features I have to contend with in Suffolk, while in previous Staffordshire and Warwickshire gardens it was too often wet and humid.

POTATOES FROM SEED

For one or two years the Ipswich seed firm Thompson & Morgan offered potato seed, instead of seed potatoes. It wasn't a successful project for them, but it could be an interesting and rewarding one for you. I asked Patrick Hughes, the organic seed expert, how to set about it and he recommended collecting ten to twenty seed heads or berries from a mature maincrop plant. Desirée is a good variety for the purpose because it makes seed very freely.

Each of the berries or plump pods contains fifty to sixty seeds and a mass of pulp. Pop the lot into a plastic bag and squash them. 'They should be left to go mouldy for about a week,' advised Patrick, 'because this breaks down the pulp of the berry, allowing the seed to be extracted and cleaned. More importantly, the mould can actually destroy any viruses on the seed coat.

'Avoid stirring the mixture, so allowing the air to get in, or else the seed may germinate while the pulp is present. If some of the seeds grow tiny roots, test it by letting some remain warm and damp. If the protuberances grow, they are roots. If not, they are the seeds' umbilical cord.'

After a week the mould is washed off, using several rinses. Spread out the seed onto a sheet of glass and dry it in the sun. When thoroughly dry, the seed should be stored in a paper bag and kept cool and dry. Sow the seed in February in trays of compost in a propagator at about 15°C (60°F) or somewhere warm indoors, and, when large enough, prick out the seedlings into 8cm (3in) pots. In April pot on the plants into half-filled 12.5cm (5in) pots and top up with compost as the plants grow. Plant them out in late May. The crop will mature later than that from seed potatoes, so dig up the potatoes only when the leaves have died away completely.

Finally, because there should always be an element of fun and excitement in gardening, you should elect to grow something either extremely expensive when bought from the shops or intriguingly unusual: globe artichokes or asparagus, or the gourmet root crops salsify and scorzonera, or the poor-yielding but top flavour potato Golden Wonder.

This section is in three parts and should be used in conjunction with the advice on crop rotation on pages 132–3. (For detailed advice on a wide range of crops refer to *Organic Gardening*, the author's previous book.)

ROOT VEGETABLES

These are the crops most readily tainted by chemicals, so the organically grown ones generally have a superior flavour. They also occupy a smaller growing space than the other groups of vegetables and a surplus from the fresh crop can usually be stored over the winter without involving the deep freeze. Priority crops in this group are beetroot, carrots, kohl rabi and turnips.

Pull baby beetroot for salads and pickling when golf-ball size

Beetroot Aim to grow two lots of this easy-to-grow crop: one for use as baby beet, the other as a maincrop for use throughout the autumn and winter. Allow for three rows, each 4.5m (15ft) long and 30cm (1ft) apart or in a deep bed a band 1m (3ft) wide and 3m (10ft) long, sowing seed 1.25cm (½in) deep and 7.5cm (3in) apart. Sow first lot of seed in mid to late April, depending on district, and the maincrop about four weeks later. Alternatively, sow a cluster of three to four seeds in pots or soil blocks indoors and plant out.

Pull the baby beet when they are no larger than golf balls and use them for salads or pickling. This will be about twelve weeks after sowing. The maincrop roots are pulled as required, but for winter storage should be lifted before the first hard frosts. Drought causes the crop to bolt or become woody.

DIETARY VALUE: Rich in niacin, vitamin A and fibre, and contains betain, a substance that is said to protect against cancer.

TOP FLAVOUR TIP: Mulch in late spring with chopped seaweed or give a dressing of seaweed meal.

Carrots Carrots are an excellent crop for light, rich soil that has not been freshly manured. You can either grow one variety for use throughout the season, pulling immature roots as delicious new carrots and allowing the bulk to grow to maturity, or you can grow an early variety followed by a maincrop one. If your soil is very heavy or full of stones, you can grow a small-rooted variety, such as Stuko, in windowboxes or other containers filled with compost and fed with liquid manure.

Sow the seed from late March to May, 1.25cm (½in) deep in rows 15cm (6in) apart, when each 30cm (1ft) of row should yield about 450g (1lb) of mature carrots or, in a deep bed 1m (3ft) wide, sow in bands giving a total length of about 3m (10ft).

Carrot fly can ruin the crop so follow the precautions detailed on page 77. In hot, dry weather water the rows and occasionally spray with soapy water to prevent a build-up of carrot aphids.

DIETARY VALUE: Carrots contain more vitamin A than any other vegetable, along with useful amounts of B, C and E vitamins and calcium.

TOP FLAVOUR TIP: Juwarot is considered to be the outstanding variety for flavour when eaten fresh or used for juicing.

The turnip-like stem of the kohl rabi is the edible part. When small, it can be cooked whole and has a delicious nutty flavour

Kohl rabi Light land with a neutral pH of 7.0 suits this delicious vegetable. It is actually a brassica, although it is the turnip-like stem that is eaten, so fit it into the brassica group for rotation. A humus-rich soil and an open site give the best results, and two sowings will give a summer crop and a winter one. Sow the summer-maturing crop in late March or April to pull in July or August. For the winter crop sow a purple variety in late July. Sow 1.25cm (½in) deep in rows 30cm (1ft) apart, or in bands in the deep bed, thinning to 10cm (4in) apart. Spray with soapy water if aphids appear.

DIETARY VALUE: Vitamin C content is highest when the young bulbs are grated and used in salads. Leaves may also be cooked and eaten like spinach, and have good fibre content.

TOP FLAVOUR TIP: Best when the bulb is the size of a tennis ball. Do not peel, but cook whole or sliced, preferably in a pressure cooker or steamed to preserve the nutty flavour, or use raw. The winter crop

should be left in the ground, covered with a mulch, until needed.

Turnips Turnips are part of the brassica family, so rotate them with that group. As with kohl rabi, sow two lots for summer and winter use and cook the leaves as a tasty alternative to spinach. Two rows 4.5m (15ft) long sown in late March or early April for summer use, and two sown in July for winter use, give self-sufficiency for a family of two adults and three children. Alternatively, sow in a deep bed by broadcasting the seed in bands and thinning the early seedlings to 10cm (4in) apart and the late ones to 15cm (6in) apart. The maincrop roots can be lifted and stored for winter use. Flea beetle can be a problem on young seedlings. If it is, use the controls recommended on page 78.

DIETARY VALUE: The leaves can be cooked and used as greens, providing carbohydrate, calcium, iron, lots of vitamins A and C, as well as fibre. The roots also offer potassium, sodium, trace elements, vitamin C and fibre.

TOP FLAVOUR TIP: Young turnips need not be peeled, simply washed thoroughly and cooked whole. Older roots should be peeled as thinly as possible, diced and cooked until tender. If the flavour of turnip is a turn-off with your children, try mixing it with carrot, mashing both together, or adding it to winter stews.

GREEN VEGETABLES

This group, the brassica family, is more demanding of space than the root vegetables and is usually moved around the garden each year. Because the edible part of these crops is the leaves, commercial growers are able to bulk up the crop with nitrogenous fertiliser and large amounts of water, and this may mean a considerable loss of flavour, so any brassica crop grown organically and eaten the same day it is harvested will have a superior flavour and higher nutritional value than the shop-bought equivalent. A ten-rod (250 sq m) allotment, properly planned, should be able to provide self-sufficiency in year-round cabbages, winter cauliflowers, Brussels sprouts, calabrese, sprouting broccoli and spring cabbage for a family of four. Priority crops in this group are Brussels sprouts, calabrese and purple sprouting broccoli.

Brussels sprouts Once Britain's most popular winter vegetable, the Brussels sprout has been slowly declining in sales. The reasons aren't clear, but one of the villains in the act is the frozen sprout. If your introduction to Brussels sprouts is via the fla-vourless buttons from the deep-freeze cabinet, you are very likely to believe that all sprouts are similarly tasteless. The growers must take the blame for con-centrating on high-yielding varieties that, too often, have very little flavour whether fresh or frozen. The flavour of organically grown sprouts is a very sound reason why this superb vegetable should be given priority in the garden or allotment.

In exposed areas, wind rock can cause Brussels sprouts to produce open buttons. The remedy is to secure each plant to a stake

Any reputation this crop has acquired for being difficult to grow by the amateur is undeserved and is due, probably, to failure to give it organically-enriched soil and very firm planting. In exposed areas wind rock of the mature plant will cause open rosettes instead of solid buttons; firm planting should prevent this, but it may even be necessary to stake each plant and draw soil up the stem. For self-sufficiency for a family of four you will need about fifteen early, fifteen mid-season and fifteen late-maturing plants, although much depends on your choice of varieties. Most experienced growers agree that sprouts are at their best from November to Feb-ruary, but with a comprehensive range of varieties to select from, it is possible to extend the sprout sea-son from September to April. Sow in a seed bed or cold frame in March for early varieties, April for mid-season or late ones, and transplant to their growing position when large enough. The site should have firm soil, not newly dug, and be well supplied with compost or well-rotted manure. Water the plants before transplanting and water them into their permanent home, then place a brassica collar round them to deter the cabbage root fly.

Whitefly can be a nuisance because the honey-dew they secrete causes a sooty mould on the but-tons. Pull off yellowed leaves and collect any fallen ones.

DIETARY VALUE: Raw sprouts have the highest nutritional value and can be used grated in winter salads. Both raw and cooked sprouts provide good amounts of vitamin C, carotene, carbohydrate, pro-tein, minerals and fibre. The important thing is not to overcook them. When all the buttons have been gathered use the sprout tops as spring greens.

TOP FLAVOUR TIP: Many people reckon that the old, open-pollinated varieties have a superior flavour to the newer F1 hybrids. If you live near the coast, try giving the sprouts a mulch of chopped seaweed; inland you could give a light dressing of seaweed meal teased into the top few centimetres round the plants.

Calabrese This is a particularly useful crop because it is ready about sixteen weeks after sowing and needs very little space compared with its big brothers in the brassica family. It will also tolerate soil that is unsuitable for the hungry feeding cauli-flowers. A row of fifteen plants, 30cm (1ft) apart, should yield about 7kg (15lb) of broccoli spears. Sow in April in a seed bed or cold frame and trans-plant in late May. Ensure that the plants never want for water. After cutting the main shoot in July, give a feed of liquid seaweed fertiliser to encourage production of side shoots.

DIETARY VALUE: Should be cut and eaten the same day for maximum nutritional benefit from its high vitamin C, B2 and A content and other major nutrients. However, this crop freezes particularly well when young and tender.

TOP FLAVOUR TIP: As with other brassicas, the flavour is enhanced by dressing with seaweed meal, or regular foliar feeding with liquid seaweed extract, such as SM3 or Maxicrop.

Purple sprouting broccoli is a fine crop for the green gardener. Highly nutritious, it gives a rich return yet needs little space. Cut the young shoots at about 15cm (6in), when the flower buds have formed

Purple sprouting broccoli A superb subject for the amateur grower on several counts. It is easy to grow, matures at a time when other green vegetables are in short supply (what used to be called the Hungry Gap), is highly nutritious and gives an excellent return from very little space. Give it an open site with plenty of air movement, well-manured soil and a 4.5m (15ft) row of six plants will give self-sufficiency for the average family. Sow in late April or early May and transplant the seedlings to the permanent site when they are about 10cm (4in) tall, putting a brassica collar round each plant. Stake the plants if they are liable to wind rock. Cut the tender shoots, beginning with the central one, when the flower buds are still in a tight bunch and continue taking the shoots for about six or seven weeks.

DIETARY VALUE: Must be eaten as soon as possible after cutting the shoots, but it must not be overcooked. Has nutritional value that puts it at the top of the brassica league.

TOP FLAVOUR TIP: Always cut and cook the shoots with some of the young leaves attached. Regular foliar feeding with liquid seaweed extract is beneficial.

LEAD IN LEAFY CROPS

In areas of high traffic density, leafy crops can contain unacceptably high levels of lead and that's bad for adults but exceptionally so for children who have to eat the tainted crops. Spinach, cabbage and lettuce absorb most lead pollution, while peas, beans and root crops the least.

The lead from road traffic exhausts reaches the plant tissue in two ways. It is deposited in the soil and is taken up by the plant roots. It is also carried in the air in micro-particles and deposited on the leaves. Fortunately, emissions are being reduced as the use of lead-free petrol grows. However, you can reduce to nil the amount of lead taken up by the edible crops you grow by digging in composted organic matter at the rate of 25 per cent by volume into the top 15cm (6in) of soil.

Vegetables grown in this organic medium have the ability to filter out not only the lead but also cadmium, the other commonly occurring pollutant. The lead deposited on the leaves and stems of leafy vegetables and lettuce can be removed entirely by simply adding a tablespoonful of vinegar to each pint of water used for washing the crop prior to cooking or serving it.

BEANS, PEAS AND OTHER CROPS

This section includes crops that are rather demanding in terms of space, such as peas, broad beans and courgettes, and those which, when taken dew-fresh to the kitchen, are far superior to the shop-bought equivalent. All of them, when grown organically and with varieties selected for flavour rather than yield, are very rewarding items for growing in the garden, offering an excellent return for very little outlay.

Broad beans Try to make room for this fine vegetable. It is tolerant of most soil conditions, easy to cultivate, gives a fairly long succession of tender succulent beans and, when they have all been picked, the plants can be chopped and dug in as a green manure. For best results rotate the crop each year. Prepare the site by working in plenty of compost, followed by a dressing of calcified seaweed. Allow for three 4.5m (15ft) rows, 45cm (18in) apart, with the plants 30cm (1ft) apart. In mild parts, seed can be sown in November and the plants will overwinter, or sow in trays in a cool greenhouse in February, or direct into the site in late March. When you see the first small beans, pinch out the growing point of each plant just above the top cluster of flowers. This helps the beans to swell and gives some control over blackfly. Use the tops as tender spring greens. When you find a variety that suits you well, allow a few plants to mature without picking any of the pods. Harvest the seed in August for next season's use.

DIETARY VALUE: Excellent source of protein, carbohydrate, vitamin C and iron, as well as dietary fibre. The tops have a particularly high vitamin C content.

TOP FLAVOUR TIP: Very young beans can be cooked and eaten in the pods; otherwise don't pod the beans until minutes before they are to be lightly cooked. Eat the beans when they are young; when you open the pod the beans should have a white scar between the segments, not a brown or black one.

French or dwarf beans This crop is frost-tender and comes into bearing after the main flush of broad beans, but before the start of the runner beans. To germinate, the seed must have a minimum soil temperature of 10°C (50°F), so a good plan is to sow in paper pots indoors, and plant out under cloches or after the danger of frost has passed. A site that has been well supplied with compost and is never lacking in moisture gives the best results. Give the young bushy plants twigs to protect them from lodging or falling over, and a mulch of compost or grass cuttings is appreciated. Start picking the crop when the pods are about 10cm (4in) long.

DIETARY VALUE: Good source of vitamin C, carotene, iron, mineral salts and fibre.

TOP FLAVOUR TIP: Cook the beans whole, having just topped and tailed them. Flat pod or English varieties have the best flavour but become stringy more quickly than the pencil-pod types.

Runner beans Shares with peas the distinction of being the most popular of summer vegetables and, happily, has a season that starts in August and goes through to the first frosts of autumn. Fortunately, too, this is an ideal subject for even the smallest garden because it can be grown up fences, poles or wigwams, while on exposed sites it can be grown 'on the flat'. This crop repays extra care in preparation of the soil, and the old idea of digging runner bean trenches in late autumn and winter and filling them with farmyard manure and compost is worth copying, if you can. Sow the seeds when the frosts have finished, but only then if the soil is warm and not sodden. For self-sufficiency you will need to have a double row 4.5m (15ft) long which should yield about 45–68kg (100–150lb) of beans. Sow the seed about 5cm (2in) deep, spacing them 30cm (12in) apart with the rows 38cm (15in) apart.

For growing on the flat, space the rows 60cm (2ft) apart and when the plants have made about 45cm (18in) of growth pinch out the growing points to encourage the laterals that make bushy plants. In dry summers this method often gives a heavier yield of beans over a longer period than from plants grown up supports.

DIETARY VALUE: When very young, runner beans can be eaten raw in salads, offering a good content of vitamin C, which decreases when cooked. They also supply fibre, minerals, carotene and protein.

TOP FLAVOUR TIP: Add the herb savory to the water to enhance the flavour, and always eat the beans within a few hours of harvesting and preparing them.

GOOD COMPANIONS FOR THE RUNNER BEANS

Runner bean plants sometimes produce plenty of flowers, only to have them drop before they have been pollinated. It seems to be worse in hot, dry summers. One remedy was reckoned to be spraying with plain water in the evening, although evidence nowadays is that this is only marginally effective. Since oil seed rape became a major crop in cereal-growing areas the pollen beetle has become a troublesome pest to gardeners, and this may account for some failure of the runner bean crop. You can minimise premature blossom fall by encouraging pollinating insects, particularly bees. Try growing your beans closer to bee-haunted groups of annuals, such as nasturtium and candytuft, or perennials, such as delphiniums. Even better, grow sweet peas with your runner beans and let them share the climbing supports to bring lots of bees to set the bean flowers.

Grow sweet peas with runner beans to help pollination of the bean flowers

Courgettes Often classified as marrows (or squashes in the United States) although there are zucchini varieties bred specifically to produce courgettes. My preference is to grow a small-fruited bush marrow and take the crop as courgettes while immature, allowing other fruit to develop to a handy size for a single meal. The plants are half-hardy, so time the sowing to enable you to plant out when all danger of frost has passed. You can raise the seedlings indoors in spring, one seed to a 7.5cm (3in) pot placed somewhere warm. Germination at 24°C (65°F) is rapid and the plants can go out in a sunny, sheltered position in early summer, after they have been hardened off. Alternatively, sow outdoors at this time and put a jam jar or half a plastic bottle over the sowing site to hasten germination. Six plants 1m (3ft) apart each way will give self-sufficiency in courgettes; or four plants for marrows.

Plenty of well-rotted farmyard manure or compost worked into the top 15cm (6in) of the soil and regular feeding with a liquid manure will help the plants to give an abundance of fruit. As courgettes, the fruit should be cut before the skin hardens. Test marrows with a thumbnail and if you can score it, the marrow is tender. A few can be left, however, at the end of the season and stored in a cool, dry place for use up to December.

DIETARY VALUE: The belief that this vegetable has little food value is misplaced. Both courgettes and marrows contain only about twelve calories per 100g (3½oz), but provide vitamins A and C, mineral salts, carbohydrate and trace elements.

TOP FLAVOUR TIP: Don't peel courgettes or young marrows because the peel enhances the delicate flavour. Don't overcook either: sliced courgettes need only parboiling. They can be served cold with an oil and vinegar dressing. Steamed marrow benefits from a fresh parsley sauce.

Cucumbers Try growing a couple of outdoor bush cucumbers in a sheltered but sunny spot where the soil has been enriched with organic matter, or in an organic growing bag on a sunny patio, and you will be rewarded with a gastronomic delight. The fruit have a far superior flavour to the commercial greenhouse types. Sow the seeds on edge in small pots in mid-April and place in a warm place, such as above the boiler. Plant out after hardening off at the end of May or early June. Alternatively, sow in situ as for courgettes. Keep the plants well watered and mulch with compost or thick layers of newspaper. When the fruits have started to swell, feed weekly with liquid manure.

DIETARY VALUE: Only ten calories per 100g (3½oz), but contains a good dollop of vitamin C, some folic acid, fibre and mineral salts.

TOP FLAVOUR TIP: Very fresh outdoor cucumber has the finest flavour, particularly if it has been grown with the help of liquid seaweed extract (Maxicrop or SM3). A surplus of the crop can be used to make cucumber soup, pickles or chutney.

STOPPING PLANTS

Stopping a plant means pinching out the growing tip or tips. Carried out at an early stage in the plant's life, it encourages it to produce side growths, and this is especially important with fuchsias, dahlias, chrysanthemums, marrows, cucumbers and grape vines. More side shoots means more fruit or flowers. When the stopping is applied to a greenhouse tomato plant, it is intended to stop it making further trusses of flowers and fruit.

Leeks Unlike onions, leeks cannot be lifted and stored over the winter, but providing the soil isn't gripped tight by frost, the leek crop can be used fresh from late autumn through to late April, and needs a correspondingly long growing season. Sow under glass in February, or outdoors at the end of March, and set out the plants in June or early July. Sow the seed about 1.25cm (½in) deep and thin the seedlings to 2.5cm (1in) apart. Before lifting the young plants, water thoroughly both the seedbed and the site they are to occupy.

Planting simply involves making 15–20cm (6–8in) holes with a dibber and dropping the leeks in, allowing about 15cm (6in) between them. Fill each hole with water and set the plants so that the leaves are aligned along the row. Allow one well-grown leek per person per meal to determine the number of plants you will need for self-sufficiency. When lifting the crop trim off the roots in situ, turn them into the top few centimetres of soil and use the site for an early lettuce crop.

DIETARY VALUE: Rich source of fibre with useful amounts of vitamin C, mineral salts and protein.

TOP FLAVOUR TIP: A fortnightly feed of liquid seaweed fertiliser enhances the flavour.

Lettuce When grown organically, all outdoor lettuce taste better than the force-fed commercial greenhouse efforts. Cos types are generally considered to be the best for flavour and are ready to eat about twelve weeks after sowing, sooner if given cloche protection. Two 4.5m (15ft) rows, or the equivalent in deep-bed bands, will give self-sufficiency, but the sowings should be made half a row at a time from late March until mid-June. Sow the seed thinly and only 6mm (¼in) deep. Thinnings can be used as sandwich filling, or sow a leaf lettuce type specially for this purpose. Throughout its growth this crop should never go short of water.

DIETARY VALUE: An important source of vitamins A and C, potassium, protein, trace elements, mineral salts and fibre.

TOP FLAVOUR TIP: Eat within an hour of harvesting for the best flavour. If you like crisp texture with a nutty flavour go for the baby cos type Little Gem or the full cos Erthel. Good butterheads are Avoncrisp and Avondefiance. Recommended leaf varieties are Salad Bowl and Red Salad Bowl. Red varieties of lettuce are recommended for those who prefer a tangy, bitter-sweet flavour.

Peas Commercial production of peas for selling fresh has declined quite dramatically in Britain as the frozen pea industry has claimed the lion's share of the pea market. But if you can find space in the garden to grow this crop, pick the pods young and eat the tender, sweet peas within an hour, you will appreciate why this is one of the earliest vegetables grown by man, and one of the most nutritious. Because it offers such a rich reward, this crop deserves special attention. Give it an open, sunny site with deep, well-drained soil that has been enriched with organic compost or well-rotted farmyard manure, allowing a good two bucketsful to each metre/yard run of trench. Prepare the site by digging a trench as soon after Christmas as possible, a spit deep, that's about 23cm (9in), and a spade's width. In light land you can line the bottom of the trench with a thick layer of soaked newspaper. Mix

OVERSIZE ONIONS AND MONSTER MARROWS

On 16 September 1989, at the Harrogate Great Autumn Show, an onion grown by Vin Throup, of Silston, Yorkshire, became the world's heaviest onion at 4.37kg (9lb 11½oz), winning a cash prize of £2,000 for its proud grower. But, tell me, what do you do with an onion that size? What's the point of growing massive marrows, grotesquely large pumpkins, 51.3kg (114lb) cabbages or 21.6kg (48lb) swedes? These are all edible crops that, when grown to record-breaking proportions, become valueless in the kitchen. If they are not fit for their intended purpose, their size becomes senseless. Perhaps it's time we blew the whistle on these contests to grow the biggest vegetable because they do nothing to improve the quality of the crop, however much they boost the vanity of the growers.

variety should give up to 5kg (10lb) of peas, picked young, and for maincrop about 6kg (13lb). Allow up to 450g (1lb) of peas in the pod for each adult when picking the crop. For a fully detailed description of sowing and management techniques and advice on selection of varieties of pea, please refer to my book *Organic Gardening*.

DIETARY VALUE: Garden peas have a higher protein content than that of cereals. They also contain a worthwhile amount of vitamins C and A, carbohydrate, dietary fibre, mineral salts and trace elements.

TOP FLAVOUR TIP: Wrinkled or marrowfat peas are far sweeter than the hardier round varieties. Never overcook fresh peas: three minutes in a pressure cooker or fifteen minutes in lightly salted boiling water is sufficient. Add a sprig of fresh mint to the water before cooking.

Radishes This might seem a strange choice to be given priority, but it is an unfussy crop that can be fitted into a shady spot in the garden where the soil has had a good dressing of compost. The spring sowings can start in March and continue at three-weekly intervals until the end of May. Winter radishes are sown in August for use from October onwards. This crop should never go short of water, and a feed with liquid manure will help to ensure rapid growth.

DIETARY VALUE: A rich source of vitamin C, calcium, folic acid, iron and potassium.

TOP FLAVOUR TIP: Hot, woody radishes are the result of too slow growing and a shortage of water. Sweet, crisp radishes should be eaten on the day they are harvested.

Shallots Where space doesn't allow a crop of onions, try growing shallots. The crop keeps better than onions, is more versatile in use, and you can save bulbs for planting year after year. This means, for a very modest outlay on, say, a 450g (1lb) bag of virus-free 'seed' shallots, you will consistently get a crop worth up to twenty times more than the seed, especially when used as pickled onions. Start the bulbs off in a tray of moist soil as early in the year as possible. When the bulbs have made about 2.5cm (1in) of roots, plant out with a trowel, placing them 15cm (6in) apart in rows 22.5cm (9in) apart. Each

the compost or manure with the soil as you return it to the trench. Before sowing the seed add a top dressing of a balanced organic fertiliser.

Sow the seed into a flat-bottomed drill about 15cm (6in) wide and 6.75cm (3in) deep, allowing space between the trenches roughly equivalent to the height of the crop, that's to say, anything from 45cm to 1.5m (18in to 5ft). The seed should be placed in staggered fashion in two rows, each seed about 5cm (2in) apart each way. Cover with about 5cm (2in) of soil and then place a wire pea guard over the row to prevent the birds from taking the seedlings. Alternatively, you can stretch three or four lines of black cotton along the rows. Mice can be a problem and suggestions on how to deter them are given on pages 84–5.

Sowing times will vary, of course, according to the region, although an important point common to all areas is not to sow when the soil is cold and sodden because the seed will rot. Given a mean soil temperature above 12°C (47°F), the early crop could go in from late March onward, and the first meal off it could be expected in early June. The maincrop seed would be sown in late April or early May and be ready in early August. To estimate your approximate yield, a 4.5cm (15ft) row of an early

continued on page 116

MAKE ROOM FOR HERBS

Herbs thrive in an organic environment that is open to the full sun, and as close to the kitchen as possible so that their fragrance can be enjoyed every day in the summer, and gathering them doesn't involve a tiresome trek. Ideally, they should have an island site to themselves, but in a small garden that may not be practical. Because most herbs have attractive foliage and flowers, as well as a strong scent, they can be fitted in as part of the ornamental border, in window boxes or other outdoor containers. You can even set some of them, such as a low-growing thyme and pennyroyal, in the gaps of the crazy paving – the rich perfume of the leaves is released when the plants are brushed against.

Prepare the site for the herbs early in the year by digging a spade's depth and working in compost, spent peat and leafmould. Rake the surface to a fine tilth, then mark out a pattern for planting, using squares, diamonds or circles for planted and unplanted areas. Remember that the taller subjects should not be allowed to overshadow the shorter ones. The unplanted areas can be covered with gravel, bark, old bricks or crazy paving, and lawn-edging strips, bricks or tiles can be used as retaining walls for the gravel or bark.

Go to a specialist herb nursery, preferably an organic one, for your stock of perennial plants, choosing the varieties that you will want for the kitchen first. Hardy annuals, such as borage, chervil and dill, can be bought as seed by mail order from, say, Suffolk Herbs, and sown in late March, while the half-hardy ones should be sown towards the end of April.

Remember that the mints are very invasive, so much so that you would be well advised to isolate them from the herb garden and give them a patch where the roots can be kept within bounds. Parsley is another herb that needs individual treatment. We use so much of it that I grow it as an annual crop in the vegetable plot.

For those with the space and the wish to be adventurous, the basis for a modern herb garden might be bay, borage, chervil, chives, coriander, dill, fennel, garlic, horseradish (but give it the mint treatment to deter its territorial ambition), marjoram, mint, parsley, rosemary, sage, sorrel, tarragon and thyme.

Add lavender as the best of all herbs for scenting linen, and those crushable beauties, the creeping thymes, chamomile and pennyroyal, where they will release their heady aromas at high summer.

thyme

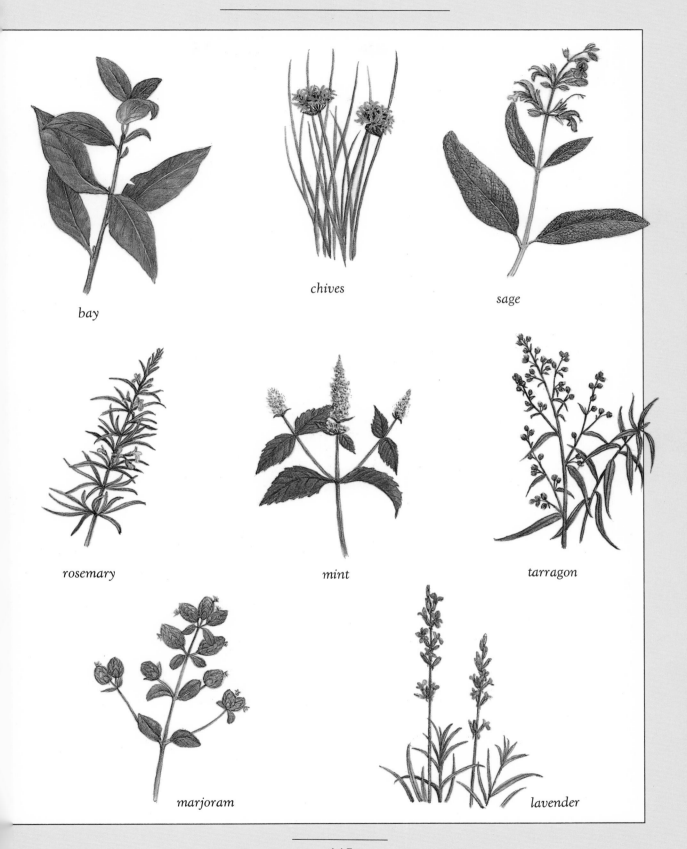

bay

chives

sage

rosemary

mint

tarragon

marjoram

lavender

bulb produces a cluster of up to ten new bulbs. When the foliage has turned yellow, they can be eased from the soil and allowed to dry off thoroughly. The shallots can be stored in old tights or on trays somewhere cool and dry.

DIETARY VALUE: A very nutritious vegetable that can be used raw, baked, braised or pickled. Shallots contain some vitamin C and fibre, and provide carbohydrate, potassium, calcium, mineral salts and trace elements.

TOP FLAVOUR TIP: Bake with the skins on, then peel before serving to enjoy the full flavour.

Tomatoes You will discover the true tangy flavour of the old-fashioned tomato when you grow an outdoor variety organically. Standard varieties can be given a south-facing wall or fence, while bush varieties that need no support can be given a sunny spot virtually anywhere in the garden, including a growing bag or large pot on the patio. Six plants will give you self-sufficiency all summer long. It is a good plan to raise your own plants because the choice at nurseries or garden centres is usually very restricted. Old favourites Ailsa Craig and the cherry-size Gardener's Delight are top-flavoured standards, while Red Alert and the Amateur are good bush ones. Sow the seed in early March in a seed tray and place somewhere warm, such as the airing cupboard. When the seeds emerge, place them in a light, draught-free position. At the two true-leaf stage they can be pricked out into 8cm (3in) pots and go onto a sunny windowsill or into the cool greenhouse. Harden off gradually so that the plants are ready to be planted out after the last frost. Give the standard plants a cane for support and space them 60cm (2ft) apart. Allow 1m (3ft) each way between the bush types. Standard or cordon plants will need the side shoots removing, while the bush varieties should be given a mulch of straw, bark or black polythene to protect the fruit from splashes and to speed ripening. All outdoor tomatoes benefit from foliar feeding with liquid seaweed extract.

DIETARY VALUE: The most important salad crop for its nutritional value, containing good amounts of vitamins C, A and E (when raw), folic acid, calcium, potassium, dietary fibre and trace elements.

TOP FLAVOUR TIP: Flavour in tomatoes is heightened when the right variety has restricted watering, but weekly foliar feeding.

A FRUITFUL SMALL GARDEN

To satisfy the demand for blemish-free, uniform apples, the commercial grower has to give the trees a mind-boggling programme of spraying and carefully controlled dosing with artificial fertilisers.

All the chemical sprays, we are assured, have been individually tested and given safety clearance, although the frequency with which previously declared 'safe' chemical sprays are withdrawn because of doubts about their hazard to health in the long term makes one wonder how safe is safe. There is the added worry of the cocktail effect on our bodies of all the chemical residues left not only on the fruit, but also in almost every item of food we buy. No wonder, then, that there has been such a boom in back-garden fruit growing. Grown organically, we can be confident that home-produced fruit will be entirely wholesome and health-giving, because even airborne pollutants can be washed off.

The problem then becomes what to grow. Just as with vegetables when space restrictions force priorities, this can best be solved by a family discussion. Take account of location, soil, climate, the availability of commercially grown organic fruit, the family's preferences, and the relative values of the various crops. Few things can match the fragrance and flavour of that first bowl of sun-warmed strawberries, picked and eaten the same day, although the ultimate in blissful luxury in our home is the dessert gooseberry, wine red and walnut size and with a sweetness and flavour that defies imitation or description. Dessert gooseberries are not found in supermarkets and you might have a fruitless search for plump, shining cultivated blackberries, ripe, juicy raspberries, loganberries and tayberries, and those special delights of summer the white-, red- and blackcurrants.

Dwarfing rootstocks have enabled fruit breeders to produce varieties of top fruit – apples, pears, plums and cherries – that fit happily into quite small gardens. In fact, the arrival of columnar apple varieties, such as the Ballerina and Minarette types, means that you can even grow them in extra large pots on the patio, providing you have made provision for more than one variety. Self-fertile varieties are advertised, but are seldom successful. For those gardeners prepared to spend a bit of time studying the technique involved in their training and pruning, cordon or espalier fruit trees occupy very little space, give a good yield of top quality fruit and can be made a most decorative feature of the garden, whatever its size. Cordons can be used to line a pathway, while espaliers can be trained over a bare wall or fence, and your choice of fruit could include apples, pears, cherries, plums, peaches, figs, nectarines and apricots.

Perhaps the most important point to make about fruit trees and bushes in the small garden is that they don't have to be given a set-aside plot. Their beauty of foliage, blossom and fruit makes them worthy candidates for sharing borders and beds with the ornamental shrubs and perennials, providing the special requirements of the fruit-bearing trees are given some priority. For example, avoid a known frost pocket, usually the lowest part of a garden that slopes, and don't use cordons or espaliers as wind breaks because that could result in damage to the leaves and blossom, along with poor pollination.

Buy the stock in winter from a fruit specialist, preferably one that you can visit to discuss your requirements, and prepare the site in your garden for your fruit trees and bushes with at least as much care as you would give to ornamental trees. With cordons and espaliers you will need to erect post and wire supports before the trees arrive, or are collected from the nursery, while those to be grown fan-trained against a wall or fence will have to have an extra helping of humus-forming material incorporated in the planting hole, because until their roots grow large enough to move away from the wall they will be extra thirsty.

Well before you are ready to plant, check the pH value of your soil. For most tree and bush fruits the range from 6.0 to 6.5 is ideal and you need to make a correction only if the pH reads below 6.0 (page 33). Reserve a good measure of your homemade compost, worm-worked compost, well-rotted farmyard manure or bought-in organic compost for incorporating into the planting site. For one- or two-year-old trees and shrubs dig two spits deep, that's about 45cm (18in), and mix in about a wheelbarrow load of the compost as you return the soil at planting, leaving enough to provide a mulch around the firmly planted tree. Give established trees and shrubs about 150g (6oz) of fish, blood and bone meal annually, followed by another mulching layer of manure or compost. A twice-yearly spraying with liquid seaweed extract, in the first year or two, is also beneficial in light soil where there might be a trace element deficiency.

GUIDELINES FOR BACK-GARDEN FRUIT

- Whether you are planning to plant apples and pears or soft fruit such as raspberries and strawberries, plan the positioning of the plants with care. All fruit needs a sunny, open position yet with protection from harsh winds. Birds that at other times are welcome in the garden become a nuisance when the soft fruit is ripening, so you may well have to allow for protective netting.

- Choosing the right rootstock and varieties to suit your garden is an important factor in successful cropping. Go to a specialist nursery and check your choice with the experts there. With apples the smallest-growing rootstock is M27, which eventually reaches about 1.8m (6ft) tall, M9 grows to 3m (10ft) and M26 to 3.6m (12ft). There isn't a dwarf pear rootstock: Quince C grows to 3m (10ft) and Quince A to 3.6m (12ft). Plum trees are available on Pixy rootstock, gowing to 2.4m (8ft) tall, while the smallest cherry rootstock is Inmil or GM9 at 3.6m (12ft) tall.

- Remember that apples and pears need cross pollinating with another variety in bloom at about the same time. Check with the nursery about suitable pollinators.

- In the first few years after planting, apple and pear trees are winter pruned to mould a good, balanced shape without overcrowding and to remove any diseased or damaged branches. From about the fifth year onward, apple trees generally need pruning only every fourth winter, while pear trees will need pruning every other winter. Plums and cherries need only dead wood removing, not drastic pruning.

- Raspberry canes are cut to ground level after fruiting and five or six of the new canes are tied in to the supports. Gooseberry, red and white currant bushes are pruned at any time to keep an open inverted umbrella shape, while blackcurrants and the hybrid berries can be cut back after pruning, like the raspberry canes.

- You can delay the ripening of the currant family by adapting a Victorian practice. To achieve a spread of ripe fruit over four or five weeks, instead of one or two, selected bushes were given a wigwam of straw on a framework of canes. You can use the same technique, substituting old carpet or matting for the straw, and the same technique again in the winter to protect semi-hardy shrubs in hard weather.

The soft fruit plants will need protection from birds. Just a few can be given individual cover as the fruit ripens with plastic netting or disused net curtains, or you can spray with a harmless deterrent such as Hoppit. But if you are growing a range of soft fruit in a large garden, then the most satisfactory arrangement is to erect a fruit cage large enough to walk in without having to bend double.

Raspberries, blackberries and other briar fruits will need a wire-and-post structure to support them and on which they are trained. As well as mulching the plants to provide nutrients you will also need to put down a dense mulch to deter weeds and suckers. A thick layer of newspapers or black polythene sheeting, followed by a cosmetic covering of straw or bark, will do the trick. The raspberry beetle is the major pest of raspberries, blackberries and the hybrid berries and here prevention is the best weapon. In June and July this tiny beetle lays its eggs in the blossom and after about fourteen days they hatch into larvae which eat into the embryo fruit. After about four weeks of feeding, the grubs drop to the ground and pupate in the soil throughout the winter. You can achieve a fair degree of control by using the methods described on page 80.

Strawberries, like asparagus, have a short season, take up a fair amount of space for the yield and yet are offered in any number of gimmicky ways by mail order firms. True, you can grow them in barrels or strawberry towers, but you need a lot of luck and a fair bit of skill to make the effort worthwhile. True also that you can grow them as a decorative feature at the front of a sunny border, but you must overcome the problem of slug and bird damage. You can also buy the so-called perpetual-fruiting varieties, but my bet is you will be disappointed to find the berries are very small and the far from generous yield in high summer is prematurely terminated by the first frost. On the positive side, strawberry breeders are constantly introducing new varieties that have overcome some of the major snags, such as virus infection and sterility, and once you have bought your initial stock from a reputable grower your plants will produce infants in the form of runners to enable you to increase or replace the parent stock.

Columnar apple trees, such as the Ballerina and Minarette types, can be grown in even the smallest garden, but more than one variety is needed to ensure proper fertilisation

GROW YOUR OWN ORGANIC MUSHROOMS

Most commercially produced mushrooms are grown with the protection of insecticides, although it is perfectly feasible and more profitable to produce them organically. It just requires a bit more skill. Cultivated mushrooms don't have the pronounced flavour of the field mushroom but, as you can buy mushroom kits requiring very little space and a modest temperature of about 13°C (55°C), even the flat-dweller has the opportunity of growing a steady supply of mushrooms over a ten- to twelve-week cropping period, and any surplus that can't be eaten fresh can be frozen.

If you have a little-used part of the lawn that isn't going to look too unsightly left uncut for a while, it's good fun, though a bit chancy, to grow your own mushrooms in the garden. For this you will need an area at least 1m (3ft) square.

Plan to have your mushrooms cropping in the autumn because this is the natural season for them. Make a start in June or early July by marking out the site, somewhere shaded for preference, but not too overshadowed. Carefully remove the turf, cutting it in easy to handle strips about 5cm (2in) thick. Dig out about 10cm (4in) of the soil and replace it with well-rotted farmyard manure, or a proprietary manure, mixed 50-50 with the soil you have removed. It should be moist but not saturated.

You can now seed the patch with either spawn pellets or small pieces of block spawn, then replace the turf. Continue to cut the grass as normal until about the first week of September; after that the site should be left undisturbed and not walked on.

The tiny button mushrooms should show through about twelve weeks after spawning. Depending on whether you want buttons, cups or the larger flat mushrooms, let them mature for a day or two. Pick them by twisting and gently pulling. Don't leave the stalk in the ground. With luck, you should be able to gather mushrooms in batches every ten days or so for as long as ten weeks.

Put a little-used part of the lawn to productive use by growing your own mushrooms

WHY NEW ISN'T ALWAYS BEST

In the National Fruit Trials at Brogdale in Kent there are more than 1,800 varieties of apple. Yet the majority of British shoppers buy only French-grown Golden Delicious and home-grown but often immature Cox's Orange Pippin. So why bother to build up and maintain a collection of old varieties of apple?

Come to that, when there are so many 'improved' varieties of vegetables and flowers available today why was it thought important in the late 1980s to establish a gene bank of varieties at the Institute of Horticultural Research at Wellesbourne, Warwickshire? The answer, briefly, is that without an investment bank of varieties whose antecedents stretch back hundreds of years, our stock of breeding material could have become bankrupt and be lost for ever.

One result of Britain joining the European Community was the requirement in the 1970s to conform to new plant patenting laws. A national list of seeds was drawn up and it became illegal to sell seeds of varieties that weren't listed. Independent seed firms were quickly snapped up by the oil and chemical companies who could see big profit potential in patented varieties.

Since 1973 we have lost many hundreds of traditional vegetable varieties, many of which were regarded as synonymous with other varieties. But, too often, their removal from the list was made entirely for commercial considerations with the knowledge that patented varieties, which must be 'uniform, stable and distinct', could earn fat royalties.

Organic growers and gardeners are more concerned with good flavour, quality, disease resistance, weather tolerance and suitability for local conditions. In short, the very factors that have kept old fruit and vegetable varieties firm favourites over the centuries could become superseded by the commercial desire for maximum yield, cosmetic finish and good handling and travelling characteristics, because, of course, plant breeders work primarily for farmers and growers, not amateur gardeners.

For this reason alone all gardeners, whether organic or not, should cherish the old varieties. This is not to say that many modern hybrid varieties aren't worth growing. On the contrary, some offer very significant benefits over the open-pollinated types (see page 59). One way to ensure that old varieties don't disappear for all-time is to keep on buying them. Another is to save one's own seed or get together with friends to form a seed-saving co-operative.

There are signs of a swing back by consumers to flavourful food rather than the bland quick-fix stuff of recent years. It happened with bread. It's happening with tomatoes and apples. Safeway, the supermarket chain, conducted tasting trials of old varieties of tomato, such as Ailsa Craig, Gardener's Delight and Tigerella, and they handsomely beat newer hybrids developed for commercial growers. The same supermarket re-introduced a very old English lettuce called Wallop and oyster mushrooms as alternatives to ordinary commercial ones. About the same time Marks & Spencer introduced old varieties of apple in selected stores and were 'delighted' with the result.

Flavour in fruit and vegetables is far more important than mere good looks and that alone is justification for keeping old varieties on active service. Here are some that I've found have a superior flavour when grown organically:

Apples: Blenheim Orange, Charles Ross, D'Arcy Spice, James Grieve, Kidd's Orange Red, Sunset.
Beans, broad: The Sutton. *Climbing French:* Blue Lake. *Runner:* Scarlet Emperor.
Beetroot: Detroit Globe.
Brussels sprouts: Cambridge No 5, Fillbasket.
Cabbages: Golden Acre, Minicole, January King, Winnigstadt.
Carrots: Early Nantes, Autumn King.
Celery: Giant Pink, Giant White.
Gooseberries: Bedford Red, Crown Bob, Leveller, Whinham's Industry.
Leeks: Musselburgh, The Lyon.
Lettuces: Little Gem, Paris White.
Parsnips: Hollow Crown, Tender and True.
Pears: Beurre Bedford, Bristol Cross, Doyenne du Comice.
Plums: Blaisdon Red, Coe's Golden Drop, Victoria.
Potatoes: Early: Arran Pilot, Duke of York. *Maincrop:* Dr McIntosh, Golden Wonder, King Edward.
Raspberries: Lloyd George, Malling Admiral.
Strawberries: Cambridge Vigour, Royal Sovereign, Talisman.
Tomatoes: Ailsa Craig, Gardener's Delight, The Amateur, Tigerella.

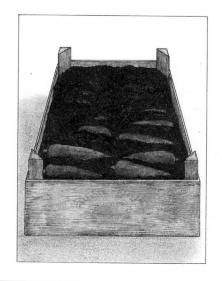

LAWN CARE
WITHOUT CHEMICALS

 Given the difficult choice of growing grass or vegetables, the organic gardener would probably choose the edible crops, while the hard-pressed or utterly lazy gardener would prefer a paved patio. But if there are children, then a hard-wearing lawn gives an area where they can play in relative safety and where the parents can relax in relative peace. Yet grass is a very demanding crop, taking up what some would say is an inordinate amount of time and energy, whether it is the perfect green-striped foil for a backcloth of handsome trees and shrubs, and borders of immaculate flowering plants, or a patch of old turf that has the daylights kicked out of it by the youngsters from April until October.

MAKE A MARK

When marking out a new lawn, flower bed or sites for sowing annuals, use a length of rope to make the required shape, then sprinkle flour or fine sand to mark the outline.

To keep a lawn in reasonably good condition you need four things: a garden fork to admit air into the roots of the grass, a mower, a lawn rake and your own man- or womanpower. There's absolutely no need for chemicals, such as weedkillers or specially formulated grass fertilisers, and in terms of the velvety striped effect that the TV commercials reckon we should insist on, there's little difference between the least expensive hand mower and the ultimate in lawnmower luxury: the ride-on job with electronic ignition and accessories to hoover the cuttings and collect fallen leaves.

In fact, experiments carried out by Reading University's Department of Agriculture and Horticulture proved conclusively that leaving the clippings on the lawn is far better for the health of the grass than collecting them for compost making. Grass clippings do not lead to a build-up of thatch or an increase in weeds. Allow them to return to the soil and they recycle the nutrients, and in only about fourteen days the nitrogen taken up by the grass is returned to the soil by the clippings.

If you have children or pets or both it is especially important to avoid using chemicals on your lawn. Problems with grass usually arise because of bad drainage, inadequate aeration, overshadowing by trees or tall shrubs, cutting the grass too short too often, drought, and poor growth through insufficient nutrients.

On light soils the lawn might drain too quickly for strong, lush growth. Ideally, this problem should have been anticipated before laying down the lawn by incorporating plenty of humus-rich material in the soil. But better moisture-holding property can be worked into the lawn by adding organic matter such as well-sieved homemade compost, worm-worked compost, spent compost from growing bags, leafmould or composted bark. Brush it into the grass in early autumn, and early in the following year apply a top dressing of fish, blood and bone meal at the rate of 56g (2oz) to the sq m/yd, or give it a monthly feed from March to June of a liquid seaweed extract, such as SM3 or Maxicrop, or a manure-based one, such as Farmura, or one made by the method described on pages 51–2. Whether the feed is a dry one or liquid it is important that it is applied to moist soil.

On heavy soils the lawn can become waterlogged if the drainage is poor. Like any other crop, grass must have adequate air at its roots. Waterlogging drives the air out and the roots literally drown. Regular aeration is necessary on any lawn, but essential on a badly drained one, and the simplest method is to use an ordinary garden fork. Once a month drive the tines deep into the soil, then work the handle back and forth a bit to widen the holes. Sprinkle a generous quantity of medium grade builder's sand or gravel over the entire lawn after the final mowing in the autumn. A lawn on clay or sandy soils may be too acidic for healthy grass growth and this would allow the encroachment of moss. Check the pH with a meter, or a soil test kit, and if it is below 6.0 sprinkle hydrated lime early in the year at 225g (8oz) to the sq m/yd on clay, or carbonate of lime at the same rate on light soil.

The way you mow is an important factor in lawn care. Too close mowing brings problems of weeds and drought. Prostrate weeds such as clover, medicks and pearlwort can survive close mowing, which further weakens the grass and encourages moss, while in hot, dry weather close-mown grass roots can be mortally exposed to scorching by the sun and shrivelling by drought and wind. When adjusting the height of cut on your mower give a coarse-grass lawn a cutting height of 2–3cm (¾–1¼in) while fine grass can be gradually lowered to a short 1.5cm (½in), with both the first few cuts of the season and the last few cuts made with the cutting height higher.

THE PROBLEM OF MOSS

A healthy lawn with vigorous grass will keep moss at bay, but if your lawn is already moss-ridden, there are various steps to overcome the problem. Don't cut the grass too short and give regular dressings of homemade compost or fish, blood and bone. Improve drainage by regular aeration and raking. Try to avoid having plants and shrubs that overshadow parts of the lawn.

Raking the grass with a lawn rake in early spring will remove the thatch that has accumulated over the winter. Worm casts are an indication of a healthy organic lawn, but they are a nuisance when mowing. Don't use a chemical preparation to kill the worms, simply brush the casts gently with a bristle broom or

Regular aeration of the lawn is necessary to keep the grass healthy. All you need is a garden fork pushed well into the turf every few inches

LEATHERJACKETED LAWNS

Leatherjackets, the larvae of the daddy longlegs or crane fly, can do an annoying amount of damage to a lawn by eating the roots of the grass and so causing bare patches to appear. Starlings are especially fond of leatherjackets and a flock of them will descend on the lawn after a heavy shower to feed on them. You can help matters along by giving the lawn a thorough soaking in the evening, then cover it with a bit of old carpet or black polythene. In the morning the leatherjackets will be on the surface for you or the birds to pick off.

besom to scatter them. Weeds such as the plantains, dandelions, thistles and daisies can all be hand weeded.

In autumn and winter it is a good plan to keep off the lawn as much as possible, especially when it is frosty, apart from raking to remove fallen leaves.

Finally, if you really can't stand the tedium of looking after your grass patch, remember that you can make a lawn out of other plants. A non-grass lawn won't be a practical proposition where there are children or dogs, but can be a very attractive way of filling in the space between the borders. Thyme and chamomile are good choices and will require only infrequent mowing. They are colourful if allowed to flower and are fragrant when walked on.

FREE-RANGE EGGS FROM YOUR GARDEN

 If, like my family and many, many more, you are sickened by the manner in which factory-farmed eggs reach your breakfast table, there's a choice of actions. You can give up eating eggs altogether, or find a supplier of genuine free-range eggs. Or you can keep a few hens in your garden, humanely, yet with the reward of a regular supply of wholesome fresh eggs and nitrogen-rich manure.

Garden hen-keeping can make good sense both in reducing food waste and relieving our dependence on factory-farmed eggs. We waste something like 25 per cent of food in the kitchen before it reaches the table – the potato peelings, outer leaves of cabbages and cauliflowers, the pods of peas and beans, pieces of stale bread, biscuits and cereals, the heads and tails of fish.

Another 4 or 5 per cent of food is wasted after it has been cooked. It leaves the table as scraps and goes straight into the waste bin. Some of us save vegetable waste for recycling as compost, while the cooked scraps go into the worm farm or dustbin. Those scraps could, instead, go to the hens in the garden.

The statistics are impressive. Just two hens will produce a total of at least 400 eggs a year, or rather more than one egg a day, fed on the waste from the kitchen with about 60g (2oz) of corn, and 170g (6oz) of layers' mash daily. The bonus is the annual production of 50–100kg (110-220lb) of excellent manure with about four times as much plant food as farmyard manure (page 34). Providing a suitable hen house is a fairly simple DIY task, or you can buy one ready-made for easy assembly.

Generally, the traditional breeds are more suitable for garden keeping. My parents kept the handsome Speckled Sussex with chestnut-brown plumage splashed with white and black, while my wife's people favoured the beautifully marked Speckled Maran, the small Silkies, White Leghorn and Rhode Island Reds, all sturdy breeds for the garden.

Two points cannot be emphasised too strongly. Keeping hens is out of the question unless you are prepared to learn about their needs and their welfare. An excellent guide to chicken craft is *Chickens at Home* by Michael Roberts, available for £3 from the author at Honeybourne Pastures, Evesham, Worcestershire WR11 5QJ. The second vital point is that hens need attention twice a day, every day, even when you are away from home. So before you make the commitment to become a hen owner, ensure that a friendly neighbour or close-by relative can take over whenever holidays or illness prevent you from caring for your charges.

Finally, a word about the Ministry of Agriculture regulations concerning regular testing for salmonella. If you keep fewer than twenty-five birds and produce eggs only for your family's consumption, you are exempt from the regulations.

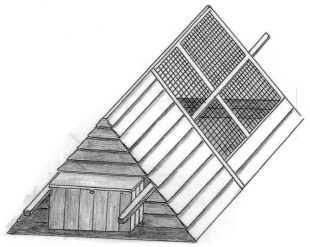

Two hens can be housed in a mobile ark and moved progressively over the lawn

HOLIDAY
SURVIVAL GUIDE

 He was seventy-odd and gloomy, despite the heavenly summer. 'I haven't had a holiday in fifty years, not since I married. Can't leave the garden to anyone else to look after. Not for a week. Not in the summer.' I know how he felt.

If you've spent a lot of time and lavished love on your plants, leaving them in foster care or, worse still, unattended when they are in their prime, is a wrench. Happily, there are ways to make your absence from the garden less distressful for you and your plants, so that you can take off to the over-rated sunspots of the Mediterranean with the confidence that when you return, your garden is still the beautiful, fragrant haven it was before you left. You'll appreciate the peace and quiet, the greenness even more.

There are two main areas that need your attention well before your departure, and if you own a greenhouse or conservatory there's an important third.

First, the houseplants. Some, such as the cacti, succulents and bromeliads, can safely be left where they are without water for a couple of weeks. Many others can be stood outside for their own summer holiday, and you could ask a neighbour to give them an occasional watering if the rain fails. Choose a sheltered spot for them, out of direct sunlight and where they can't be knocked over by marauding moggies.

Plants that have grown too big to move outside, such as a monster Swiss cheese plant, will have to make do with a thorough watering on the eve of your leaving, and if you can cool the room down by pulling the curtains part way, and provide some ventilation, so much the better.

The problem plants are the ones that can't be placed outside and that require adequate water and humidity to keep doing well: African violets and many foliage plants are in this category. Fortunately, there's a very effective way of caring for these plants using capillary matting.

If you have more than half a dozen or so pot plants, the best plan is to buy a length of the matting from your local garden centre and use your bath as the watering hole. You'll also need something to stand the plants on, about 15cm (6in) tall. A dozen house bricks and a sheet of hardboard would be just the job.

Put newspaper down to protect the bath's surface, then the bricks and board, then lay the capillary matting over the lot and tuck the ends under the bricks. Fill the bath to within 2–3cm (1in) of the top of the bricks, and place your pots on top of the capillary matting. While you are away your plants will be kept nicely moist but not saturated.

Instead of the matting, if you have just a few potted plants to worry about, you can buy a capillary watering mat shaped to fit the draining board of your kitchen sink. It is long-lasting, re-usable and washable. You simply place the plants on the mat, leave the end hanging down into the partly filled sink or, if you prefer, a bowl of water in the sink, and the capillary action of the mat keeps the compost in the pots moist.

PLANT FOOD STICKS

Feeding pot plants organically is simple if you use a liquid seaweed extract, such as SM3 or Maxicrop. Alternatively, you can buy Finnish-made organic plant food sticks made from chicken manure and seaweed. The manufacturers claim that the sticks provide slower-release macro-nutrients, trace elements and other growth stimulants. You stick them in the compost and water the plants in the usual way.

The second area for attention is the garden, especially the vegetables, soft fruit and the lawn. For the most part the flowers and shrubs will survive without attention for a fortnight, but any newly planted items, such as the hanging baskets and other outdoor containers, will need watering every day in dry weather, so you will have to arrange for a friend or neighbour to do the honours. If the arrangement is a reciprocal one, it would be a sound idea to include one mowing of the lawn in the deal if you plan to be absent for a couple of weeks.

Newly planted shrubs and trees will benefit from a thorough watering, not just a trickle from the watering can, followed by a mulch of bark, leaf-mould, compost or even a thick layer of newspaper weighted down with bricks.

Some annuals, notably sweet peas, will need to be picked every other day because if they are allowed to form seeds their flowering period is shortened. Similarly, in the vegetable department ask your minder to harvest crops such as courgettes, outdoor cucumbers, radishes, lettuce, peas, dwarf beans, runner beans and turnips. As well as being picked over, all these crops, along with the celery, celeriac, marrows and outdoor tomatoes, would all benefit from a good watering mid-term through your fortnight away.

Soft fruits, such as the strawberries and raspberries, should be gathered daily – and eaten, of course, as the minder's reward for picking.

Capillary matting is an effective way of providing water for your plants when you are away from home

The greenhouse is the problem place because as well as the need for watering the plants, there's the vital requirement of adequate ventilation. According to the experts, on a hot day in July in southern England three tomato plants in a growing bag take in 6l (11pt) of water and that means giving them a long drink at least twice a day.

The most satisfactory answer, although admittedly a somewhat expensive one, is to install a trickle system of watering your greenhouse plants. Kits are available for DIY installation, either fed from the mains water supply or from a large capacity reservoir. These trickle systems feed the water direct to the growing bags or plant pots, or they can be used to keep capillary matting moist. There's even a computer-controlled system, which is linked to a mains supply, and can be programmed to turn the water on and off two or three times a day.

Any greenhouse watering system must be supported with adequate automatic ventilating. Any day during the summer months the temperature in a greenhouse can shoot up to 38°C (100°F) or more unless the air can be moved. At temperatures over 27°C (80°F) plant growth slows down or stops altogether.

Automatic vent openers for greenhouses are inexpensive and very effective, although in small greenhouses extra ventilation is often necessary, along with shading of the glass by a product that you paint on. It is opaque when dry, but becomes clear when it rains. If you leave the greenhouse door open, remember to cover it with netting to keep out birds and cats.

HOUSEPLANTS

Watch out for early signs of attack by insect pests. Whitefly and aphids, both sap-sucking insects, are the most commonly encountered ones on flowering plants indoors. They can be controlled with a soft soap solution or one of the other safe insecticides detailed. Use a fine misty spray to cover both sides of the leaves and growing points. With some small plants it is possible to invert the plant and dunk it into a bowl or bucket of soapy water, although several treatments may be necessary as aphids and whitefly breed at a rapid rate.

Red spider mite should not be a problem with plants that are sprayed with water regularly, but an infestation can be checked with liquid derris. Mealy bugs can be picked off with tweezers or dabbed with a cotton bud dipped in methylated spirits. Scale insects can be scraped off the leaves and stems using a lollipop stick or similar wooden spatula.

OPPOSITE
Pests are seldom a problem on this group of houseplants:
Cactus, African violet, geranium, palm and impatiens.

ALLOTMENTS AND FOSTER GARDENS

If you haven't the space to grow as much of your own food in your garden as you would like, the answer is to rent an allotment. If that's impossible or inconvenient because of where you live, seek out someone, such as a disabled or elderly house-owner, who would welcome your help in their garden. In return, you could grow organic vegetables, salads and, maybe, some fruit. It's what I call foster gardening and, providing there is a very clear understanding between both parties as to what is involved, it can be mutually rewarding.

Allotment gardening in Britain peaked during World War II, and for about fifteen years afterwards. In the Dig for Victory campaign, the contribution allotments made to wartime self-sufficiency was massive. Together with vegetable production from private gardens, possibly as much as 50 per cent of all the vegetables consumed in the United Kingdom were home grown in this way. During the war there were at least 1,500,000 allotment plots in full production. In 1990 there were probably fewer than 500,000 plots, and many of those were under pressure from local councils who are told by Whitehall to realise their assets and flog off land to the property developers.

Back in 1969 an official enquiry into allotments culminated in the 460-page Thorpe Report, which made scores of recommendations to try to change the politicians' indifference to allotments, but neither Labour nor Tory administrations since then has paid the slightest attention to the report – yet all the evidence is that people in densely populated areas do want allotments.

The reasons are not hard to find. Gardens are shrinking, so the space just isn't available to grow more than a token amount of food. Allotments simplify gardening. You aren't competing with the Joneses and, providing you keep the plot reasonably

well cultivated, no one is going to criticise your standard of gardening. Yet even the average ten-rod plot is capable of providing enough fresh vegetables and some soft fruit to keep a small family provided for most of the year, and it is food that is far fresher and far less expensive than can be bought at any greengrocer or supermarket.

What's more, allotment gardening doesn't call for a shed full of costly tools. In ourselves we have the most efficient green machine ever devised, the most economical source of energy and one with an inbuilt system for recycling waste. Putting that machine to work as an allotment tenant gets you back to the fundamentals of the soil, fresh air, the sun, rain and the sweat of the brow. You can make your own small but important protest against this plastic age of take-away tastelessness and junk foods.

Before taking an allotment or fostering someone's garden, you'll need to decide if you can spare enough time to tend it properly. Bringing back land to a reasonable state for growing crops after a long period of neglect can be daunting, and there's no doubt many vacant plots throughout Britain can't be relet because of that.

Some councils plough up vacant plots to keep the weeds under control, but that can be a mixed blessing. If there's couch grass or bindweed among the weeds, ploughing or rotavating simply distributes the roots throughout the plot and eradication becomes even more of a problem.

By far the most thorough way is to cut off the top growth before it re-seeds and use it to start a compost heap. The remaining growth is then dug over or forked over and all the weed roots are removed and stacked for drying. They then, I'm sorry to say, have to be burned or disposed of through the refuse collection service. Couch grass, bindweed, nettle, dock, dandelion, thistle and ground elder roots, the bulbs of oxalis and bulbous buttercup, and any

THE LAW ON ALLOTMENTS

Allotments in Britain came about because of the effects of enclosure, although the principle of providing poor people with plots of land to grow food had been advocated well before the Enclosure Acts.

The Allotments Act of 1887 gave local councils power to acquire land by compulsory purchase and there was an extension to the Act in 1908. The major statute came in the Allotments Act of 1922, after World War I had shown how dependent Britain was on home-grown food and how big a contribution the allotment tenant could make. The outbreak of war in 1939 gave the allotment movement another tremendous boost. In 1990 it was estimated that one in forty households had an allotment and many councils had waiting lists.

Do we have a right to an allotment? The law says yes, we do. The 1922 Allotments Act gave everyone, not just the poor or jobless, the right to cultivate a plot for food crops, and from 1925 local councils were required to decide how many allotments were needed to meet local demand. In 1950, following a recommendation by the Allotments Advisory Committee, it was decided there should be four acres (1.6 hectares) of allotments per one thousand people, or one plot for every twenty-five people.

If a local council wants to sell off an allotment site or to use it for other purposes, it must assure the environment minister, through an inspector, that there are no longer any plots being worked or that other plots elsewhere are available for the tenants who would be dispossessed. Obviously, where an allotment site is under-used and there is a desperate shortage of housing, the land is too valuable to remain idle. Even so, the deal between the existing allotment tenants and the council should be struck amicably and the alternative site offered to tenants should meet statutory conditions of size and ease of access.

As an allotment tenant, whether you rent from a local authority, from British Rail or a private landlord, you have rights and obligations and these should be set out in a tenancy agreement. It should cover such things as how much rent you pay and when you pay it; who is responsible for keeping headlands and pathways tidy; whether you will be allowed to keep livestock (chickens and ducks) on the plot; and the provisions made to keep the site free from vandals and other pests.

If a tenant is unable temporarily to cultivate his plot because of injury, illness or absence, it's prudent to let the council know. Some councils have increased their rents to the point where jobless tenants and pensioners find it difficult to pay. Before giving up a tenancy in these circumstances, the tenant should seek advice from the council or Citizens' Advice Bureau.

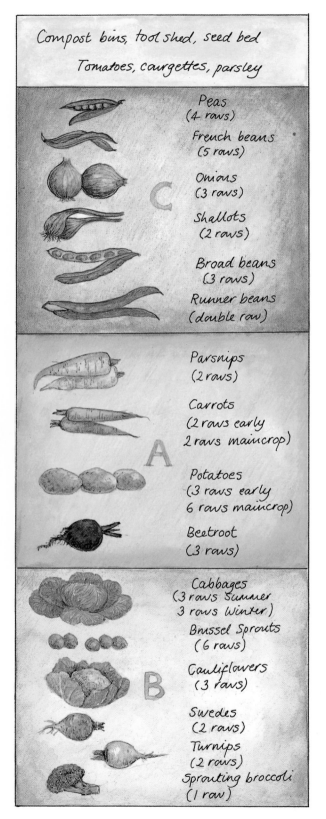

Compost bins, tool shed, seed bed

Tomatoes, courgettes, parsley

Peas
(4 rows)

French beans
(5 rows)

Onions
(3 rows)

Shallots
(2 rows)

C

Broad beans
(3 rows)

Runner beans
(double row)

Parsnips
(2 rows)

Carrots
(2 rows early
2 rows maincrop)

A

Potatoes
(3 rows early
6 rows maincrop)

Beetroot
(3 rows)

Cabbages
(3 rows Summer
3 rows Winter)

Brussel Sprouts
(6 rows)

Cauliflowers
(3 rows)

B

Swedes
(2 rows)

Turnips
(2 rows)

Sprouting broccoli
(1 row)

diseased plant material, are best kept out of the compost heap. Some expert compost makers chop and dry these pernicious weeds and add them to their aerobic heap, where the heat finishes the process of recycling them. But I find it safer to keep seeded perennial weeds and their roots out of the composting materials.

How long will it take to keep a ten-rod plot in good condition, once the initial clearance has been done? The major element in this estimate is the time spent getting to and from the plot. If the allotment is within comfortable walking distance of your home, or a quick cycle ride, frequent short trips to the plot are feasible and desirable. If, however, getting to the plot involves a bus ride or car journey, a weekly trip of longer duration should be planned. Routine work on the plot can be estimated accurately enough to judge whether it's within your capability to cope without too much stress on other family commitments. Few activities are more worth doing than growing your own organic food, but it should be done with the enthusiastic support of everyone in the family.

On my Cowpasture allotment plot in Felixstowe I know it takes 7 minutes to dig a row 4.5m (15ft) wide and about 15cm (6in) deep. Allowing for pauses to admire the scenery, ease the back or to chat up the attendant robins, thrushes and blackbirds, I can dig 8 rows in an hour. That's roughly 5.5sq m (60sq ft). So to dig 10 rods or 250sq m (300sq yd) requires an outlay of about 40 hours, bearing in mind that when the plot is in production part of it will be carrying winter crops and will not require attention until late spring.

Of course, you can take an easier route to getting the land ready for crop production and that's to hire a rotavator. The plot is allowed to lie fallow during the winter, then top-dressed with manure and compost in early spring and rotavated, weeds and all. A ten-rod plot can be churned up in a morning's rotavation, so the method is certainly a great time-saver. What it does to the earthworm population I shudder to think, and, in the long term, rotavating on the more clayey soils creates a condition called panning where the top 15cm (6in) remains fairly open-textured but below that there's compaction of the sub-soil that can lead to drainage problems.

Many green gardeners find great satisfaction from digging not only because of the healthy exercise it involves but also because it brings the gardener and

YEAR 1	YEAR 2	YEAR 3
(Dig in manure, compost, organic fertiliser before sowing) Miscellaneous crops Peas, beans Onions, Celery Spinach Courgettes etc. **C**	(Apply organic fertiliser 2 weeks before sowing <u>Brassicas</u> **B** or planting out)	(Apply organic fertiliser 2 weeks before sowing) <u>Roots</u> **A**
(Do not manure or lime. Organic fertiliser two weeks before sowing) **A** <u>Root Crops</u> Beetroot, carrots Parsnips potatoes	(Dig in manure, compost. Apply organic fertiliser 2 weeks before sowing <u>Miscellaneous</u> **C** Check pH and lime if necessary)	(Dig in manure, compost. <u>Brassicas</u> **B** Apply organic fertiliser 2 weeks before sowing or planting)
(Dig in manure or compost, lime if needed. Org. fertiliser) <u>Brassicas</u> Brussels Sprouts Cabbages Cauliflowers Swedes, Turnips Kohl Rabi Kale, Broccoli **B**	(Apply organic fertiliser 2 weeks before sowing) <u>Roots</u> **A**	(Dig in manure, compost <u>Miscellaneous</u> **C** Apply organic fertiliser 2 weeks before sowing)

Rotation of the crops in the vegetable garden or allotment helps to prevent attacks by soil pests and diseases and enables groups of crops to secure maximum benefit from regular manuring

(Left) A cropping plan for a ten-rod allotment plot based on the wartime Dig for Victory campaign

the soil into a more intimate contact than is possible with machine cultivation.

Ideally, one should take on an allotment garden at the start of a family when, with all four cylinders firing smoothly, one can put maximum effort into supplying wholesome, home-produced food taken dew-fresh to the kitchen. It can give a healthy satisfying form of exercise that, eventually, every member of the family can join in. Later, allotment gardening will have become a way of life, with deep satisfactions that hold as good in retirement as they did in the first youthful burst of enthusiasm. In between, the allotmenteer will have undergone subtle changes, because in managing a plot you become tolerant, patient and forward-looking.

The allotment holder with young children will have them with him as often as possible so that they can learn with their parents the joys of working the land to provide food to take home in triumph. Our four children each shared in the work and pleasures of raising crops, both on our three-acre Cherry Place smallholding and our allotment plots. They were environmentalists even as toddlers because an allotment is an excellent place to find out about the other inhabitants who share the plot: the wild flowers, insects, and the visiting birds and animals. If you take the family to the plot, remember these guidelines:

- Make sure the children do not wander to the annoyance of other plotholders.
- Take a good supply of soft drinks and make sure of shade when the going gets a bit warm.
- Keep a first-aid kit in the hut to cope with minor cuts and stings.
- In your hut keep bottles of pesticides, organic or not, and bags of fertilisers, along with knives, secateurs and other potentially damaging tools out of reach of the children.
- Try to organise something constructive for the children to do, perhaps tending a part of the plot themselves where they can grow a few crops of their own choosing, and some flowers for cutting or drying.

If your town or district has an allotment holders' association, then join it because it gives you that bit of public muscle in brushes with bureaucracy, and, if it comes to a fight, enlist the support of your local papers and radio station. Unfortunately, the National Society of Allotment and Leisure Gardeners, to which many allotment associations are affiliated, while offering valuable advice, has insufficient funds to fight local battles to retain threatened allotment sites.

Good local associations encourage family participation by providing special play areas for the children when they tire of helping. Membership also enables one to buy seed potatoes, lime and fertilisers, compost and bark in bulk at trade prices. If bulk orders are given, seed firms offer very attractive discounts – up to as much as a third off –

and local stockists and garden centres will usually give members a discount on tools.

Many of Britain's allotments are the most fertile and productive pieces of land in the country. Some sites have been in continuous use for hundreds of years, and generations of gardeners have tended them, mucked them year after year, and passed them on that much better than when they took them over. Partly because of tradition, increasingly because of the mounting costs of pesticides, allotment gardeners are generally either practising organic gardeners, or nearly so. Today's allotment gardener is just as likely to be a bank manager or green-fingered GP as a manual worker, and on my plot at Cowpasture the age range is as wide as high school pupil to octogenarian.

In some areas allotment associations are in the forefront of the fight for a better environment. At Bristol, for example, where there are 150 allotment sites covering 242 hectares (600 acres), representatives of the allotment tenants presented the city council with a report and proposals, with the aim of clearing up all derelict sites, protecting and enhancing the wildlife habitat and nature reserve aspect of allotments, creating organically sound management of plots and pressing for the removal of all artificial chemicals from allotment sites within twelve years.

Allotment gardening, says the report, 'provides a valued and useful facility particularly for the disadvantaged members of our society – the poor, the elderly, the unemployed, single parents and those living in the inner city. It also acts as a huge nature reserve within the city, providing space for trees and bushes, as well as a huge range of wildlife, which is of benefit both to allotment holders and the rest of the city.'

The proposals called on the Bristol parks department to adopt a policy of recycling all available organic waste, such as leaves, grass mowings and weeds, for composting by the department staff, and for regular testing of plot soil for chemical pollutants.

Even when an inner city allotment site becomes derelict, there's every reason why it should not be promptly sold off to line a developer's pocket. Inner cities have far too few breathing spaces, too few public parks and far too few nature reserves to allow highly fertile pieces of land to become yet more building blocks.

STORING YOUR SURPLUS CROPS

 Home-grown fruit and vegetables are at their nutritious best when eaten within hours, preferably an hour, of picking. The flavour, too, often falls off considerably the longer the produce is kept. Take, for example, Brussels sprouts. That nutty, sweet flavour peaks after a frost or two but can become progressively more bitter each day after harvesting. But sprouts have more than just a distinctive flavour going for them. Eat them on the same day that the buttons are gathered and you have a crop with as much vitamin C as freshly picked oranges. Indeed, new sprout varieties in the pipeline for the mid-1990s will have up to four times the vitamin C content of present-day varieties.

Both the flavour and the nutritional value of sprouts suffer when the buttons are frozen and many commercially grown ones are gathered for freezing while still immature and before the flavour has become assertive. Even so, it's better to freeze your surplus sprouts and other organic vegetables rather then have them go to waste.

Happily, most winter vegetables can be stored without freezing. Carrots, beetroot, parsnips, turnips, swedes, onions, shallots and maincrop potatoes all store remarkably well for use over the winter. Unless yours is a notoriously hard-winter area, carrots and parsnips can be left in the ground, although it is prudent to give them a covering of straw, bark, bracken or even shrubby prunings to keep the hardest frosts at bay.

On my very exposed east coast allotment, where the north and east winds blow virtually unchecked all the way from Siberia, a winter seldom passes without a spell of very hard frosts and the occasional deep snowfall, so storage of root crops out of the ground after harvesting them in October is the normal drill.

STORING FOR WINTER

Marrows and pumpkins If you are passionate about pumpkins or mad about marrows, you'll be glad to know they store well over the winter providing they have been harvested with tender care. The method is to leave both pumpkins and marrows on the plants until the skins are hard, then cut them with a piece of stem as a handle. They can then be suspended in nets or cradles of cloth in a cool, airy but frost-free place.

Potatoes Setting the skin is also a feature of successful storage of maincrop potatoes. If you have to lift the spuds a bit prematurely, maybe because there's blight about, the skins might not have toughened enough naturally to prevent internal bruising, or promote healing of any grazes made during lifting. In store, such damage can lead to rot.

You can toughen the skins, or cure them as the Americans call it, by spreading them out under cover for about a week, then turning them over to give the other side exposure for a week. This sets the skins as surely as if they had been left in the ground for another three or four weeks.

Potatoes store best in hessian or paper sacks, not plastic ones. They should be kept in the dark somewhere frost-free, so if a shed or garage is used, it's a good idea to cover the sacks with old blankets or carpet. Commercially grown potatoes, unless they are from an organic source, are usually treated in store with a chemical dressing that inhibits sprouting. Your home-grown crop will not be doctored in that way, so from early spring onwards the stored spuds will send out shoots that gradually dehydrate the tubers. Once they show signs of sprouting you can take out enough tubers to provide the seed stock for the next crop.

FRUIT

Damaged or bruised apples or pears should not be put into store. Pick those you want to keep for storage, with the stalks intact, before they are over-ripe. Medium-size fruit store better than oversize ones, although you can make an exception with that king of cooking apples Bramley's Seedling.

Ideally, dessert apples should be wrapped individually in oiled paper wraps and placed in wooden fruit trays in a store at 2–4°C (35–40°F). It should be dark, humid and airy. However, most of us have to compromise and use a shed, garage or under the bed in the spare room. A small crop of apples can be stored very successfully in polythene bags, each holding about 1kg (2lb) of fruit. The bags should have holes punched in them and the tops turned over or loosely tied, but not sealed.

Pears are best stored unwrapped on trays so that the individual fruits are not touching each other, but don't expect your stored pears to keep for anything like the length of time of the stored apples.

Plums, cherries, peaches and nectarines cannot be stored for more than a few days, so any surplus should be bottled in Kilner jars or made into jam. Dessert grapes can be left on the vine, or you can copy a very old method of cutting the bunch and inserting the stalk into a jar of water.

Strawberries, raspberries, blackberries and the hybrid berries go mouldy if you try to keep them for longer than a couple of days or so after harvesting, while gooseberries and the currants will keep in good order for a week or more in the salad compartment of the fridge.

Peppers and cabbages These can also be stored over the winter, or rather, part of the winter. Cabbages of the late autumn and winter types can be kept in good condition for up to eight weeks if lifted, roots and all, and hung up in an airy shed, garage or cellar. Alternatively, cut the cabbage when fully mature but before the hard frosts arrive and leave on about 25cm (6in) of stalk for handling, and the outer leaves, making sure they are dry and caterpillar-less. The cabbages can now be stored in nets suspended in the cellar, shed or garage.

With peppers the plan is to lift the whole plant and hang it up with the fruit still attached. You'll need a cool place where the air can circulate. This way the peppers should keep well into the New Year.

Onions and shallots The ideal storage condition for onions and shallots is 0°C (32°F) and 70 per cent relative humidity. The nearest we can get to that is the cellar of our Victorian house where the winter temperature averages 7°C (45°F) and the humidity is normally 75 per cent. The onions are hung up in the traditional strings and the shallots in nets or old tights and they keep in perfect condition from early autumn right through to the following June. Long storage life of shallots, onions and garlic does depend on their ripeness at harvesting. The skins should be brittle dry. Garlic, by the way, is best stored in strings in a warm, dry place such as near the boiler.

Root crops Root crops intended for storage should not be washed. They should be allowed to dry off after lifting, then have the loose soil brushed off. The leaves should be trimmed off to leave just a little green at the neck. With beetroot one should always twist off the leaves, rather than cut them off, as this is said to prevent the beet from bleeding. Shorten the roots but don't hack too much off or rot might set in from the base.

Carrots, swedes and parsnips can be stored in sand, the used peat from growing bags or, I imagine, coir fibre or composted bark. Deep wooden boxes

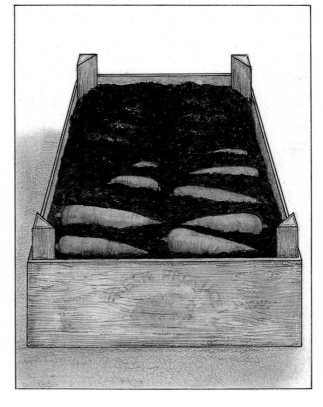

Store onions in strings once the bulbs have dried thoroughly

Carrots, swedes and parsnips can be stored in boxes of peat or sand

are ideal and the roots are positioned in layers with the largest ones at the bottom and the smallest at the top. The reason for this is that the small roots dehydrate quicker than the larger ones, so should be used first. The stored crop needs a cool store with high humidity, up to 98 per cent. They should remain in good order right through to springtime, when the warmer conditions will trigger them into growth and blanched leaves start sprouting.

Beetroot and turnips can be stored in a similar way but tend to shrivel rather more speedily than the other roots and the flavour of the beet goes off fairly rapidly in store after about Christmas.

All crops in store should be readily accessible not only for the convenience of the cook but also because they should be examined regularly for signs of rot. Onions with thick soft necks or the dreaded white rot at the roots deteriorate very rapidly and the whole crop can be contaminated. Potatoes that have been touched by blight and carrots that have had attention from carrot fly grubs also rot very quickly in store.

SUMMER AND AUTUMN CROPS

An important point to remember is that when we harvest an edible crop we are interrupting a cycle of growth that would terminate in seed production. With vegetables and some fruits the crop is still growing when we pick, cut or lift it to take it to the kitchen. Quality quite rapidly fades from that moment on, as witness the limp lettuce, tired tomatoes and uncrisp cabbage of many a high street greengrocer.

You can preserve the quality of your home-grown crops by picking early in the morning, then cooling the crop to as near 0°C (32°F) as soon as possible and keeping it in the fridge. Most summer vegetables store well in the fridge at 2–4°C (35–40°F) but are badly damaged at below freezing point.

The exceptions to fridge storage are French or dwarf beans, runner beans, cucumbers, courgettes, marrows, tomatoes and sweet peppers, which should be stored in loosely tied polythene bags in a cool, airy place where they will keep quite well for a week or more. Don't try to store any items that have been damaged by pests or diseases, and do handle the crop as gently as possible during the pre-storage period. Marrows, courgettes and tomatoes are particularly susceptible to bruising if roughly handled.

Garlic is an easy crop for the amateur to grow. Harvest it when the skins have become brittle and dry, and store in a warm, dry place

Leafy vegetables Leafy vegetables, such as cabbage, spinach, lettuce and celery, can be kept cool if sprayed with water twice daily for a couple of days or so before harvesting. On sunny summer days, vegetables in full sunlight can heat up by as much as 10°C (50°F). Spraying has the effect of prolonging quality while the crop is still in the ground, and of cooling it prior to harvesting. It is sensible also to have a basket covered with a cloth when gathering your crop and to place it in the shade until you can get it to the kitchen.

Legumes Peas, broad beans and French beans retain their flavour and texture quite well after freezing, so if you have the space it's worthwhile growing extra simply to stock up the freezer. Runner beans don't react so well to freezing and we find there's nothing to beat the time-honoured method of salting them for storage. We have a large earthenware crock, well over a hundred years old, that was used up to about 1960 to store eggs in isinglass. It holds

14l (3gal) and has a close-fitting lid, and this is our bean store.

Whenever the runners are picked any surplus beans are sliced and put in the crock with a sprinkling of sea salt. The last of the crop goes into the crock in October with a final sprinkling of salt on top and we reckon on starting on these stored beans round about Christmas time as a change from sprouts and cabbage. To prepare them all that's needed is a thorough rinsing, followed by soaking for about fifteen minutes, then the beans are cooked in the normal way and are indistinguishable from those eaten fresh in the autumn.

Of course a hundred-year-old crock is not a vital item of equipment for storing runner beans in brine. Any china, glass or plastic container with a close-fitting lid would work equally well.

LIFT THE DAHLIAS

Dahlia tubers should be lifted in the autumn when they have finished flowering, and it isn't necessary to wait for a frost to cut back the foliage.

Cut off the top growth to within 15cm (6in) of the soil, label them, then lift them and trim off the soil. Turn the plants upside down to drain off any moisture in the stems. Leave for a week or so to dry off thoroughly, then dust with flowers of sulphur and store in boxes of compost or sand in a frost-free place.

RECYCLING A–Z

Aluminium foil can be re-used to line a cardboard box for raising seedlings on the windowsill. Its reflected light helps to stop the seedlings becoming leggy. Use a strip wrapped round the stem of each plant when transplanting if cutworms are a problem.

Bags Paper bags can be saved and used to store seed saved from your own plants. Clear plastic bags can be used over flower pots when taking cuttings to provide a humid warm environment, and over seed trays to assist germination of the seed.

Bottles, plastic Cut the large ones in half to make mini-cloches for protecting newly planted seedlings from wind, frost and slugs. Use the other end, with the cap, to make an apple and pear picker. Cut a V-shaped notch to push up under the stalk of the fruit. Fit a length of dowelling or cane into the mouth of the bottle and, as a finishing touch, bind the cut edge of the plastic with sticky tape. Coloured plastic bottles can be cut into 8cm (3in) collars as slug guards round small plants. Cut empty detergent bottles into plant labels.

Brassica stalks can be trench composted or cut into sections and used to trap wireworms. Bury 15cm (6in) lengths about 10cm (4in) deep and leave for four or five days in soil you know to be infested with wireworms. Dig up the sections and burn them.

Breeze blocks make inexpensive permanent walls for cold frames, and the base for timber and aluminium greenhouses.

Bricks Secondhand bricks make attractive pathways, walls for cold frames and raised beds. Damaged ones can be broken up and buried to improve drainage of bad patches of the garden. Keep some small pieces as crocks for flower pots.

Brown paper can be used in a thick layer to blanch trench celery and leeks.

Cardboard panels are useful as mulching for weed suppression. Cover the cardboard with gravel or bark.

Carpet There are numerous uses in the green garden for old carpet. Use it as a long-term mulch to get rid of weeds or to keep borders or beds weed free, adding a covering of bark, gravel or spent peat to improve the appearance. Cut holes in it for plants and shrubs and you'll find the cool, moist environment is much appreciated by earthworms as well as the plants. Cut a square of carpet as a cover for your compost bin to keep heat in and rain and snow out. Use it also between the rows of raspberries to stop inter-row suckers and weed growth. First put down a thick layer of newspaper, then cover it with the carpet, finally add a layer of straw, bark or spent peat. Carpet underlay or foam-backed carpet can be cut into 15cm (6in) squares to protect brassica plants against cabbage root fly. Larger squares of old carpet are useful for covering the lights of cold frames and for wrapping round outdoor containers of overwintering plants whenever a hard frost is forecast. Dry them off thoroughly before re-using them in this way. When preparing a pond, use foam-backed carpet as a base for the butyl liner instead of sand. It should last the life of the liner and is far less abrasive than sand.

Credit cards cut in half make good scrapers for your mud-encrusted spade and for removing the green

---

A clear plastic bag creates a warm, humid environment for propagating cuttings. Use half a plastic bottle with a length of dowelling to make this useful apple and pear picker. Thick brown paper can be used to blanch trench celery. Remove any side shoots and slugs, wrap the stalks with the paper and tie loosely, then gradually earth up. Egg cartons are ideal for sprouting seed potatoes prior to planting them

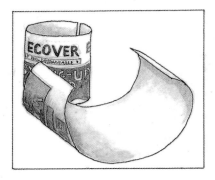
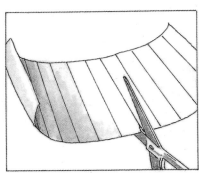

Cut the top and bottom off an empty detergent bottle, then cut it in half, open out each half and cut plant labels to the required length

algae from between the panes of glass in the greenhouse. Soften the algae first with a squirt of diluted washing-up liquid.

Cycle inner tubes, cut into 30cm (12in) lengths, make excellent tree ties. Twist into a figure of eight with one loop round the tree trunk, the other round the supporting stake.

Egg cartons make good holders for chitting seed potatoes. Afterwards they can be returned to the supplier.

Eggshells washed, then popped into the bottom of the oven when baking, will become brittle and easily crushed. Sprinkle them around slug targets in spring, such as hostas, lupins, delphiniums and lettuces.

Energy is wasted if you can't find a particular garden tool when you need it. Keep tools tidily in the

Make a carrier for small garden tools out of a large soft drinks container – by cutting out a side panel

garden shed or garage (not the greenhouse) and return them to the same positions after use. Keep potentially dangerous tools out of reach of children. Take secateurs, string or raffia, plant labels, a penknife and hand trowel whenever you pop into the garden, even for a short stint. Dodging back and forth to the garden shed for tools wastes time and energy. You can buy a gardener's apron with special pockets to carry all your bits and pieces, or you can make a carrier out of a large soft drinks plastic container, the square type with a handle. Cut out a panel from the side and carry it around with you in the garden complete with accessories. Paint handles of small hand tools a bright colour so they are less likely to be mislaid or lost.

Expanded polystyrene used to pack electrical appliances and household goods, can be re-used as a heat insulating base for your electrically heated propagator. Small pieces can be placed in flower pots in place of crocks.

Film holders The little cylinders that 35mm film is sold in make good containers for saving seed. Stick a label on, giving type of seed and variety and date.

Fork without its shaft can be given a new lease of life as a crome, a sort of heavy-duty rake. Take the fork to a metalworker or blacksmith to have the tines heated and bent at ninety degrees to the shaft and a new handle fitted.

Friends Ask your non-organic ones to save their lawn mowings, weeds and kitchen waste for your compost making. Give them some of your organically grown fruit and veg as a reward: it's the quickest way to make converts.

Glass bottles should go to your local bottle bank, but hold on to a few if you are troubled by pigeons or moles.

Gooseberry prunings can be used as cuttings. Simply trim them to about 30cm (12in) long and

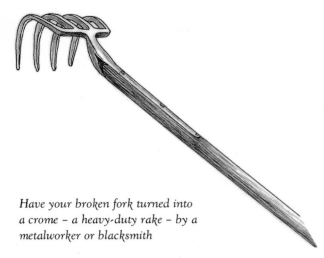

Have your broken fork turned into a crome – a heavy-duty rake – by a metalworker or blacksmith

push them about 8cm (3in) deep into a soil-sand mixture in a cold frame or sheltered spot in the garden. They should have made enough roots to transplant after about six months, but leave longer if necessary.

Grass cuttings should be recycled on the lawn or composted, but you can also use them as a mulch round roses and shrubs, or to make a nest when planting seed potatoes and so avoid scab. Some people use just grass cuttings and soil to make good compost using the Bio Recycler method.

Greengrocer Ask your friendly local one to save his waste produce for you to add to your compost-making materials instead of putting it out for the dustmen.

Growing bags whether organic or not, contain only small residues of plant nutrients after you've cropped them. Nevertheless, you could try sowing and growing some annuals in them. Alternatively, use the compost for storing root crops over the winter, for mulching round newly planted shrubs or for lining the seed potato trench.

Hair from grooming your pets can be added to the compost heap or dug into the soil.

Hessian sacks are becoming rare. Use hole-free ones to store potatoes; damaged ones can serve to hold the manure to make liquid manure.

Holly Save the holly after Christmas and allow it to become brittle dry. When sowing peas put a barrier of the dried holly each side of the drill to deter mice.

Hot water bottle that's no longer serviceable can be stuffed with fabric scraps and used as a kneeling pad.

Kitchen paper roll inners can be used for blanching leeks.

Kitchen waste that is vegetable and uncooked should be saved for compost making. Cooked scraps can help to feed your free-range hens or go to the worms in the worm farm. In winter save bread, cereal and biscuit scraps for the birds.

Knife Don't discard an old kitchen knife. Use it as a spot weeder for the lawn or crazy paving.

Leaves in the autumn should be collected and made into leafmould, not burned.

Lolly sticks make good labels for the seedbed.

Net curtains draped over the raspberry rows will protect the fruit from birds, and fan-trained apples, pears and peaches from late frosts.

Newspaper can be shredded and added a little at a time to the compost container or soaked in a bucket of liquid manure and placed at the bottom of the pea and bean trenches. Use two sheets of tabloid size paper to make paper pots. Wrap them round a rolling pin, paste the edge and when dry, slide off and

Use two sheets of newspaper to make paper pots for raising bean plants. Wrap the sheets round a rolling pin to form a cylinder. Paste the edges and, when dry, cut into 10cm (4in) lengths

cut into 10cm (4in) lengths. Use with a peat-based or Natgro compost for raising French, broad and runner beans, one seed to each paper pot. When ready, plant out pot and all and keep watered. Use thick layers of newsprint for mulching no-go areas for weeds, such as between the raspberry rows and shrubbery. Cover with a coarse grade of bark to improve the appearance and hold the paper in place.

Nylon typewriter ribbon, cut down the centre, tied to sticks a few centimetres above the rows, will protect newly sown seeds such as peas.

Onion nets can be re-used to store spring-flowering bulbs over the summer and can be tied over choice apples and pears to protect them from birds and wasps.

Paint Old, thick oil-based paint will repair small holes in the bottom of metal or plastic buckets or watering cans. Pour it in and allow it to set hard. Paint the handles of small hand tools with a bright colour.

Petals When dead-heading the roses and other fragrant flowers, save the petals, spread in the sun to dry and use for pot pourri.

Railway sleepers make excellent retaining walls for deep beds

Plastic cups from the office machine can be re-used as pots for raising seedlings. Make a hole in the bottom for drainage. Use them also as slug guards by cutting out the bottom and slipping over young plants. Seeds can be sown into plastic trays if you first make drainage holes. Use the larger plastic containers as punnets for your soft fruit.

Prunings of roses and many shrubs will often take if trimmed as cuttings and placed in a sand–soil mixture in a shallow trench in a cold frame or sheltered part of the garden.

Railway sleepers make permanent walls for deep beds.

Seaweed washed up by the autumn gales, can be collected and used as a valuable natural fertiliser, although watch out for any contaminated with oil or sewage. Stack it for a few weeks, then spread it and turn it into the soil during the winter. Used as a mulch, it does wonders for the flavour of beetroot, Brussels sprouts and purple sprouting broccoli, or chop it and spread it over the asparagus bed in early spring, or dig it into the site for the outdoor tomatoes. Small amounts make an excellent activator for the compost heap.

Seed saving falls into two categories: the seed you save from the bought packets, and that you save from plants allowed to bolt or run to seed. Seed left after the current season's sowing should be stored in its original foil and paper packets with the year clearly marked. Keep all such used packets in a cold, dry place, preferably in a seed organiser (page 15) and test for germination when you want to use them. Seed you save from your own plants should be from open-pollinated sorts and, having been carefully selected, cleaned and dried, should be stored in paper bags, clearly marked with type and date. Test these also for germination.

Soot Use it when it has been weathered for warming the soil and for the onion bed.

Straw bales that have been allowed to rot can be used for growing tomatoes, as the walls of a large compost heap, or to mulch between the raspberry rows and the pathways between deep beds.

Tights The legs of discarded tights, cut into strips, make useful plant ties, strong but not harsh enough to cause chafing. Use the legs complete to make ties for securing newly planted trees to supporting stakes. Loop the material round the trunk, then give a few twists before looping round the stake and tying firmly. The material stretches to accommodate

Bladderwrack and other seaweeds make valuable fertilisers

Discarded tights can be used for securing newly-planted trees to stakes

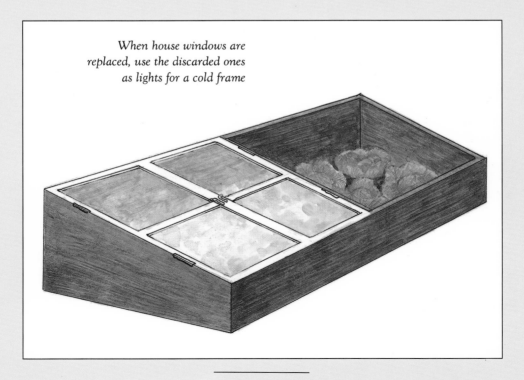

When house windows are replaced, use the discarded ones as lights for a cold frame

the growth of the young tree. You can store shallots, onions and bulbs in the legs of discarded tights. Hang them in a cool, airy place. You can cut pieces from the tights to use in flower pots to block off the drainage hole. Water drains away, but the compost doesn't. If you have a petrol-engined mower, cultivator or paraffin-powered flame gun, stretch a piece of fine-gauge stocking material over the mouth of the funnel when filling the tank to stop debris getting into it. You can use the seat of the tights, cut into an oblong panel, when planting out tulip bulbs. First dig the planting hole, then line it with the panel cut from the tights. Plant the bulbs and fill in the hole with soil, allowing enough spare material from the panel to be turned up so that it is just level with the surface. After flowering you can simply excavate soil from the hole and lift out the bulbs, using the panel to carry them to a corner of the garden where they can be lowered into a shallow trench until the foliage has dried off. Hang the dried bulbs in the legs of the tights until ready to plant out again in the autumn. If you have a dwarf cherry tree, you can protect the fruit from birds by covering them with the legs of tights while the fruit is still green. Gently thread the legs of the tights over the branches and watch while the cherries ripen, safe from the birds. Cut pieces from old tights or stockings and tie them round choice apples, pears, plums and peaches to protect them from birds and wasps.

Tins filled with stale beer or sugary water make slug traps when sunk to the rim near to target plants.

Turf Old turves should be stacked face side down. They become valuable loam after about six months for use in homemade composts.

Urine In times past the contents of the chamber pot were used as an activator in making compost and as a winter wash for currant and gooseberry bushes.

Water is precious: save it whenever you can to re-use in the garden.

Wellies Cut the legs from an old pair of wellington boots and use as arm guards when pruning prickly subjects like pyracantha, roses and gooseberry bushes. Always wear stout gardening gloves, preferably of leather, when pruning prickly items. Quite often it's not the puncture from the thorn or prickle that causes infection, it's the dirt that's taken into the skin from the surface of the thorn.

Windows Re-use replaced windows as the lights of cold frames.

Wool scraps can be dug in to the soil in winter to provide a slow-release source of nitrogen. Wool waste is sold as shoddy.

FURTHER READING

GENERAL

Companion Planting Gertrud Frank (Thorsons, 1983)

Composting Dick Kitto (Thorsons, 1984)

Cowpasture: Everyday life of an English allotment Roy Lacey (David & Charles, 1980)

Down to Earth Stephen Nortcliff (Leicestershire Museums Publication No 52, 1984)

Fruit Garden Displayed (Royal Horticultural Society, 1986)

Green Manures (Elm Farm Research Centre, 1982)

Organic Gardening Roy Lacey (David & Charles, 1988)

Pests, Diseases and Disorders Stefan Buczacki and Keith Harris (Collins, 1983)

Salad Garden Joy Larkcom (Windward, 1984)

Vegetables from Small Gardens Joy Larkcom (Windward, 1976)

Vegetable Garden Displayed (Royal Horticultural Society, 1961)

Working the Land Charlie Pye-Smith and Richard North (Temple Smith, 1984)

WILDLIFE

The Backgarden Wildlife Sanctuary Book Ron Wilson (Penguin, 1987)

Garden Life Jennifer Owen (Chatto and Windus, 1983)

Gardening with Wildlife (RSPB, 1982)

How to Make a Wildlife Garden Chris Baines (Elm Tree Books, 1985)

The Living Garden Michael Chinery (Dorling Kindersley, 1986)

The Natural History of the Garden Michael Chinery (Collins, 1977)

Theft of the Countryside Marion Shoard (Temple Smith, 1980)

Wild Flower Gardening John Stevens (Dorling Kindersley, 1987)

Every month *Organic Gardening* magazine gives advice on all aspects of the subject, along with news of interest to green gardeners.

Both the Soil Association and Henry Doubleday Research Association publish leaflets on aspects of organic gardening.

USEFUL ADDRESSES

Cottage Garden Society, 15 Faenol Avenue, Abergele, Clwyd LL22 7HT.

Friends of the Earth, 26–28 Underwood Street, London N1 7JQ.

Greenpeace, 30–31 Islington Green, London N1 8XE.

Henry Doubleday Research Association, Ryton-on-Dunsmore, Coventry CV8 3LG.

Men of the Trees, Crawley Down, Crawley, Sussex RH10 4HL.

National Society of Allotment and Leisure Gardeners, Hunters Road, Corby, Northants NN17 1JE.

Nature Conservancy Council, Northminster House, Peterborough PE1 1UA.

Royal Horticultural Society, Vincent Square, London SW1P 2PE.

Royal Society for Nature Conservation, The Green, Nettleham, Lincoln LN2 2NR.

Royal Society for the Protection of Birds, The Lodge, Sandy, Bedfordshire SG19 2DL.

Soil Association Ltd, 86–88 Colston Street, Bristol BS1 5BB.

Tree Council, 35 Belgrave Square, London SW1X 8QN.

Wild Flower Society, 86 Outwoods Road, Loughborough, Leicestershire LE11 3LY.

Women's Environmental Network, 287 City Road, London EC1V 1LA.

Woodland Trust, Autumn Park, Dysart Road, Grantham, Lincolnshire NG31 6LL.

SUPPLIERS

BIOLOGICAL CONTROLS

English Woodlands Ltd, Burrow Nursery, Cross-in-Hand, Heathfield, East Sussex TN21 0UG.

Koppert (UK) Ltd, PO Box 43, Tunbridge Wells, Kent TN2 5BX.

Oecos, 130 High Street, Kimpton, Herts SG4 8QP.

Steel & Brodie, Stevens Drove, Houghton, Stockbridge, Hants SO20 6LP.

COMPOSTS, MANURES AND ORGANIC FERTILISERS

Camland Products Ltd, Fordham House, Fordham, Cambs CB7 5LN.

Cowpact Products, Adstock, Buckingham MK18 2RE.

Early Bird Worms, 17 Hill Cottages, Flag Hill, Great Bentley, Essex CO7 8AG.

East Anglian Organic Products Ltd, Green House, Timworth Green, Bury St Edmunds, Suffolk IP31 1HS.

E. J. Godwin (Peat Industries) Ltd, Meare, Glastonbury, Somerset BA6 9SP.

Fertosan Products (Wirral) Ltd, 2 Holborn Square, Birkenhead, Merseyside L41 9HQ.

Goldengrow Ltd, Court Farm, Llanover, Abergavenny, Gwent NP7 9YD.

Humber Fertilisers plc, PO Box 27, Stoneferry, Hull HU8 8DQ.

E. W. King & Co Ltd, Monks Farm, Coggeshall Road, Kelvedon, Essex CO5 9PG.

Leggar Organics, Knapp Farm, Chadshill, Cannington, Bridgwater, Somerset TA5 2BR.

Maxicrop Ltd, 21 London Road, Great Shelford, Cambridge CB2 5DF.

Norfolk Farm Composts Ltd, Docking Farm, Oulton, Norwich NR11 6BR.

Organic Concentrates Ltd, 3 Broadway Court, Chesham, Buckinghamshire HP5 1EN.

Organic Worm Products, 43 Francis Road, Ashford, Kent TN23 1UP.

Skirza Horticultural Products, Roadside, Skirza, Freswick, Wick, Caithness.

Stimgro Ltd, Bridge House, 97–101 High Street, Tonbridge, Kent TN9 1DR.

Uza Frenly Organic Gardening, Stallard Common, Great Ellingham, Attleborough, Norfolk NR17 1LJ.

Warner Knowles, 67 Queensway, Great Cornard, Sudbury, Suffolk.

Worm Firm, Ryehurst Farm Cottage, Cabbage Hill Lane, Binfield, Berks.

EQUIPMENT AND SUNDRIES

Fieldspray Ltd, Cuckoo Hill, Bures, Sudbury, Suffolk CO8 5JH. (Slug killer, bird, rabbit, cat and dog repellents.)

Fyba Pot Company Ltd, Malvern Road, Knottingley, West Yorkshire WF11 8EG. (Biodegradable pots.)

Garden Rewards, 104 Branbridges Road, East Peckham, Tonbridge, Kent TN12 5HH. (Protection netting.)

Growing Success Organics, South Newton, Salisbury, Wiltshire SP2 0QW. (Slug killer.)

Hydrocut Ltd, Sudbury, Suffolk CO10 6HB. (Agryl P17, Hortopaper.)

Impregnated Tapes Ltd, Lower Penarwyn, St Blazey, Par, Cornwall PL24 2DS. (Slug tape and pads.)

Metro Products, 98–102 Station Road East, Oxted, Surrey RH8 0AY. (Capillary matting.)

Monro, Alexander & Co Ltd, Newleaze, Great Somerford, Chippenham, Wiltshire SN15 5EN. (Vegetable and tree guards.)

E. J. & V. A. Moran, 60 Ridgedale Road, Bolsover, Derbyshire S44 6TX. (Humane traps.)

Netlon Ltd, Kelly Street, Blackburn BB2 4RJ. (Protection netting.)

Pan Britannica Industries Ltd, Britannica House, Waltham Cross, Herts EN8 7DY. (Pepper dust.)

Sinclair Horticulture & Leisure Ltd, Firth Road, Lincoln LN6 7AH. (Cat repellent.)

Two Wests & Elliott Ltd, Unit 4, Carrwood Road, Sheepbridge Industrial Estate, Chesterfield, Derbyshire S41 9RH. (Greenhouse equipment.)

Wilson Grimes Products, Corwen, Clwyd LL21 0DR. (Soil test kits.)

GENERAL
ORGANIC PRODUCTS

Chase Organics (GB) Ltd, Addlestone, Weybridge, Surrey KT15 1HY.

Cumulus Organics and Conservation Ltd, Two Mile Lane, Highnam, Gloucester GL2 8DW.

Dig and Delve Organics, Fen Road, Blo' Norton, Diss, Norfolk IP22 25H.

East Anglian Organic Products Ltd, Green House, Timworth Green, Bury St Edmunds, Suffolk IP31 1HS.

HDRA (Sales) Ltd, Ryton Gardens, Ryton-on-Dunsmore, Coventry CV8 3LG.

Pan Britannica Industries Ltd, Britannica House, Waltham Cross, Herts EN8 7DY.

SEED FIRMS

Denotes suppliers of organic seeds.

J. W. Boyce, 67 Station Road, Soham, Ely, Cambs CB7 5ED.

*Chase Organics (GB) Ltd, Addlestone, Weybridge, Surrey KT15 1HY.

Chelsea Choice Seeds, Notley Road, Braintree, Essex CM7 7HA.

Samuel Dobie & Son Ltd, Broomhill Way, Torquay, Devon TQ2 7QW.

Mr Fothergills Seeds, Kentford, Newmarket, Suffolk CB8 7QB.

*HDRA (Sales) Ltd, Ryton Gardens, Ryton-on-Dunsmore, Coventry CV8 3LG.

Hursts Seeds, Stepfield, Essex CM8 3TA.

W. W. Johnson & Son Ltd, Boston, Lincs PE21 8AD.

*Kings Crown Quality Seeds, Grange Hill, Coggeshall, Essex.

S. E. Marshall & Co Ltd, Regal Road, Wisbech, Cambs PE13 2RF.

W. Robinson & Sons, Sunny Bank, Forton, Preston, Lancs PR3 0BN.

*Suffolk Herbs, Sawyers Farm, Little Cornard, Sudbury, Suffolk CO10 0NY.

Suttons Seeds Ltd, Hele Road, Torquay, Devon TQ2 7QJ.

Thompson & Morgan Ltd, London Road, Ipswich, Suffolk IP2 0BA.

Unwins Seeds Ltd, Impington Lane, Histon, Cambs CB4 4LE.

Van Hage Seeds, Great Amwell, Ware, Herts SG12 9RP.

My profound thanks to my editor, Vivienne Wells, for her diligence and encouragement, to Tricia Newell for her magnificent contribution as illustrator, to the many correspondents to my gardening pages in the 'East Anglian Daily Times', who sent me their favourite gardening tips and, not least, to David St John Thomas who asked me to write this book.

INDEX

Lacey, Roy.
The green gardener.

632
L11

Date Due

DEC 0 4 1992		
FEB 1 0 1993		
APR 2 4 1993		
JUL 3 1994		
Sept 10/94		
MAR 0		
MAR 1 1 1997		
MAR 1 1 1997		
JAN 2 3 2002		